ECONOMIC POLICIES OF THE COMMON MARKET

Also by Peter Coffey

EUROPEAN MONETARY INTEGRATION (*with John R. Presley*)
THE SOCIAL ECONOMY OF FRANCE
THE WORLD MONETARY CRISIS
THE EXTERNAL ECONOMIC RELATIONS OF THE EEC
EUROPE AND MONEY

ECONOMIC POLICIES OF THE COMMON MARKET

Edited by

Peter Coffey

First published 1979 by
THE MACMILLAN PRESS LTD
London and Basingstoke
Associated companies in Delhi
Dublin Hong Kong Johannesburg Lagos
Melbourne New York Singapore Tokyo

British Library Cataloguing in Publication Data

Economic policies of the Common Market
 1. European Economic Community
 I. Coffey, Peter
 338.91′4   HC241.2

ISBN 978-1-349-03655-4   ISBN 978-1-349-03653-0 (eBook)
                           DOI 10.1007/978-1-349-03653-0

Contents

List of Tables

Preface

Many different factors have prompted the writing of this work. Ever since his arrival at the Europa Instituut, the editor has been painfully aware of the absence of a text concerning the economic policies of the EEC which could be used by more advanced students and their counterparts in business, finance and government.

Equally, the presence in Amsterdam, each year, of so many experts in different fields of economic activity related to the Common Market encouraged the preparation of a work which might be used as a basic economics course-book by the Europa Instituut and similar institutes elsewhere. Then it has become increasingly obvious that the European Economic Community has now arrived at a crossroads where it must take fundamental economic structural decisions about the future. Such a situation implies that independent experts should offer proposals to the Community. Hence the editor felt that the contributors to this study should make their own proposals for future structural changes in the EEC.

All these considerations suggested a fairly logical plan for this book. Basically, the most important areas of the Community's economic activities, past, present and future, should be included. Also, in order to satisfy both academics and practical people, each economic sector includes basic theoretical considerations, an examination of Community policy in that area (together with the results of the policy applied) to date, and proposals for future policy changes. Further, the aim of the editor is to revise this work approximately every two years, thus providing readers with an up-to-date economic guide to the EEC.

Amsterdam   PETER COFFEY

Acknowledgements

The editor wishes to thank colleagues and friends who have collaborated in this work. Also, in the Europa Instituut, he wishes to thank Miss S. Stevens, Miss J. M. Baarspul, Mr. B. Kotman and Mr. R. Bijlo for assistance with typing, translation, tables and the index.

A number of institutions and journals have placed material at our disposal in the preparation of this book. Thus the editor wishes to thank the journal *Annual Energy Review* for allowing the article by Messrs Brondel and Morton to be reprinted, and the editor of the *National Westminster Bank Review* for permission to reprint Table 4.1 from the May 1977 issue of the review. Lastly, special thanks are given to the Commission of the European Communities, the OECD and the United Nations Organization for the use and reproduction of statistics in the preparation of tables which appear in this book.

Notes on the Contributors

PETER A. BROMHEAD is Professor of Politics at the University of Bristol. He has lectured and published widely in different parts of Europe.

GEORGES BRONDEL is the Director of the Directorate for Hydrocarbons, Directorate-General for Energy, Commission of the European Communities, Brussels.

PETER COFFEY is a Senior Research Fellow and Head of the Economics Section at the Europa Instituut, University of Amsterdam. He has published many works on monetary and European questions and has lectured in most countries of the Common Market as well as in Portugal and the United States.

ALEXIS P. JACQUEMIN is Professor of Economics at the Centre for Economic and Legal Studies at the University of Louvain. He has lectured and published widely in Europe and North America on industrial economics.

TIM JOSLING is Professor of Agricultural Economics at the University of Stanford. He has been an adviser to governments and international bodies and has lectured widely in different parts of the world.

WILLEM MOLLE is an associate of Professor Paelinck at the Erasmus University, Rotterdam.

NOEL MORTON is a member of the Oil and Natural Gas Directorate, Directorate-General for Energy, Commission of the European Communities, Brussels.

JEAN PAELINCK is Professor of Regional Economics at the Netherlands National Institute of Economics at the Erasmus University, Rotterdam. He has undertaken projects in different parts of the world and has published several works about regional problems.

ALAN R. PREST is Professor and Head of the Economics Department at the London School of Economics. He is an acknowledged international authority on fiscal questions and has advised national and international authorities about fiscal matters. Professor Prest has lectured in all parts of the world and has published several major classic works on fiscal issues.

1 Agricultural policy

TIM JOSLING

INTRODUCTION

The Common Agricultural Policy is not easily contained within a single chapter. No brief treatment can do justice to its complexity. It is a policy for European agriculture, influencing the output and profitability of a diverse and populous industry. It is a building block for European integration, and hence a manifestation of common decision-taking among a group of sovereign states. It contains the Community's trade policy for temperate-zone agricultural products, and hence is part of the external face of the EEC. It accounts for a large part of the common budget, and thus represents the only significant way that the Community effects large-scale financial transfers at the European level. It is a food policy, influencing the wholesale price of staple products. It has elements of regional policy, of social policy, and of employment policy. Such a policy can only be tied down by making the conscious choice to emphasise one aspect and resolutely avoid the temptation to follow all the hares that are raised in the process.

This chapter will take the position that the CAP can be studied as an example of how the Community has reacted to a set of problems, faced by all industrial countries and regions, of the regulation of agricultural markets to the long- and short-term satisfaction of the rural and urban electorate. As such, it can be compared with the successes and failures of other countries, as well as with the standards of independent policy analysis. Any such evaluation is bound to be contentious. In a fundamental sense, a policy enacted by due process in a democratic system can never be 'wrong': it is the best that the people elected could come up with given the information at their disposal. The CAP exists as a result of cumulative decisions by democratic administrations. The reason for examining past decisions is not to judge them but to see whether such an exercise assists with present and future problems.

The CAP developed rapidly. It was originally devised to sweep away the debris of economic nationalism which had persisted throughout post-war reconstruction. It emerged over the decade of the 1960s from the bland pronouncements of the Rome Treaty to a comprehensive set of marketing regulations covering most major agricultural products. It achieved the major objective of liberalising trade among the original six Member States and harmonising the treatment of imports and exports at the frontier. It imposed relatively uniform domestic market support procedures in a group of countries that had previously used every variety of such policy instruments in pursuit of their objectives. It established joint decision-making as an essential element of Community policy, and shared-financing as both a symbolic and a practical part of such integration. But the policy also acquired a life of its own, somewhat separate from its various functions. It became an object, to be defended, criticised, or reformed. It became endowed with principles, inviolable, indisputable, and self-justifying. Discussion of agriculture in Europe became discussion *about* the CAP. It had indeed, for many people, become a problem in its own right. The tendency for policies which have lost their relevance to emerge as problems is common in all aspects of public decision-making. In the case of the CAP it is not clear whether the underlying problems have in fact changed significantly since its inception, but the policy has shown an impressive propensity to attract attention to itself and divert discussion from the fundamental issues.

To illustrate this, and to distinguish the problems of agriculture from the problems of the CAP, it is necessary to review the context within which all farm policies in industrial societies operate. The types of policy choices available can then be considered, and the strengths and weaknesses of each assessed. This forms the subject of the first section of this chapter; subsequent sections deal with the more detailed application of the policy and then the possible options open to the Community in the future.

I THE AGRICULTURAL PROBLEM

The development of any sector in an economy is the result of a variety of influences. The conditions governing the demand for the product or service provide the opportunities and constraints. A 'young' and expanding industry is characterised by a strong growth in demand and a keen attitude by entrepreneurs to fulfil and exploit that demand. Temperate-zone agriculture produces, in the main, a set of products where domestic demand often grows little faster than the increase in population and where overseas demand is limited by serious constraints of purchasing power and foreign exchange availability even when underlying needs are great. In general, 'new' products are rare, and further opportunities for product differentiation to exploit taste variations seem few and far between. Individual producers, except in a small number of cases, sell a homogeneous product, indistinguishable from that of their neighbours, in an anonymous market over which they have little control. The signal to the farmer emanating from the market is the level and stability of the price he receives. It determines his gross income from particular production decisions, and influences his investment pattern and his view of the future. As a small businessman, the farmer is under normal commercial pressures. He buys farm inputs from a relatively well organised supply sector, which also provides most of the technical advice that goes with the use of purchased inputs. Inflation and high interest rates hit his costs, and attractive wages in other sectors make labour scarce. The farmer himself typically provides most of the capital needed for his enterprises, uses family labour at a rather low implicit wage, and lives 'over the business'. He is under pressure to adopt new techniques which expand output or reduce costs: he cannot afford to drop too far behind his neighbours in farming practices. The application of science to farming is continually opening-up technical improvements, often allowing labour force reductions and yield increases. But the net effect of such technology may be to put farmers with limited acreage and inadequate borrowing power at a disadvantage in the race: the small farmer's self-image of resilience, self-reliance, and dedication is severely tested, since modern agricultural methods seem always to favour the big, adaptable, and purely commercial farm business.

The result of these factors, in all industrial countries, has been to promote a run-down in the number of such small farms, the increase in the average size and the degree of capitalisation of holdings that remain, a tendency toward polarisation of agricultural structures into the modern and the traditional, the release of hired labour to work in the towns, and the growing tendency of farmers themselves to take part-time employment elsewhere. Governments have accepted the social responsibility for presiding over these changes and ensuring that the degree of social hardship is kept to a minimum. Since the problem, though common to most countries, has its specific manifestations in different situations, the attitude of governments varies from a relatively 'hard' line, allowing market pressures to encourage adjustments, to a 'soft' approach of cushioning those most affected from these trends.

It is difficult to generalise about the approach of European governments to this problem. Some countries, notably Denmark, the Netherlands, and the U.K., emerged in the postwar period with agricultural systems that were relatively sophisticated and well poised to take advantage of new technology without undue social hardship. The major adjustments in the labour force had in fact been achieved before the days when governments saw such developments as within their responsibility and competence. In other countries, such as Ireland, Italy, and France, the major adjustments in agriculture have been much more recent and as such have become a part of the responsibility of the European Community. Looking to the future, the accession of Portugal, Greece and Spain would add to the community three countries where the painful adjustments in rural life may yet have to be faced. The main question that this poses for policy makers is how the modernisation of agriculture can be accomplished within the constraints of social equity, and, on the assumption that an answer to this question is forthcoming, to what extent Community policy should be made responsible for such a task.

If this is the essence of the agricultural problem, it has many more facets. The most apparent of these is the inherent instability of agricultural output, arising from variability in weather and in the incidence of plant and animal diseases. Large corporations might be able to take the risks involved and cover losses in the bad years with profits in the good. Small family businesses will tend to be harder hit, though the very smallest, with modest cash outlay and little borrowed capital, may appear to be more secure. Governments have reacted to these problems by attempting to manage agricultural markets to dampen the impact of natural hazards. Thus in addition to lessening the social burden of economic change over a period of years, national administrations have taken on the responsibility for short-run 'burden-sharing' by underwriting in various ways the value of year-to-year farm output. The balance between these two activities is one of the most crucial aspects of government decision-making in agriculture. This balance differs among countries, and the establishment of the correct policy mixture within the CAP and between national and Community authorities is a major continuing matter for discussion.

Besides the stability of agricultural markets, a number of other aspects of the production and distribution of food products have attracted government attention. These range from basic research into agricultural production techniques, usually premised on the assumption that the farming industry itself will not be in a position to finance such research, through to quality standards for food products reflecting the ideas of the day as to the degree to which governments should protect consumers from their own ignorance or bad habits. In between are two important areas where policy is often formulated and government involvement extensive. The first relates to the structure of marketing farm products as they enter the food industry. A common theme running throughout policy in this area is that the framework should be established for the improvement of the bargaining position of individual farms through the establishment of institutions which can coordinate their marketing decisions. Two common forms of such institutions are farmer cooperatives and para-statal marketing boards, though in practice there exists a continuum of structures from small local associations of farmers to monolithic state trading agencies. Once again, historical, geographical, and political factors influence the attitudes of individual governments in their legislative response to marketing problems.

The second area of special interest relates to the question of the price of food, either in general or in relation to specific groups of consumers. A steady change in food prices over time, in line with those of other products, causes no particular alarm: a rapid rise galvanises administrations into action. Sometimes action is taken at the retail level to inhibit price increases through subsidies or direct controls, but governments have also viewed the influence of their own farm policies on the wholesale price of agricultural goods as offering a further anti-inflationary device. Though the leverage that agricultural price restraint has on the overall cost of living is not great, there are several reasons why such action is attractive. Food prices have an undoubted political importance not shared by, for example, the price of cars. They also figure prominently in wage negotiations, both in the workplace and also in the domestic context of the amount of 'housekeeping' money needed to feed the family. Low-income households are proportionately disadvantaged by steep price increases for foodstuffs, as are those with large families. Fixed income groups, such as pensioners, often find food price increases particularly burdensome. Such considerations explain the intense interest in food price levels at times when agricultural prices are rising rapidly, and the involvement of governments in the agricultural pricing process leads naturally to the formation of policies to contain such inflationary pressures. Experience in the period 1972–4, when farm prices for many goods rose suddenly, illustrates the measures that governments can take when concerned about food price developments.

It is useful to distinguish between the underlying problem of the long-term adjustment of employment in agriculture, coupled with a tendency for farm incomes to be below those of other groups, and these other concerns of market stability, distributional structure, and food price levels. The first, for instance, is of little relevance in the United Kingdom. Farmers, in common with other small independent businessmen, have to make decisions on investments and the hiring of labour in the light of their appreciation of underlying market trends, modified by the policies of governments. But there is no distinct 'rural problem' in a country where social and educational facilities are relatively uniform and where the labour force is mobile. However, the other problems remain even when agriculture represents less than three per cent of employment and of the national product. Indeed, some aspects of government concern with agriculture, such as the level of food prices and the impact of fluctuation in world markets on the balance of trade, may even become more significant despite the 'solution' of the long-term adjustment problem. The different emphases put by various governments on these aspects help to explain not only many of the difficulties encountered in discussions at an international level on agricultural policies but also some of the problems faced in the formation of a Community policy acceptable to all Member States.

POLICY INSTRUMENTS

Before turning to the specific mechanisms used by the European Community for dealing with the range of economic and social problems facing agriculture, it is as well to recognise the range of options open to governments. Although no one-to-one relationship exists between particular measures and particular objectives, it is possible to relate typical policy actions to the main motive for the policy's introduction. The striking feature of government policy toward agriculture, as in other aspects of economic policy, is the relative inability of countries to resist and deflect underlying secular changes in the balance of the economy. Even countries which have engaged in the transfer of considerable funds to the agricultural sector have seen the outmigration of labour continue and relative income disparities persist. Some countries have pursued policies of substantial redistribution of productive assets, primarily agricultural land, as part of an agrarian reform programme. In others, state controlled output and employment decisions under the heading of centralised planning have had a marked effect on rural economic activity and incomes. But in the main, the 'Western industrial democracies' have allowed the dynamics of adjustment to be dictated by economic forces tending to attract fewer people from each successive generation to work on the land. Policy has been confined to influencing the speed of such adjustment, and to the amelioration of the impact on the remaining rural communities. In fact, with respect to the process of adjustment itself, non-farm policies have generally been of greater significance.

Among these more general policies, the maintenance of full employment through macroeconomic management is perhaps the most important—even though conditions of the last two years cast doubt upon the universal success of such policies. Along with the provision of non-farm jobs in the economy as a whole has come the attempt specifically to create employment in rural or semi-urban areas to pre-empt the drift to the major conurbations. Success has been patchy, but has been greatest where a relatively scattered settlement pattern already existed. In countries where industry and service activities are already dispersed, the pull of non-farm employment has shown up as a striking increase in the number of part-time farmers. Such a social system may well be a stable and constructive compromise between rural depopulation and urban crowding, on the one hand, and extensive and expensive programmes to provide adequate incomes from agriculture alone, on the other. The spread of adequate educational facilities to rural areas has also played a major part in the adjustment in agriculture, as has the extension of social security schemes to include farm families, and indeed the improved communications which have influenced both the attitudes and aspirations of rural people and their physical mobility.

Against these forces, the policies strictly related to agriculture have been relatively inconsequential. The provision of credit on concessional terms to farm businesses, together with amalgamation grants, facilitates the rationalisation of holdings; particularly necessary where inheritance laws have led to excessive fragmentation of farms. Extension services spread knowledge of new methods of husbandry and encourage more formal accounting techniques. Personal and property taxation concessions often relieve the farm family of a share of the financing of the modern corporate state. Retirement pensions and annuities and schemes for retraining have been introduced in some countries. But it remains true that the lure of the non-farm job and its financial rewards, despite attempts at farm price support, largely determine the employment pattern and the relative income levels in agriculture.

Policy instruments which operate directly to influence the market conditions for agricultural products are somewhat easier to assess. Their impact, at least in the short run, is fairly predictable. Two types of market policies predominate. The first raises the demand for domestically produced agricultural goods, in the sense of increasing the price at which any given quantity will sell. This is done through restricting imports, either by taxes or quotas, by subsidising exports, by separating various product uses to gain from price discrimination, and by the granting of various subsidies on consumption. The second method is to restrict the level of production or the quantity marketed in a particular period to take advantage of a demand relatively unresponsive to price, and hence to increase income. In addition to these two direct methods of market management, similar effects on farm returns can be obtained by financial outlays in the form of subsidies paid over and above market prices. Some policy instruments are less easy to classify, depending on the way in which they are used. Support buying, for instance, can either be a mechanism for facilitating the payment of export subsidies, as when the purchasing agency releases the commodity on overseas markets at a loss made good by government funds, or it can represent a form of storage when the product reappears on the domestic market at a later date. In this case it either increases the average farm price, if resold at a loss recouped from public funds, or reduces it if the support buying agency makes a profit on the resale—thus denying the producer the financial benefit of such intertemporal arbitrage.

This range of policies can be used in two ways. Policies can either aim to raise farm prices and farm returns over time whilst still allowing variability from season to season, or they can be themselves varied with circumstances to stabilise farm prices. The distinction is clearly seen in the case of import taxes, which can either be fixed at a particular level or be related to a minimum import price. In the first case instability in world prices is transmitted to the domestic market, whilst in the second it is absorbed in the variable level of import tax. The development of price policies which divorce domestic conditions from world price variations is particularly significant in the understanding of conflicts arising from the interplay of industrial countries' farm policies.

THE CAP AS AN AGRICULTURAL POLICY

In the light of the discussion of problems and policy alternatives, it is now possible to categorise the approach taken under the Common Agricultural Policy. Looked at as a response by the emergent Community, certain characteristics stand out. First, the adjustment problem for the agricultural sector in individual member states has remained primarily within the province of each government. In spite of directives to Member States on structural reform, backed up by a proportion of the funding of such programmes from the Community budget, the major responsibility still resides at the national level. This is perhaps inevitable in view of the different nature of the problem in various regions of the Community, but serves to highlight the distinction between European policy and that to be found in federal systems, such as the United States, Australia, and Canada, where a greater degree of responsibility in these matters has passed to central government. Progress towards Community-wide policies to ease social adjustment in rural areas will probably await the strengthening of regional and social measures as yet in their infancy.

It is in the realm of price and market policies where the Community has developed, in a remarkably short period, a comprehensive set of arrangements applicable to all member states. Nearly ninety per cent of farm output is covered by common marketing regulations, most of these incorporating common price systems. Only sheep and potatoes, together with some fruits and vegetables, are not subject to such regulations. It is not easy to compare the CAP with the welter of national price-support measures which preceded it: at the risk of ignoring the constraints imposed by such history, it is more convenient to think of the policies as having arisen *ab initio* during the period up to 1967. Support mechanisms vary from product to product, but certain themes emerge. First, the demand for Community produce has been kept at a level significantly higher than would otherwise have been the case: there has been a positive and in many cases a substantial degree of protection for Community producers over most of the last decade. Secondly, the theme of price stabilisation has also been dominant, protecting farmers from fluctuations in the local as well as in the general level of world prices. Thirdly, the decision has been made, in true federal fashion, to finance jointly expenditure on the market and price policies, raising the money through the revenue accruing to the Community in the form of import taxes and duties as well as by through general fiscal channels.

Two types of market support policy characterise the CAP. The first is a tax on imports which are offered below a predetermined price level in order to raise their levy-paid price to the 'threshold' level. This variable-levy system is applied to a number of products, notably cereals, dairy products and sugar. A slight variation applies to beef, where there is an additional fixed tariff in common with other meats, and where the amount of the potential supplementary (variable) levy actually charged itself varies on a sliding scale depending on the state of the internal market; the levy is abated somewhat when internal prices are high and increased when they are depressed. For livestock products which rely on grain imports (pigs and poultry) the variable element in the levy is linked to that for cereals, with an additional fixed degree of protection added for good measure. The import regimes for fruits and vegetables also make use of variable import taxes based on reference prices set in relation to domestic costs. The second major policy instrument is the payment of export subsidies either directly to firms or indirectly through losses made by support-buying agencies when disposing of purchases on third-country markets. The level of export subsidy varies with world market conditions, and keeps pace with the height of the variable levy. These subsidies are in operation for most of the products for which there is an import levy regime. The reason for employing both instruments in the same market is twofold. First, some commodities, such as wheat, sugar, and dairy products are both imported and exported by the Community: protection therefore has to be given by both levies and subsidies. Second, commodities benefiting from an export subsidy would tend to re-enter the community market if a levy of at least an equivalent level were not imposed. In this case the levy is not the main protective device, but a necessary back-up for the export policy.

Although these two policies are the mainstay of the CAP system, a number of other instruments are in use. Direct producer payments operate in the markets for durum wheat, tobacco, olive oil, and some specialist products such as grass seeds, natural fibres, and silk. Aids for private storage are also given particularly for sugar and beef, whilst public storage, again through the intervention agencies, is practised on an *ad hoc* basis. Subsidies, for consumers and for livestock feeders, have become increasingly common. They can take the form of selective aids to particular groups (pensioners, or institutions) or more general consumer subsidies financed in part from Community funds. In the case of animal feeds, they can be in the form of premiums to encourage the use of a particular product in livestock rations, such as wheat, or skimmed milk powder, or in the form of direct subsidies to stimulate the retention of the product on the farm of origin.

The system of domestic and export subsidies for the disposal of products purchased by intervention agencies, and indeed for the sale of products by private firms, can be viewed in another way. Imagine the Community to have 'purchased' the entire output of a particular sector. It can, by means of differential prices operated through selective subsidies, direct the disposition of this output to different markets. The 'normal' home market will absorb a large part of such production, but the use of subsidies can divert sales to the export market, to particular domestic consumer groups, and to special outlets where the product would not otherwise be competitive. Careful manipulation of such subsidy levels can increase the cash return from sales and hence reduce the budgetary burden. There is evidence that the Commission views policy in the market for milk in this way: the variety of end uses for milk products makes this sector particularly amenable to this type of management. The problem with such an apparently admirable marketing strategy is that, without effective control over the total supply of milk, the budget cost rises even with the most skilful manipulation of subsidies.

The only major product for which direct supply control is in operation is sugar. In this sector a series of quotas, allocated at the national level and subsequently to beet factories and individual farms, limits the quantity over which the full support price is paid. A levy is placed on above-quota production up to a certain level, beyond which extra output is sold without subsidy. Some indirect attempts to control supply have been applied to fruit and wine production, by giving grants for 'grubbing' orchards and in the milk sector by giving grants for conversion to beef. No major crop retirement programmes have been instituted or contemplated, in contrast to the policies of the U.S.A., Canada, and Australia.

The comparison with other industrial countries with major agricultural sectors is worth pursuing further. The Community in general relies to a greater extent on protection at the common frontier to stabilise and raise farm prices. In spite of being a significant exporter of many products, its attitude is very much that of an importer, able to pursue independent domestic objectives and viewing the world market as a residual supplier of products or a repository for unwanted surpluses. Despite the consistent support in international meetings that the Community has given to the concept of commodity agreements to govern world markets, internal policy has rarely exhibited the responsibility which a successful organisation of world markets requires of major producing regions. The counterpart to a dependence on trade barriers and subsidies is the lack of organisation of domestic marketing, either in terms of supply control or the establishment of marketing institutions with the ability to develop and expand sales. Producer cooperatives abound in Europe, and are encouraged by Community policy. They even have a role in the administration of price policy in the case of certain products, mainly fruits and vegetables. But these cooperatives and producer groups generally have very specific localised functions and do not exercise significant control over the broader market. Some marketing boards do exist, such as those in the U.K. for milk, hops, and potatoes, but more as a relic of past national policies. No Community-wide marketing agencies exist, and indeed they would be in direct conflict with the general competition policies of the EEC. However admirable such devotion to competition might be, the lack of a counterpart to the Australian or Canadian marketing agencies complicates the problem of output control, sales distribution, and market development, and leaves a greater burden on the general price level for the maintenance of market balance.

II THE CAP: AN EVALUATION

The last section described the CAP as if it were a reasoned response to a set of problems facing agricultural producers and markets in a group of industrialised countries. This is the viewpoint taken in this chapter as a whole, and this section will attempt to evaluate the policy in those terms. But a discussion of the constraints under which the CAP operates is an essential part of this evaluation, just as a consideration of, say, federal — provincial relationships would be important in evaluating Canadian agricultural policy. Farm programmes are rooted in the political and social psyche of a country, rather than emanating purely from the cerebration of government officials. The context in which the CAP developed is unique. A group of developed countries attempting a substantial degree of economic integration is itself rare, and the problems that this poses for common policies were largely unexplored. In one sense, the Community has been learning from year to year. What once must have seemed a relatively straightforward process of applying common marketing regulations and common prices to Europe's farm sector, now looks to have been a constant struggle for harmony in the face of all manner of disintegrating forces.

There are a number of factors which make agricultural policy in a single country much simpler than a common policy for a regional group. Perhaps the most fundamental of these relates to the political process, including the formation of decisions and the resolution of conflicts. Where the authority of the government is not challenged, difficult decisions can be taken by administrations with a fair prospect of acquiescence if policies prove to be effective. Different views will still abound, but the parliamentary process ensures that these have an outlet which questions government decisions whilst rarely being able to impede their implementation. The political structure within a country thus tends to subdue and reconcile divergent views and lead to a reasonable measure of consistency in policy making. There is, however, no reason why a group of neighbouring countries, all with their own political history, should arrive at similar views on major policy issues. And since progress towards a rational common approach to agriculture, as to any other sector, requires a coincidence of view as to the important problems and their solutions, the precondition for a 'federal' agricultural policy may not exist. The CAP could still survive as a negative set of measures designed to prevent 'unfair' and wasteful national policy practices, but it would have failed as an agricultural policy for the EEC. There could still be harmony in relations with third countries, attempting to use the collective power of Member States in international negotiations, but such concerted action would again not constitute a convincing common policy internally. Progress in developing the CAP can only attend the convergence of national views on agriculture, a process which has been undeniably slow over the past two decades.

The second major advantage that an individual country has in formulating an agricultural policy is the existence of a unified monetary system and the consequent economic policies which preside over the macroeconomic development of the country. There is only one rate of inflation within a country and one set of exchange rates against other currencies. There is one credit market, one tax structure, and one commercial environment. Agricultural policy objectives and instruments are formed and employed with these specific constraints in mind. A group of countries can, as has been dramatically shown in recent years, exhibit very different economic trends even though they are all at much the same level of development and share the same economic goals. This again casts serious doubt on the very possibility of a common approach to agriculture, or at least on the adoption of an approach which is 'federal' in the sense of being appropriate for the whole of the Community, whilst such divergent trends exist. A common policy, in such circumstances, may again take the form of a tacit agreement among governments not to attempt to force adjustments on particular sectors in view of national circumstance. Or again, it might develop as a mechanism itself for extracting economic gain from partner states to solve domestic problems.

This last aspect, the transfers inherent in policy decisions, emphasises a further distinction between national intergovernmental policies. Where a comprehensive tax system exists in a country, budget transfers are in general scrutinised on their merits in terms of equity and effectiveness of government spending programmes. Among a group of countries, sympathies rarely extend across the frontier. To the home government the foreigner has no vote, and to the domestic taxpayer he has no presumptive right to benefit from the transfer. Scrutiny of the effect of the payment stops at the border. Since agricultural policies are largely implemented through direct and indirect transfers, it follows that the preconditions for a 'federal' policy towards agriculture may be much more stringent than at first sight appear. A common policy in a regional grouping where transfers among partners are resented may once more be constrained, this time by the need to balance benefit flows.

A final difference between national and Community policies is that trade cannot in normal circumstances be hindered among firms and individuals within the nation. Common markets have to struggle to maintain the principle of free internal trade against forces which would divide and discriminate. The establishment of free trade involves a commitment to allow adjustment in resource use and a greater degree of specialisation in production. A 'federal' approach to agricultural policy takes such developments for granted: an intergovernmental policy can resist changes in the location of production and processing, using as an excuse the effect on the balance of trade and the need to maintain incomes and employment. So long as these objectives are the responsibility of national governments, the spatial implications of trade liberalisation will be politically sensitive. A common policy towards agriculture in such a loose form of economic integration will be constrained by such factors.

The task of evaluating the CAP as an approach to the agricultural problem has to take into account the extent to which the original commitment to a reasonably close form of economic and political integration in the Community still obtains. Much of the momentum of the early years of the EEC has been lost, but the objective remains however uncertain the time-scale. In one important sense the CAP went too far and too fast towards the goal of a common policy. The instruments used, as described in the previous section, assumed free internal trade, a common political attitude towards agricultural adjustment and market management, reasonable convergence of economic trends, a common financial structure that would facilitate transfers, an acceptance of such transfers on their merits, and a willingness to live with the consequences of regional specialisation and changes in trade flows. Few of these conditions have prevailed over the past decade. A policy so premised is bound to have suffered. But it is still worth pursuing the question of the appropriateness of the policy *if* all had gone smoothly in the course of integration. For if the answer to that question is in the negative, then even within its terms of reference the CAP is deficient. If the conclusion is favourable, then the blame for the current problems of the CAP lies elsewhere than in its conception and implementation.

Western European agriculture has undergone a remarkably rapid transformation in the past thirty years, adopting modern methods, increasing productivity and shedding labour. It was suggested above that this process goes on in all industrial countries almost regardless of the agricultural policies they pursue. It would be as misleading to credit the common agricultural policy with stimulating this restructuring as it would to accuse such a policy with having inhibited these changes: the link can go both ways. Price stability encourages new investment and expansion of commercial farming, but a steady, if low, income from a small dairy herd may just as easily cause a small farmer to stay in business. Cheap credit and capital grants, similarly, help both the small farmer and the larger concern. In fact there is little evidence that any government policy has materially influenced the adoption of technology and the increase in the average size of holding. All one can safely say is that a part of the substantial transfer from the non-farm sector arising from agricultural policies has undoubtedly been spent on new investment in farming; that another part has been absorbed in the form of improved living standards for low income rural families; and that the rest has gone to increase the affluence of those already well-off. The measure of a policy of agricultural protection lies in the balance of these three transfers in the light of objectives. The evidence suggests two weaknesses: much of the new investment stimulated by price support has not proved a defensible use of Community resources; and the proportion of transfers attracted by larger and more affluent farm businesses relative to the poorer farms is too high to qualify the policy as being efficient in correcting inequities in income distribution. The reason for the first failure is the setting of prices at too high a level for several major commodities, and for the second the excessive, almost obsessive, use of price policy rather than other instruments.

It is probably true that one can employ almost any instrument of agricultural market support so long as the price level implicit in that policy is reasonable. The criterion of reasonableness is itself quite clearly defined, though often difficult to measure. The producer of a commodity should receive a price approximating the value that others put on his output; valuing one's own output is self-delusion. By extension, a country, or the Community, should aim to establish price levels in line with the value that farm commodities have in international exchange—

not because of any particular political philosophy of liberalism but because that represents the only reliable guide to resource use within that country or community. Domestic prices may, for a variety of reasons, differ at any particular time from world market values, which are in any case difficult to derive from the erratic price levels on international trade markets. But any divergence in the long term represents a cost in the form of lower living standards for the country as a whole. The Community has suffered not by isolating farm prices in the short run, but in failing over a period of fifteen years to make any significant attempt to link domestic and world market price trends. The situation is as bad now as it was when the question of price levels was first discussed in the context of the CAP, between 1961 and 1964.

The reason for the poor record in the setting of prices is, as has often been pointed out, that the burden put on the pricing system to act as a form of income guarantee for the farm sector has precluded its effectiveness in directing production and resource use. The reliance on border protection and export subsidies has inhibited consumption by raising domestic price levels. The combination of new investment stimulated by high producer prices and reduced consumption has led to the symptoms of growing budget cost and the regular occurrence of physical surpluses. It has also distributed the burden of farm support in such a way that families spending a high proportion of their income on food will tend to pay more in relative (and sometimes absolute) terms— and all this to favour the farmer with the most to sell. The present price structure in Europe illustrates the problems associated with such an agricultural market policy. Among Member States the highest price levels are to be found in West Germany, where a combination of high non-farm incomes and a relatively poor agricultural structure has led to pressures to maintain prices in the face of a strong currency. The system of 'green' currencies, used to convert commonly agreed prices in units of account into national prices, has allowed the German government to accede to such pressures by maintaining an undervalued 'green' mark. At the other end of the scale, British prices are some 40 per cent below those in Germany. Slower income growth, a greater concern with consumer interests, and the absence of a significant structural problem in farming have led to a lower desired price level. By declining to devalue the 'green' pound the U.K. government has been able to keep prices from rising to the extent that the weakness of sterling might otherwise have suggested. Even in the U.K., prices are maintained generally above international market values by means of import levies. So prices paid to farmers in some parts of the Community, in particular those whose currencies have been strong over the last decade, exceed the value to the Community of their production by a considerable margin. This margin differs from product to product: It is particularly high in the case of dairy products, with cereals, sugar, and beef also supported at a price above their economic value. The spread of margins of protection among countries and products, however understandable in political terms, must in itself cast doubt upon the CAP as a reasonable answer to agricultural problems faced by the Community.

III PROSPECTS FOR THE FUTURE

In line with the general argument of this chapter, there are two ways of approaching the future development of the CAP. The first is to assume that the preconditions for a 'federal' agricultural policy will increasingly be met and that the task is to improve the present arrangements governing the management of agricultural markets and the modernisation of production. The second is to manipulate and adjust the CAP to accord with the constraints placed on a policy where such preconditions do not exist. The latter problem is for politicians in Member States for whom the CAP represents a set of constraints and opportunities facing their own agricultural programmes. The former is more in keeping with the spirit of a book on economic policies of the Community, as well as with the fundamental responsibility of the European Institutions such as the Commission and the Assembly. Member States, coming together in the Council, will ultimately decide which approach is adopted.

The key to a viable policy for Community agriculture lies in the improvement in the quality of information given to farmers with respect to the value to others of their production. The main source of such information is the price that they realise when selling their output. At present such information is quite confusing. Price levels differ widely, as mentioned above, as a result of the re-emergence of national control over 'green' rate changes. Prices for surplus commodities are raised regularly from year to year with only a cursory reference to price moderation and market balance. The Commission in deciding on its annual price proposals examines cost changes in Member States and trends in non-farm incomes. Such a procedure might be reasonably appropriate if starting from a defensible level of prices, but it gives no indication as to the major shifts in such price levels that would correct present market imbalances. Sooner or later such major adjustments will have to be faced. The essence of an information system through prices, rather than by the control of quantities produced, is that expectations on future market conditions are well founded. This may need a new approach to price-fixing. At present the Community decides annually on a set of institutional prices for the coming marketing year, in particular the target prices for regulated commodities and the derived intervention and threshold price levels. The concept of a target price may have to be extended to become a realistic target for farmers to help them to plan investment decisions and farming systems. It would relate to a future price level considered by the Community to be defensible with respect to the better use of resources. Such targets would of course be modified if conditions changed in an unforeseen way—good information must always be up-to-date—but would be less susceptible to short-run considerations of expediency.

The prospect of radical changes in the price structure meets with the immediate problem that, even though high prices are not of great benefit to farmers with low output, price decreases will nevertheless make their plight worse. A number of schemes have been put forward to compensate small farmers for the income loss which would follow a price decrease, and many more would follow if such a course were to be actively contemplated. But income compensation may not in itself be an adequate approach to the problem. It is probable that a full social cost − benefit appraisal of the contribution of the small farm sector in Europe would indicate that their social costs were lower than those of many 'commercially viable' farms and that the benefits of maintaining people in productive activity, as opposed to involuntary retirement or unemployment, may be quite substantial. The solution may not be to soften the blow to small farms by income compensation but to encourage producion in this sector at the expense of the more input-intensive commercial enterprise. The transfer of funds to agriculture would, in this way, be consistent both with equity considerations and with social efficiency.

The market regulations themselves would of course be much more easily administered if the price levels to which they were related were more appropriate. Current concerns with surplus disposal and high budget cost would be of much less political moment and intercountry transfers would be less sensitive. The policy could be sold to consumer interests, at present highly sceptical about the operation of the CAP. It would also transform the relationship with other countries, both developing and developed, who at present see the high levels of protection in agriculture as an unnatural impediment to the normal flow of trade. But some modification of market regulation instruments is desirable. The preoccupation with border controls and the associated export subsidies effectively preclude domestic consumers from benefitting from temporary domestic oversupply, as well as limiting their access to lower-priced world market produce. Such prices have, of course, had a stabilising influence on Community prices as a whole. The question is whether present policies are the only or the best way of achieving stability. There are two aspects to this question. If instability arises from external events then there is some logic in employing the traditional CAP instruments of variable levies and export subsidies in periods of low prices so long as the consumer can be assured that corresponding action to keep down prices will be taken when world market prices are high. This did indeed happen in the market for grains and sugar three years ago, but the procedures were of an *ad hoc* nature. An indication by the Council of Ministers that such action would be a normal response would go some way towards assuring consumers that the policy was not stacked against their interests. Such 'pure' stability policies, however, can only fulfil this condition if the level of prices within Europe is realistic. Alternative policies, such as a system of producer and consumer subsidies or the holding of stocks, also have their place in particular product markets. But they too must be tied to reasonable price levels in order not to involve excessive budget costs. The most direct way of alleviating the impact of fluctuating world prices is to take action, in concert with other trading countries, to improve the stability of the international trading system.

Price fluctuations occur additionally through variations in the balance on domestic markets. The choice of policies to counter these events is somewhat different. The major instrument is already to hand, embodied in the Treaty of Rome as the free movement of goods among Community Members. In spite of the obstacles to intra-EEC trade represented by monetary compensatory amounts, the principle of non-interference by governments in such trade has remained remarkably secure. The consumer has benefited from the broadening of the market and from the security that alternative supply sources bring. The main problems arise when many regions in the Community suffer similar supply problems, such as poor sugar or grain harvests, or when the pig or cattle cycles are coincident in the various Member States. In such circumstances, the existence of a wider international market holds out the best means of providing stability. The Community must be prepared to make more use of the capacity of the world market to provide food products when internal supplies are short as well as looking for overseas markets when excess production exists.

It is in these cases of domestic market instability that the choice of policy instruments becomes more problematic. Of particular importance is the balance between intervention buying and the payment of producer subsidies in the form of variable premiums or deficiency payments. One approach is to say that, once an optimal degree of stock management has been achieved, any further fluctuations in price can then be offset by financial subsidies. The financial interventions, in the form of producer and consumer subsidies, would underpin a market which itself took care of 'normal' variations in production. An alternative is to allow more price variation in normal times, stabilising farm incomes with variable premiums, and to retain support buying as the 'long-stop'. There exists scope for a rational discussion of the modalities of market management using a variety of policy instruments; dogmatic adherence to any particular mechanism is most unlikely to solve the basic problems.

An important, though often neglected, aspect of the development of the CAP has to do with the relationship between Community policy and the global problems of trade, development and poverty. A high level of agricultural production in Europe is sometimes thought to be a buffer against world supply shortages and an implicit contribution to meeting world food needs. It is certainly true that Community food aid policies can help in the alleviation of malnutrition in other countries. It is also arguable that high levels of European production can reduce the foreign exchange impact of price increases. But it is much more difficult to maintain that these by-products of Community surpluses are really the most satisfactory way of relating to overseas food problems. Legitimate food aid schemes must be tied to the requirements of recipient countries, not to the *ad hoc* existence of surpluses. They should, for instance, be increased when supplies are tight. In the same vein, the needs of developing countries are as often as not met more directly by the opening-up of markets, agricultural and manufacturing, to the products of those countries. The Community has made some notable progress in this regard, but the CAP must be made to react positively to such a challenge rather than place obstacles in its way. And with respect to world price stability, the Community must play its part in developing a more secure trading system, including the holding of reserves where appropriate. Again, the CAP is seen by many as inhibiting action on this front. The general Community interest requires that policies relating to food prices be based on a broad acceptance of these responsibilities. The prime concern throughout the Community should be to establish the basis whereby all the interested parties in the food system, the grower, the processor, the distributor, and the consumer can have confidence that the policies are both equitable and viable. Such confidence can only come if the price levels set are reasonable and credible, and if the CAP itself is made more consistent with overseas responsibilities. The CAP was once a strong force for integration within Europe: it can become so again if present problems are tackled with foresight and imagination.

2 European industrial policies and competition

ALEXIS P. JACQUEMIN

BACKGROUND

It is a well-known fact that the creation of the Common Market and the accompanying removal of the diverse obstacles to competition—whether they were tariffs, import quotas, or the right of establishment—have produced a profound change in European states. These countries have been confronted with a mass of liberalising forces which were unknown since the moves towards free trade of the years 1860–70. For instance, by 1969, intra–EC exports had increased to 48 per cent of the members' total exports, compared to 32 per cent in 1958, while exports by 'the Six' to non-EC nations rose by a multiple of 2.5.

New attitudes have appeared which favour changes in the structures of economic sectors and businesses, the launching of new industrial initiatives and the acceptance of an automatic and continuous process of adjustment to changing national and international market conditions, on the demand side and on the supply side. This acceptance was facilitated both by the economic situation and by the policies of the European Authorities. On the one hand, the high levels of demand and the rates of growth of the European economies reduced the social costs of this process of adjustment. On the other hand, European competition policy, based on Article 85 of the Treaty of Rome, which has effectively attacked cartel agreements (intended to restore the old protective walls of national markets), has consequently sustained the dynamism of an enlarged unified market against private restrictive practices.

Nevertheless, this new climate has shown itself to be delicate, and it has been shaken by the economic crisis and its attendant social consequences.

In the year 1975 there was a reduction of 2.5 per cent in the EEC gross

TABLE 2.1   General indices of industrial production
(1970 = 100)

	1968	1969	1971	1972	1973	1974	1975	1976
Netherlands	82	91	106	111	118	122	116	125
Ireland	89	95	104	108	119	122	115	126
France	85	94	106	112	119	123	114	124
Denmark	87	97	101	107	111	110	106	117
W. Germany	84	94	102	106	114	112	105	113
Italy	91	94	100	104	114	119	108	121
Belgium	88	97	102	109	116	121	109	119
U.K.	96	99	100	102	111	108	103	104
Luxembourg	88	100	99	103	115	119	93	99
EEC 9	87	95	102	107	115	115	108	115
U.S.A.	99	104	100	108	118	117	107	−

Source: Eurostat, *Basic Statistics*.

national product (expressed in real terms). This decrease also appears in the indices of industrial production: Table 2.1 shows that, for the nine EEC countries, the index has declined from 115 in 1974 to 108 in 1975, the level of 1973 being caught up only in 1976. Examination of the average annual rates of growth (1973–6) for individual industries, although revealing wide divergences between sectors, suggests that in almost all countries (except Italy), textile industry and clothing, oil refining, manufacture of leather and leather products, manufacture of paper and paper products, printing, publishing and allied industries, have all sharply declined (Table 2.2).

Such an evolution is linked with various factors whose respective influence is hard to disentangle. A first aspect is expressed by computing the changes in labour cost and productivity for the Member States.[1] Table 2.3 shows that there has been an important increase of labour-productivity for all the countries considered, with a slow-down in 1974–5; the lowest rates are those of Italy (5.2 per cent from 1966 to 1976) and the United Kingdom (3.9 per cent from 1966 to 1976). But on the other hand, the growth of labour cost has been proportionally more important, the highest growth occurring in 1974–5, with Italy recording an increase of 22.9 per cent. It is therefore not surprising that unit labour cost has risen sharply in these countries.

A comparison between the evolution of the 'average' unit labour cost

TABLE 2.2 Average annual rate of growth of manufacturing industries (1973–6)

	Nether-lands	Italy	France	Ireland	West Germany	Belgium	U.K.	Luxem-bourg	EEC 9
Beverages	7.0	-0.8	—	0.4	1.8	1.2	3.1	2.7	—
Tobacco	-0.8	2.2	5.6	—	2.1	0.6	-1.6	(1)	1.2
Textiles	-6.4	2.5	-1.9	1.9	0.1	-2.3	-3.8	—	-0.6
Clothing	-10.3	4.6	—	—	-1.7	0.3	-1.1	-8.4	-0.6
Leather	-10.9	5.2	-1.7	-2.8	0.1	-2.9	-0.8	—	0.8
Wood and wooden furniture	—	4.5	—	—	-0.6	4.7	-5.1	-0.7	—
Paper and paper products	-1.1	-0.2	-0.8	-8.2	-0.3	-0.05	-5.3	—	-1.2
Printing	-0.07	0.3	-1.7	—	-1.4	—	-3.6	-1.5	-1.9
Manufacture of rubber	0.2	1.4	0.7	—	-0.3	7.4	0.2	1.8	0.2
Chemicals	3.8	4.3	1.6	10.6	2.1	0	2.2	1.1	2.2
Oil refining	-2.3	-5.2	-2.7	—	-2.9	-9.8	-4.2	—	-3.3
Non-metallic	0.4	1.3	1.0	—	-2.1	-0.6	-3.8	-1.6	-1.0
Mineral products	—	4.3	0.3	—	-1.9	5.7	-4.3	5.8	0.7
Non-ferrous metal	—	—	—	—	-1.8	6.2	-3.1	—	—
Electrical and electronic machinery	2.7	1.5	6.5	—	0.8	3.0	-4.5	—	1.2
Non-electrical machinery	2.0	3.5	8.6	-3.1	-1.3	4.1	-1.6	—	2.4
Transport equipment	-1.4	-0.03	-0.2	-10.3	1.7	5.0	-3.0	—	-1.1

Source: Eurostat, Basic Statistics

TABLE 2.3   Labour cost and productivity changes in the manufacturing sector
(*average annual changes, %*)

	Labour cost				Productivity			
	1966–76	*1970–3*	*1974–5*	*1976*	*1966–76*	*1970–3*	*1974–5*	*1976*
Belgium	12.8	13.8	21.3	14.5	5.8	6.1	3.6	9.5
West Germany	8.8	11.1	9.9	6.7	5.0	5.0	3.5	7.9
France	11.1	11.3	18.4	14.1	5.4	6.5	−1.1	9.4
Netherlands	13.3	14.5	16.5	10.4	7.1	7.5	3.1	10.4
Italy	13.8	18.6	23.4	22.8	5.2	6.7	0.1	6.3
U.K.	10.7	9.8	21.7	16.7	4.0	4.2	−1.1	3.2
United States	6.4	6.2	8.7	8.0	2.8	4.0	2.3	4.6
Japan	15.1	17.4	20.3	11.3	9.5	10.3	0.6	11.7

Source: I.R.E.S., Universite de Louvain, 1977.

for all OECD countries and the evolution of this index for the main European countries also indicates that the 'competitiveness' of the Member States is dying down: unit labour cost in European countries increased much more quickly, the most resistant being West Germany, Belgium and the Netherlands.[2] But as these last countries have experienced an appreciation of their currency, the inverse being true for Italy and the United Kingdom, a comparison taking into account the role of the effective exchange rates shows a convergent movement.

Secondly, the energy crisis and the increased prices of crude oil, at the end of 1973, greatly affected production costs and underlined European dependence on imported energy (around 60 per cent in 1975). More generally, there is the problem of the change in relative prices of primary commodities *vis-à-vis* manufactured goods: the prices of natural resources tend to increase relative to the prices of manufactured goods, creating difficulties for the balance of payments of European countries.

Thirdly, European domestic demand, even for consumer durable goods, has stagnated, while new productive capacity in developing countries is appearing and competition from the United States and Japan[3] is increasing. The existence of a structural demand gap for private goods in the European economies may not be excluded in the future, a partial compensation coming from public expenditure. Hence a high growth rate of demand would be expected, not from the old industrialised countries, but from the Third World countries: in 1976, 36 per cent of European exports were directed towards these countries and this figure is expected to grow by 10 per cent in 1978, as compared with 7 per cent in the case of exports to the other industrialised countries.

Finally, the development of the various European sectors shows a general pattern whose implications are far from being evident for the future of the Community: the employment in industry is steadily decreasing in relative terms.[4] This phenomenon of *de-industrialisation* is also visible in the gross domestic product by sector (see Table 2.4), but to a lesser extent because of productivity growth.

Hence, after the shift from agriculture to industry, there is a shift from industry to the service/government sector. Such evidence could be regarded as showing a long-run structural feature of advanced industrial countries reaching a certain level of 'industrial maturity', and as implying necessary readjustments in the international context as well as in the domestic economies. It would then be necessary to wonder what the growth potential of these economies will be, given the dynamic role of the manufacturing sector compared with the service sector; what the effects will be on the balance of payments of these nations which are becoming less able to sell enough of their products abroad to pay for their import requirements; and what the consequences will be for safeguarding a socially acceptable level of employment.[5]

Today, the reactions of the various economic agents are still uncertain.

At the level of *national governments*, one notes an increasing degree of interference in national productive activity and in international trade which have led to a renaissance of diverse forms of protectionism.

At the level of *national enterprises*, oligopolistic structures become evident through the increase in industrial concentration.[6] These structures gradually become embedded in national and international markets just as the more traditional types of international cartels tend to lose their efficiency. Also, in order to reduce the uncertainty of the market, there is an increase in collusion between these large businesses and the public authorities. This quest for short-term security is evident from the multitude of planning agreements between state and private enterprises, and assistance for sectors and companies in difficulties which cannot be expected to cope with national, Community and international competition.

At the level of *multinational enterprises*, there is the danger of a new generation of European oligopolistic multinationals which are neither responsive to national governments nor to the EEC institutions. In the face of the crisis, these multinationals show themselves to be capable of reducing the instability of their activities—but at the price of destabilising their local environment by transferring risks to the local markets where they are operating.[7]

TABLE 2.4 Gross domestic product by sector

		Denmark	W. Germany	France	Ireland	Italy	Netherlands	Belgium	Luxembourg	U.K.
Agriculture, etc.	1973	7.7	2.8	7.4	16.5	8.5	6.0	3.7	4.0	2.6
	1974	7.9	2.7	5.7	14.0	8.2	4.8	2.8	3.3	2.7
	1975	7.1	2.7	5.1	–	8.5	5.2	2.8	3.5	2.5
Industry (including building)	1973	36.7	52.6	41.9	28.1	41.5	40.4	40.7	52.2	38.2
	1974	33.3	51.5	37.3	29.7	42.7	41.1	41.3	57.8	37.6
	1975	34.8	49.1	37.1	–	41.0	39.0	39.6	48.9	36.6
Services	1973	55.6	44.6	50.7	55.4	50.0	53.6	56.6	43.8	59.2
	1974	55.8	45.8	56.9	56.3	49.1	54.1	55.9	38.9	59.7
	1975	55.1	48.2	57.8	–	0.5	55.8	58.6	47.6	61.0

Source: Bulletin Mensuel des Statistiques des Nations Unies, Oct. 1977; and Etudes Economiques: OCDE, June 1977.

Thus today there is a shifting balance between contradictory tendencies—especially between deliberate control of European economies on the one hand, and the maintenance of competition as the principle motor of economic activity on the other.

In effect, the two movements may be observed. On the one hand, there is in many circles a desire to maintain the decentralised forces of a competitive economic system which assure a constant adaptation to changes in needs, techniques and general economic conditions and which assure the maintenance of risk-taking and industrial dynamism. On the other hand, there is a growing desire—equally among national governments, private businesses and workers—to avoid the ups-and-downs of economic activity and to reduce uncertainty through direct collaboration between the private and public sectors.

It would seem to be unrealistic to expect a clear choice to be made between these contradictory tendencies during the coming years. A realistic attitude towards European industry should rather move in the following ways. One would be to seek means of limiting the number of sectors in which competition is obstructed; equally, the duration of such obstruction should be reduced. The other way would be to coordinate, at the level of the Community—for those sectors where for economic or social reasons such obstruction is inevitable—national measures of intervention and planning agreements.

Thus it is with the preceding considerations in mind that we shall examine successively the main types of industrial policy and their limits (Section I), the evolution which may be observed in European industrial policy (Section II) and, finally, some perspectives for the future (Section III).

I MARKET AND DIRECTIVE INDUSTRIAL POLICIES

The main characteristics of an industrial policy is that it has to specify and solve the problems of structural change in the economy. Its task is to create optimum conditions for the necessary structural transformations to be carried out. The need for transformation arises from changes occuring in the process of industrial development: technological changes, shifts in demand, maturing and declining industries, and so on. The required adaptations take time, so that industrial policy is essentially long-term. Beyond this background, there are divergent views whether they concern aims or the means used.

Concerning aims, some would see them as the instruments intended to allow competition to function completely efficiently. According to L. Stoleru, industrial policy may be defined as being 'a policy of coordinating the effects of the public authorities in the direction of maximising the virtues of a competitive economy'.[8] Similarly, Toulemon and Flory assume that with regard to industrial policy, the role of the public authorities is to establish 'the framework within which the activities of producers and the choice of consumers are facilitated'.[9]

Others, on the contrary, believe that industrial policy should have a more voluntarist character. It would thus be seen as being a number of means used by the public authorities to channel industrial activity in the framework of a general economic programme towards a number of pre-established objectives.[10]

The distinction which has just been mentioned regarding the aims could be extended to the means as well.

I. 1 COMPETITION-ORIENTATED INDUSTRIAL POLICY

I. 1.1 If we accept the concept whereby industrial policy is intended to free the potentialities of the decentralised economy, its role can be seen as creating an environment that facilitates the use of the best of the forces of competition. Equally, a related automatic and continuous process of industrial adjustment will be facilitated.

Concerning industrial concentration, this competition policy favour industrial regroupings or cooperation between small and average-sized enterprises, in such a way that they grow to the optimum size for being effective partners in the market.

Regarding barriers to entry into a sector, this policy removes artificial obstacles such as differences of technical norms, discriminating fiscal charges, public markets divided into branches, and conditions of unequal financing. Also, concerning the differentiation of products, efforts should be made to improve information and to protect the consumer.

In general, it is important to reinforce the active industrialist who alone can give life to a competitive enterprise if the economic and social climate allows it. Such a system presupposes an infrastructure of quality, a professionally adapted manual labour force, accessibility of capital and credit, and a fiscal system which is not opposed to economic rationality.

This tendency, which is opposed to dirigism, does not on the contrary exclude some state action and the use of strategy on the part of the enterprises. It does not refuse the requirements of the competitive system, even if it is admitted that they must sometimes be moderated. Thus, regarding French industrial policy, H. de L'Estoile[11] speaks of a 'free muscled exchange'. But with certain reservations, industrial policy that we shall call a 'market' one rests soundly on the constraints of the competitive process. Private enterprises, by their investment and production decisions, remain the main protagonists in industrial evolution. In turn, public authorities facilitate efficient decisions and ensure an environment propitious to healthy functioning of the decentralised system.

I. 1.2 The limits of this policy are numerous and it is enough to distinguish between two types, one at the domestic level, the other at the foreign level.

At the domestic level, the market economy is beset with important failures that explain the desire for a more interventionist industrial policy. Let us enumerate the principal failures:

The regional imbalances and differences in development are less and less accepted, but could be accentuated by the free circulation of people, assets and capital. As shown by J. Meade,[12] if different citizens start with different endowments of factors of production, then the forces of competition can lead to greater inequalities in the absence of any governmental intervention to make the gainers compensate the losers.

The social costs, combined with the mobility of resources and especially of employment, are often considered to be intolerable to such a degree that only the mediation of the State is capable of safeguarding a minimum of organised institutionalised mobility.

The responsibility for the degradation of the environment is not spontaneously accepted by industry, but represents an increasing cost for society.

Linked with the preceding phenomenon, the assets and services of the community that concern urban development, green spaces, or security, are not taken into account by the market economy.

The dynamics of the system presuppose a permanent renewal of industrial services, which implies an elastic supply of business talent, when in effect at the moment one has the impression that business initiative is on the decline. Thus, firms die and are not replaced,[13] and this situation could threaten the existence of competitive self-regulation. One of the essential causes of this temporary failure is the particularly high risk of entering a market as a result of the multiple uncertainties that affect the capital and money markets, and those for raw materials, and labour.

The new technological industries are characterised by a high degree of research; increasing returns of scale and other considerations encourage a regrouping and concentration of means that threaten the competitive system.

All these aspects are reasons why the price system may fail to emit correct signals on economic scarcity and required industrial adaptation, such failures being magnified in an inflationary context.[14] Then, resource allocation processes, to be efficiently carried out, must be based upon non-price signals, alternative market mechanisms, or non-market institutions replacing the market.

Even if correct signals are emitted, economic agents could not react to them hoping to gain security in the short run. This sluggishness of reaction could be worsened by a decrease of the supply elasticity of entrepreneurial talent and of its transferability, as previously mentioned.

At the foreign level, the limits of the international division of labour present a threat. This division is confronted with the advantages of a minimum level of national autonomy below which national security would be threatened. The oil crisis, the tendency of the countries producing raw materials to reduce their supply and to transform the materials at home, the hazy character of the industrial list of initial and anticipated comparative advantages, the necessary structural adjustments and the transformation of entire sectors—all these make less realistic, at least at the socio-political level, a system that would leave to market forces the solution of such problems. Thus the interplay of these forces is henceforth insufficient to achieve the objectives of industrial development in an acceptable period of time or without intolerable social tensions.

More specifically, with regard to the traditional aim of free exchange that consists of specialisation in order to get the most out of trade and comparative advantages, two other goals become obvious: first, a political objective of independence, which aims at avoiding the inconveniences of a loss of autonomy of action as a result of being too dependent on foreign supply and demand; second, a social objective of security, that seeks to avoid the influence of specialisation bringing unemployment, worsening working conditions, and causing employment upheavals through economic changes (implying geographical and sectoral migration).

In the light of these multiple criteria and in a dynamic perspective, the acceptance of the model of free exchange and of the Pareto-optimality character of its implications is much less evident. As long as there exists no mechanism to ensure that world cooperation—leading to a maximisation of the common surplus—is possible and would be stable, in as far as this solution also gives more to certain partners and is not reinforced by systems of international redistribution of profits (side-payments) affecting transfer from the more favoured to the less favoured, it is understandable that States hesitate to adopt strategies of specialisation leading to the maximum degree of international openness. They could be tempted to adopt individual policies of the 'minimax' type—at the risk of these latter leading to results which could be fatal for the collective equilibrium.[15]

I. 2 DIRECTIVE INDUSTRIAL POLICY

I. 2.1 It is clear that there exists a place nowadays for an industrial policy of intervention which does not restrict itself to giving to the market economy its full effectiveness, but which sets a certain number of priority objectives for the industrial activity in the private and public sectors.

The means used to achieve this are many and can be coercive in nature or able to stimulate changes. In the first case, preference is given to systems of quotas, to rationing, or to imposed prices. In the second case, one attempts to make profitable the adoption by the economic agents concerned of the policies desired by the public authorities. Thus one uses subsidies, allowances, or relief from taxation. In particular, if the government is more neutral toward risk than the private investor, it subsidises the projects in order to further the level of investment. Such neutrality could be justified as long as the total cost of risk-bearing of an independent project is made negligible by the spreading of the risk over the entire population of taxpayers. It is here also that the various forms of contracts for restructuring and encouraging business management come in, ensuring that, in exchange for the subsidies transferred by the public authorities, the enterprises agree to contribute to the achievement of the sectoral, technological and regional objectives of the Plan. For example, the enterprise has to realise investments enabling it to increase its production capacity or to maintain the level of employment; and, in exchange, it benefits from budgetary credits; or an organ of the State (Société Nationale d'Investissement in Belgium, National Enterprise Board in Great Britain, Institut de Developpement Industriel in France, GEPI, IRI and ENI in Italy. . . .) will take a direct participation in the firm.

This brings us to a second level: the State, whether in collaboration with the private sector or alone, takes on productive activities, through the medium of its public enterprises or mixed enterprises; it can thus influence industrial structures directly. Apart from the sectors where the competition of the private sector is no longer applicable because the increase in production leads to increasing returns and subsequently to the formation of a monopoly, its field of action can extend to the production of strategic goods and services whose importance for the national economy is such that it cannot remain in the hands of the private sector (money, credits, energy). Besides, the sectors normally reserved for private enterprise can equally become a potential field for State participation to assure a better sectoral division of investment. In particular, this concerns investments of which the economic risk is too big for the private sector alone, or, even more, investments that have great technical importance for the whole economy (pace-making sectors).

With this in view, most West European governments have introduced new public enterprises since the late 1960s which are devoted to the management of industry. In general, these second-generation public enterprises contrast with earlier nationalisations in that governments consciously sought participation in viable and competitive rather than in failing concerns.[16]

I. 2.2 But the voluntarist industrial policy presents, in its turn, certain limits which can be summed up by the following dilemma: should one submit to the demands of efficiency generally linked with international conditions of competition and risk losing the means of control linked with the responsibility of public interest; or should one fix public objectives with the danger of misguided actions or the creation of big 'white elephants'?

More precisely, the choices for industrial redevelopment are not self-evident and—apart from some general themes such as the move towards products of great value-added, depending on an advanced technology and incorporating little energy—exact criteria are lacking.

As Malinvaud stated during the Paris colloquium on industrial redevelopment, 'You cannot expect, in any particular case, that economic studies will give incontestable indications as to which branches should be developed.'[17]

Difficulties can also arise at the level of large-scale projects. Thus, at all times, the European public authorities have encouraged large enterprises as a means of responding to the challenge of America or even of Japan. It is only recently that scepticism has appeared on the subject of the link between the size of firms and the quality of their performance.

Indeed, as far as the effects of large European size is concerned, no evidence of increasing profit, faster growth, or more intensive research activities, can be found to support the 'size mystique' that has prevailed in Europe.[18]

Equally, public authorities are too often confined to the role of giving social assistance to enterprises in difficulty. An obvious case is the conflict that arose in 1967 in Belgium between the State on the one side and the National Association of Industrial Credit (SNCI) on the other. This organisation wished, according to its initial responsibility, to give help to new industrial initiatives; instead of which it was forced to support condemned enterprises. Finally the government forced on the SNCI the conclusion of a convention (9 May 1968) allowing the granting of credits to enterprises in difficulty.

Finally, public industrial initiative can become a kind of corporate system, with nomination of employees for political reasons, lacking a sense of responsibility and initiative, and not subject to the discipline of competition and of profitability, (public enterprises which are badly managed do not usually disappear by way of the Bankruptcy Courts).

However, these reservations do not remove the need to elaborate a new industrial policy by which public and private initiatives meet and collaborate, with the aim of making socially acceptable the inevitable industrial changes.

II EVOLUTION OF EUROPEAN INDUSTRIAL POLICY

Most of the general problems which have just been mentioned exist at the European level, and certain aspects, such as those relative to pace-making sectors, are at first sight more obvious in the framework of the Community. The Commission of the EEC stated in its ninth general report: 'as regards industrial policy we must state that the list of decisions taken at Community level during the year 1975 is still as small as before, in spite of the development of an economic situation which would seem logically to call for the reinforcement of European cooperation.'

In this section, we shall briefly describe the origins of the European Industrial Policy and the passage of a 'European Industrial Market Policy' to a 'European Industrial Policy of Intervention'.

II. 1 While the Treaty of Rome explicitly prescribes the situation relative to common policies in the case of agriculture, competition, employment, commerce, transport, and fiscal harmonisation, there is no reference to industrial policy. However, the two sectoral treaties of CECA and Euratom indicate, without expressly stating it, the desire to create an industrial policy. In entrusting to the High Authority powers of supranational management, the Member States have permitted creation of a common strategy in the basic fields which, during the 1950s, meant coal and steel.

Thus, the coal crisis which arose in 1958 was solved by a systematic conversion plan which avoided the principal social tensions that would no doubt have been produced if matters had been left to market forces. Policy for the steel industry had the objective of reducing the economic imbalance between supply and demand, encouraging the reconstruction and modernisation of enterprises, as well as promoting agreements for self-limitation between European, American and Japanese producers. But some observers could also argue that such cooperation has reduced pressures for rationalisation and specialisation of these activities, making the present crisis worse.

The Treaty instituting the European Atomic Energy Community was above all intended to develop research and encourage industrial initiative in the nuclear field. According to Article 4, 'the Commission has the responsibility of promoting and facilitating nuclear research in the Member States and of complementing them by research and training programmes undertaken by the Community'. This second Industrial Treaty has not, however, had the same success as the previous one. It was concerned with the promotion of a common programme, either by direct action such as research undertaken in the 'Common Research Centre' (of which the institutions are in Ispra, Mol, Karlsruhe and Petten), or by indirect action in the form of contracts specially aimed at promoting coordination between research centres and national programmes. In fact, these efforts have not really succeeded. On the one hand, the Member States have, for the greater part, preferred to pursue a national policy and to maintain market divisions, resulting in the multiplication of non-coordinated and even competitive programmes. On the other hand, the common programme itself has not given satisfactory results: most of the research has remained at a pre-industrial stage and the actual needs of industry have had to be supplied by American technology, without even attaining a comparable level of efficiency. Besides, the Community always depends upon foreign sources for its supply of enriched uranium. The Commission in its report

of 1968 was forced to conclude: 'The Treaty which created the European
Community of Atomic Energy aimed at creating conditions favourable
to the development of a powerful nuclear industry. After ten years, we
must admit that it has only partially attained this objective.'

In the more general framework of the EEC, the first manifestations of
an industrial policy go back to 1964, when the idea of 'a medium-term
economic programme' was introduced. Since the publication of a
second programme, prepared in 1965, and covering the period 1968–70,
the Commission has insisted on the necessity of public intervention to
improve the industrial structures of the Community and has set up a
Directorate for Industrial Policy which is responsible for the preparation of orientations for the common industrial policy and the coordination of the intervention of the Member States. Besides this, sectoral
cooperation with the industrialists, trade unions, and national experts
are occasionally organised in various sectors, such as aeronautics,
shipbuilding, data-processing, paper, and textiles.

About 1970 the necessity of defining a general industrial policy was
clearly and publicly asserted: such is the aim of the Memorandum of the
Commission to the Council, entitled *The Industrial Policy of the
Community*, EEC Commission, Brussels, 1970. As the authors stated:

> Twelve years after its foundation, whilst the period of transition that
> led to the liberalisation of the common market of goods has just been
> completed, the Community approaches a new phase of its con-
> struction. The preparation of a common policy for industrial
> development favouring the constitution of what one could call a
> European industrial framework becomes indispensable to assure at
> the same time the irreversible bases for the economic, and soon the
> political, unity of Western Europe, the pursuance of economic
> expansion, and a reasonable degree of technological autonomy as
> regards its main external partners (p. 7).

But straight away the authors came up against the actual definition of
this policy. They chose a particularly non-interventionist approach: 'to
allow industry to derive the maximum advantages from the existence
and size of the 'Common Market' (p. 9). The ways they hoped to
establish this industrial policy included the following:

> The achievement of a unified market by the elimination of technical
> obstacles and the opening-up of the public sectors and the abolition of
> fiscal frontiers.

The unification of the judicial, fiscal and financial laws.

The restructuring of enterprises through the elimination of the obstacles to the formation of trans-national European enterprises, using to this end public credits for industrial development in the sectors of advanced technology.

The organisation of changes and adaptation by facilitating changing jobs, industrial exploitation of innovation, improvement in the management of enterprises, and in the recruitment of their managers and directors.

The extension of Community solidarity in economic relations with third parties, in particular, by way of the common commercial policy.

In spite of its qualities, the Memorandum gives an impression of dissatisfaction. There is a clear constrast between the wealth of information that it sheds on the situation of the Community's industry and the lack of clarity about the policies proposed. The absence of a precise political engagement did not change the fact that one had to wait until the Declaration of Paris in October 1972 for the governments to express their support for this industrial and technological policy.

Apart from the desire to coordinate policies at the Community level and to have a precise timetable and finance settled before 1 January 1974, this declaration was once again expressed in rather general terms. One may be surprised that it had taken so long to arrive at this declaration of principle. Diverse factors delayed the Community's progress in this field.[19] These may be defined as follows:

(a) The quarrel concerning the enlargement of the Community blocked all new developments not originally foreseen, in the meantime, and the negotiations of adherence received priority.

(b) Certain initiatives, especially French ones, have taken intergovernmental scientific and technical cooperation agreements outside the Community sphere (for example, Concorde and the Airbus).

(c) The traditional conflict between the States more attached to liberalism, such as Germany, and those which practise a more interventionist policy, such as France or Italy, has been complicated by a conflict in the attitude towards the United States. In this respect, France is in fact more anxious to affirm the European autonomy *vis-à-vis* the United States than are Germany, Italy or the Benelux.

(d) The refusal to make a broad approach and the insistence on the principle of the '*juste retour*' restrict progress.

(e) Finally, a common industrial policy concerning pace-making industries such as aeronautics, computers or electronics, can only be realised in so far as the European Community takes on the political dimension that it still lacks at the present time.

Despite all these considerations, on the basis of the Declaration of Paris the Commission produced, as from May 1973, the 'programme for industrial and technological policy', also called the Spinelli Report. A list of decisions of the Council and of Member States was proposed, the adoption of which the Commission deemed necessary, with a timetable lasting until 1977.

If all the propositions are not yet realised, numerous aspects have been touched upon:

(1) Regarding the elimination of technical obstacles to trade various proposals or directives aim at the harmonisation of national regulations. This harmonisation is not only designed to remove obstacles to trade inside the Community; it should also allow the achievement of qualitative objectives important in the fields of public health and for the protection of the environment. The chemical and pharmaceutical sectors are already the object of diverse measures to assure the opening-up of the market.

(2) The opening-up of national markets for purchasing by public and semi-public sectors in the Community implies that any 'preference' or 'reservation' for national production, or any exclusion of deliveries of imported products from other Member States, should be permanently forbidden. One of the propositions of the directives aims, in particular, at the cooridination of procedures concerning public tenders. This contains rules governing publicity, going as far as the publication of notification of contracts for tenders in the Official Journal of the Community. The directive concerning public works contracts has already imposed this obligation (26 July 1971).

(3) The encouragement of trans-national European enterprises is desirable and can reinforce competition. 'Concentration in the national sphere leads to competition between firms that are supported in diverse ways by their governments and that do not often come to reach the threshold of profitability. The trans-national groupings offer, on the contrary, the possibility of combining effective competition and economies of scale.' It is in this perspective that the directives concerning the harmonisation of company law should be seen (in particular that of the limited liability company, the SPRL, the cooperative society, the private company groups of companies, and

that concerning consolidated balances), and also the directives aiming to create new juridical forms, such as the European company, the European group for cooperation, and the common enterprise, hitherto reserved exclusively for nuclear field. A new directive is likewise awaited concerning the participation of workers in their enterprises. The same applies to the directives relating to industrial property, fiscal law, and capital markets.

(4) Regarding small and medium-sized enterprises, there exist 'Community development contracts designed to support innovations developed through trans-national cooperation, as well as an 'Office for Mergers between Enterprises'. This office furnishes enterprises with information and advice, informs the Community about the obstacles of a general nature that the enterprises meet in their attempts to cooperate or to merge together, and seeks partners for the enteprises of different nationalities wishing to engage in cooperation with a view to improving their competitiveness and facilitating their adaptation to the enlarged market. It can also cover cooperation agreements as well as financial integration (common branch offices, participation, merger or absorption). In its report of 23 December 1975, the Commission showed that, from May 1973 up to October 1975, there had been 2,259 requests for information, 327 requests for merger and 2,490 responses by interested enterprises. The activity of the Office resulted in the proposal of a plausible partner in two cases out of three and the contacts led to an agreement in one case in five. The most active sectors were chemicals, the metal industry, mechanical construction, the food industry and services.

(5) Concerning the sectors confronted with special problems, the Commission proposes to by-pass the distinction dividing sectors of advanced technology and sectors in the process of change or in trouble. The most serious actual problem concerns a group of sectors, namely those of the heavy investment equipment. It aims at allowing the Community to gauge, in time, the risks it runs in the field of long-term supplies of raw materials, energy and key products. The Commission has decided to undertake a systematic study of primary resources that will be necessary to the Community in the future.

(6) Finally, the necessity of coherence of industrial policy with the other objectives of the Community, in the social, regional and commercial fields is stressed, without making any concrete propositions, as such, with the exception of the work of the Social Fund and of the European Regional Fund. Those play only a marginal role, however.

In his programme speech of 8 February 1977, the President of the Commission particularly insisted on the key problem of the different stages of evolution of the economies and on the necessity of more varied and flexible means than those of the present Funds in order to reduce these divergences.[20]

II. 2 On examination of the principal aspects of the European industrial policy, it seems clear that, despite the perspective which has guided those responsible, it concerns essentially what we have called a 'competition-orientated' industrial policy. By contrast with the experiences of the CECA, and of Euratom, the means used consist of those designed to assure an integrated market. Thus one of the most recent achievements, the Office for Mergers of Enterprises, strives above all to enable small and medium-sized enterprises to adapt themselves more easily to the enlarged market.

On the contrary, M. Marjolin aims, as a start, to complete the mechanisms of the market by means of a European medium-term economic programme susceptible of controlling and influencing industrial development. But such an orientation presupposes a solid consensus of European policy, a consensus relying on the rationalisation and the reconversion of sectors in decline, as well as on the common promotion of pace-making sectors.

In reality, it has not really been possible to coordinate aid given by States to sectors in trouble. Within the context of the crisis, the national public authorities have not waited for the recommendations of Brussels to coordinate their aid, running the risk of simply preserving an obsolete industrial structure or transferring difficulties from one Member State to another. It is this which the successive reports of the Commission about the policy of competition make evident. In the 6th Report[21] one can read a long description of various aid given by States to their enterprises and the difficulty the Commission has in controlling them against a background of economic recession. The question is the more delicate since the so-called 'opaque' aids (as compared with 'transparent' ones) tend to multiply. These opaque aids that can not be expressed as a percentage of investment (fiscal aids, help for creation of new employment, and for the better functioning of enterprises) represent nearly 50 per cent of the budget devoted to regional policy by the whole of the Member States

Besides, as we have seen, European initiatives in the sectors of advanced technology have been swept away by national actions, unilateral or bilateral; for example, in the electronics industry (with the disappearance of UNIDATA), or in aeronautics as characterised by the achievements of certain countries. The result is the multiplication of non-coordinated, even competitive, programmes. However, even here, the necessity of a common industrial policy is self-evident in so far as these fundamental sectors imply enormous expenses for research and development before becoming profitable, because they must realise economies of scale which only the integrated market permits them to obtain.

In the General Report of the Commission[22] for the year 1976 may be seen the desire for a move from a competitive-orientated industrial policy to more interventionist initiatives. The Commission affirms there that in the actual economic circumstances the action of the Community regarding industrial development could not limit itself to a pure and simple application of the rules of the Treaty of the EEC. It had also to begin to orientate, coordinate and eventually to complete the measures that Member States judged indispensable at national level (p. 210). Actions have already been undertaken in the fields of the steel and computer industries, aeronautics, electronic components and telecommunications.

The two principal lines followed are:

(1) to try to arrive at a common strategy in the pace-making sectors, for which the intervention of States is often crucial;

(2) to coordinate the policies of the Member States in the sectors in difficulties, to prevent them interfering or cancelling reciprocally.[23]

A supplementary stage was reached in the final text of the proposed Fourth Medium-Term Economic Policy Programme.[24] One can read there that enterprises should have at their disposal more abundant information concerning current developments. This improved 'transparency' of structural changes will encourage a more searching attitude among the managers of enterprises. For that purpose it would be suitable to bring together and to study at Community level the forecasts available at national level concerning the sectoral evolution (p. 62). And at Point 9 of the project, it is added that 'In order to improve the transparency in certain capital-intensive industrial sectors where there exist risks of overcapacity, the Commission at regular intervals requires a notification concerning investment projects' (p. 7). Had this proposition of a preliminary notification of investment projects been accepted, it would have been an important step in the direction of concerted industrial policy. But at the level of the Council of Ministers it ran into strong opposition, emanating mainly from Germany. The case was the more difficult to defend as the steel industry was then in the middle of a crisis. In the decision of the Council of 14 March 1974, laying down the fourth programme, the paragraph in question has been replaced by the following text (point 8): 'The Commission will encourage the establishment, at national level, of sectoral analyses that will be examined together by the Member States at Community level. On this occasion, it will be assessed to what degree these analyses may lead to Community decisions.[25]

Today, the Director of the Directorate for Industrial Policy, E. Davignon, is trying to find a compromise between a 'Directive Industrial Policy' and a 'Competition-orientated Industrial Policy',[26] but in the present European situation such a compromise probably will be very unstable.

III GENERAL PERSPECTIVES

III. 1 Until the post-energy crisis and subsequent economic recession, one can say that the European industrial policy, used in the context of 'neo-liberalism', tried to play the role of a useful complement *vis-à-vis* the policy of competition in favouring the realisation of a Common Market between Member States. The sought-after industrial structure has encouraged a better internal productivity and more effective international competition. In most cases, the action of the Commission has, since then, been 'counter-interventionist', that is to say, it has avoided excessive intervention in the affairs of the Member States.[27]

III. 2 Diverse phenomena, catalysed by the crises and mentioned in the introduction, have brought this perspective into question and have led to the renewal of the call for a more voluntarist industrial policy, as was expressed in the CECA and Euratom Treaties, and as was conceived by certain promoters of European medium-term programming. Equally, the virtues of the competitive system, both inside the Community and in its relations with third parties, have been questioned, and, as a result, the industrial and competitive European policies, clashed more and more frequently, both among themselves, and with the corresponding national policies.

III. 2.1 *Within the Common Market* different elements influence the situation, and these may be listed as follows:

(a) There has been noticeable growth of the public sector and of the share of public expenditure as a percentage of national expenditure. Recent estimations of long-run elasticities of public expenditure with respect to private consumption show not only an elasticity higher than one, but also that this elasticity is increasing with time.[28] This acceleration of the collectivisation of the European economies is thus likely to continue in the future and is *a priori* more favourable to political processes of reallocation of resources than to market mechanisms. Besides, the privileged relations and cooperation between large private enterprises and public authorities have increased in such a way that the large firm, either public or private, tends to become an instrument of national economic policy and to benefit from measures of particular support with a view to favouring its leadership at the international level: this could be the origin of a dangerous new corporatism.

(b) The aids to enterprises and to sectors in difficulty increase and take on more and more of an 'opaque' character (in contrast with 'transparent' aids) that make any quantitative assessment of their importance more difficult.

(c) In the case of national economies, the increasingly divergent conditions of adaptation to international difficulties and expansion make the definition of a common denominator less easy.

III. 2.2 *Concerning third-party countries*, the advantages of liberalisation of international trade and of international division of labour are offset by the adjustment costs that result from such an opening-up of work economy.

(a) Concerning trade with other industrialised countries, especially with the United States of America and Japan, the implied consequences of such free trade (the free movement of labour or an unhindered adjustment between profits and salaries) for the EEC are less and less acceptable owing to the social conflicts that they cause.[29] Thus the pressures are increased for the European countries (Benelux, Germany, Scandinavia) that have lost, *vis-à-vis* the American partner, the advantage of low salary costs and may sometimes have to face the decline of entire industrial sectors. Besides, the question of the security of supplies and the will to maintain an integrated production structure assuring national independence have become essential. A growing dependence on external trade (with its associated risks) makes national autonomy an illusion.

(b) Concerning developing countries, the positive effects of agreements (the Convention of Lomé, Agreements of Association with the Maghreb countries and similar agreements with the Middle East), as shown by an increase in trade, are also criticised—especially where the increase is in manufactured products. Although the absolute amounts remain small, the exports of manufactured products of these countries have grown more quickly than those of the industrialised countries, and have thus increased their share of the world market. Further, the composition of their exported manufactured goods has been improved, in that they now export products with a strong income elasticity (chemicals, machines, transport material, electronic components, radios, cameras, etc.).

A complete analysis of this evolution is the subject of another study (see especially the chapter below on Trade and Monetary Policy). On the industrial policy level, however,we underline one consequence: certain developing countries exceed the limits of industrialisation orientated towards their own domestic market and compete on the markets of the industrialised countries. In the same manner, the multinationals implant themselves in countries with low salaries from which they export manufactured products competing with the local production of in-dustrialised countries. Even products which are classified as of home (European) manufacture are, more and more, made overseas. 'British-made', 'French-made' or 'Belgian-made' television sets or refrigerators contain tubes or electric motors made outside the Common Market, so that the amount of work performed by European workers on 'European-made' goods becomes less, implying a decreasing value added.

Member States have increasingly manifested the fear that this growth of trade with certain developing countries may lead to painful adap-tations in the regions with old industries specialising in products of a weak technological capacity and hence less competitive. This aggravates the difference in the economic evolution within the Community itself and reinforces national protectionist reactions. Nevertheless, there are fewer reservations than in the case of relations with third-party industrialised countries, in that complementarity is more probable. Indeed, the international division of labour with developing countries is still much more vertical (Europe imports raw materials or primary commodities and exports manufactured goods), than horizontal. Fur-thermore, enlargement of markets for European products in the developing countries is linked with access to investment in the develop-ing countries, which tends to favour European exports, whilst 'joint ventures' between the two types of countries are likely to increase.

III. 3 Faced with this upsurge of nationalism and protectionism, especially evident in the more or less autonomous industrial policies of the Member States, the attitudes that the European Authorities can adopt are threefold: *the application of a common policy* (not a cartel) between European States; *real European achievements in certain specified sectors*—showing the efficiency of a transfer of responsibility from the national level to the Community level; and the obtaining of a *better connection between the various dimensions of the industrial policy* such as the links between internal and external industrial policies and links between industrial policy and the competition policy.

III. 3.1 Since 1975, initiatives aimed at establishing a minimum of concerted action between European governments in international, commercial and industrial negotiations have multiplied. Nevertheless, one does not get the impression of a real desire for common policy but rather of the seeking of a 'cartel' between European countries. Indeed, concern has been expressed in the United States and in Japan that, when the European Community does set about agreeing on a common industrial policy, this will really involve more protection against external interests. Such a concept contains an important weakness. A protectionist cartel of European States runs the risk of having the instability common to cartels of industrial enterprises. At the level of its internal organisation there are the problems of cartel enforcement, since the temptation of Member States to cheat is strong because the returns from cheating are substantial. Also, the common policy is loosely defined and national production possibilities are not homogeneous. At the external level, the outsiders, that is to say to other industrialised States, European or others, cannot be controlled and are often capable of proposing more advantageous alternative conditions, thus causing discord among the countries of the Common Market. Eventually, bilateral agreements between certain of these countries and external countries may be concluded.

However, a common industrial policy is not a consolidation at Community level of old national protectionist habits. It requires clearly defined objectives and methods, resulting from a real policy of consensus. The creation by the European Council (10 December 1974) of the second tripartite European conference in Luxembourg and the bringing together of representatives of governments, employers and workers (24 June 1976) were important steps in this direction. These moves were extended by the consultation of social partners about the fourth medium-term programme that has especially emphasised the need for the medium-term economic policies of the Member States to correspond to the aims accepted at Community level.

III. 3.2 The demands in favour of a real transfer of responsibility in the industrial field from the national level to the Community level will remain vain hopes as long as the efficiency of the industrial policy of the Community has not been proven. Member States will only be prepared to adopt common industrial policies where the advantages to be gained from acting as a Community complement or outweigh the benefits accruing from their individual policies. This situation risks becoming a vicious circle. In order to get out of it, it is important that, besides making grandiose declarations of intent, the Commission should prove its capacity to elaborate European operational plans for the reconversion and expansion of specified sectors. It is in this way that the new officials responsible for the Directorate-General for Industrial Policy are moving: that is, concerning the steel industry, the textile industry (where it has to go well beyond the renewal of the Multifibre Arrangement), aeronautics, the shipping industry and computers. In all cases, 'action-programmes' have been worked out. At this level, however, a delicate problem arises. On the one hand, it seems that industrial redevelopment has to be conceived at a rather delicate disaggregated level of industrial activities. The question is not how to promote or to check the growth of certain major sectors, but how to favour intra-sectoral specialisation as a result of the quality of products. Thus, it is not sufficient to state that European production in such sectors as clothing, footwear, or cereal-based products, will diminish, whilst sectors such as computers, organic chemicals, or machinery, are the object of a persistent demand on the world market. One still has to note that, inside the textile sector, the sub-sector of luxury clothing will probably be little affected by the structural consequences of the economic crisis, whilst the sub-sector weaving has to meet a growing competition from developing countries.

It is indeed well known that an ever-increasing part of trade between European countries as well as with other countries corresponds with the growth of products that belong to the same branches of the industry but which differentiate themselves by their special qualities.[30]

But on the other hand, it seems very dangerous to expect of the European authorities, as well as of national authorities (see p. 33), systematic orientation of specialisation at the intra-industrial level. In effect, if in some very concentrated sectors where the products are standardised, the statistical information is strongly developed and the habits of dialogue and cooperation (even collusion) firmly rooted (as in the case of the steel industry), it is not the same for numerous other industries. In sectors such as textiles and food, firms are very numerous, the variety of products is extremely wide, and the products themselves strongly differentiated. Besides, the source of difficulties varies from one case to another, ranging from the question of commercial policy to that of financial management, taking in the production structure – *passant*. Finally, microeconomic statistics are, in general, terribly bare and unstandardised. Thus, to expect that European Industrial Policy should simultaneously stimulate, orientate and control the industrial redevelopment in these fields would be foolish. Such a policy, that would in effect tend to duplicate the competitive decentralised process by a badly-informed, badly-equipped 'visible hand' working expensively, would result in an unmanageable situation. It will not be easy for the European Authorities to find a compromise between general plans for reconversion and development, and market studies orientated toward products.

III. 3.3 One of the facts that have become clear during recent years is the danger of defining an industrial policy geared only to private industrial activities inside the Community, whilst neglecting the problems that concern their relations with public industrial activities in Europe and with activities in other countries (both industrialised ones and developing ones). The extreme interdependence of all these aspects demands a better coherence between the internal and external policies of the Community, implying that those Directorates-General in the Commission responsible for policies of direct interest to industry should be more closely grouped. Concerning the public sector, the growing roles of public enterprise on the supply side and of public expenditure on the demand side must be integrated into the orientation of the industrial policy. There should be research for more transparency of public intervention and a new examination of the competitive and complementary relations with the private sector.

Industrial trade with countries such as the United States and Japan influences the directions and the growth of European industrial activities. As we have observed, the situation is not as clear as it was some years ago when one could affirm the unconditional necessity for a liberalisation of trade. Further complications have arisen because of the Common Market's attempt to diversify its sources of supply (as in the case of energy), to rely less on international trade and to opt for complementarity rather than competition and substitution in its trading policies. These changes are likely to modify the future industrial and commercial policies of the Community and to make them more selective than general in character.

Regarding relations with the developing countries, complementarity is more assured, but for certain European regions and certain industries there are harmful reconversions to be made. The supporting role of the common regional and social policies is, in this last case, indispensable for keeping the markets open.

III. 3.4 Inside the Community itself there is, finally, the question of how much cooperation should be allowed to intrude upon the competitive process and to what extent an interventionist industrial policy has to supersede that of competition as the main regulator of economic activity.

It seems important to underline here the necessity of safeguarding the competitive process within the Common Market. At this internal level, where the costs of adjustment to the structural changes could be met in a satisfactory way by common social and regional policies, it must be possible to maintain the efficiency of our decentralised economic system founded on the spirit of enterprise, willingness to take risks, mobility of resources, and creativity. Even in the context of the modifications to the ownership of the means of production which are on their way in various European countries, the competitive system remains indispensable to safeguard the alternatives and freedom of choice, and to avoid the abuses of economic power that come from public as well as private monopolies.[31]

This view implies the continuation and the reinforcement of the European policy of competition—especially *vis-à-vis* concentration, the public sector, and multinationals. As we have frequently suggested, it also presupposes a greater degree of autonomy for the Directorate responsible for competition inside the Commission, as well as increased collaboration with the national authorities of the Member States and Third States. Action conducted within the framework of the OECD is, in our view, very positive.

Inevitably certain conflicts will result from industrial policy. Rather than being camouflaged by deceptive compromises inside the Commission and between the Directorates, these conflicts should be explained and discussed at the level of the European Parliament so as to expose fully the objectives at stake, the results of alternative policies, and the respective costs and benefits. Rather than an industrial Europe based on technocratic compromises, one must hope for the construction of a really democratic industrial Europe.

NOTES

1. See IRES, *La position competitive de l'économie belge sur le marché international*, Rapports de J. Houard, C. Ghymers et F. Prades (Louvain la Neuve).
2. See IRES, *op. cit.*
3. The share of the EEC 9 in the total Japanese exports was 8.9 in 1958, 11.9 in 1973 and 10.8 in 1976; the share of the EEC 9 in the total Japanese imports was 8.1 in 1958, 8.3 in 1973 and 5.6 in 1976. (*The Summary Report Trade of Japan*, Japan, Tariff Association).
4. From 1973 to 1975, the employment in industry decreased from 49.5 % to 46 % in West Germany; 39.3 % to 38.6 % in France; 30.7 % to 29.8 % in Ireland; 36.2 % to 34.8 % in the Netherlands; 43.3 % to 39.9 % in Belgium; 42.3 % to 40.9 % in the United Kingdom; 33.8 to 31.5 % in Denmark; 48.6 % to 47.3 % in Luxembourg. Only in Italy has the situation been stable (44 %).
5. For the case of the United Kingdom see R. Bacon and W. Eltis, *Britain's Economic Problem: Too Few Producers* (London: Macmillan, 1976). See also the very stimulating paper of A. Singh, 'U.K. Industry and the World Economy: A case of De-Industrialisation?' in A. Jacquemin and H. de Jong, *Welfare Aspects of Industrial Markets* (Leiden: Nijhoff, 1977), who shows the role of the world market conditions. For a confirmation of Kaldor's hypothesis that there is a close relationship between the rate of growth of a country's GDP and the growth of its manufacturing sector, see T. F. Cripps and R. J. Tarling, *Growth in Advanced Capitalist Economies*, (London: Cambridge University Press, 1974), who have analysed the growth process in advanced industrial countries during 1950–70.
6. See, for example, R. Linda in *Regulating the Behaviour of Monopolies and Dominant Undertakings in Community Law*, Collège d'Europe (Bruges: de Tempel, 1977), p. 62, where it is calculated that in 53 % of the 301 European markets that were analysed the principal company controlled 40 % of its national market.
7. For a general analysis of these different aspects, see A. Jacquemin and H. de Jong, *European Industrial Organisation* (London: Macmillan, 1977).
8. L. Stoleru, *L'Impératif Industriel* (Paris: Seuil, 1969) p. 186.
9. R. Toulemon and J. Flory, *Une Politique Industrielle pour l'Europe*, (Paris: PUF, 1974) p. 17.
10. A. Jacquemin, *Economie Industrielle Européenne* (Paris: Dunod, 1975) p. 324; H. Bauwens in Cepess, *Politique Industrielle* (Bruxelles, 1974) p. 7.
11. H. de l'Estoile, 'Les Objectifs actuels de la politique industrielle en France', in *Politique Industrielle et Stratégies d'Entreprise* (Paris: Institut de l'Entreprise, Masson, 1977) pp. 124–5.

12. J. Meade, *The Just Economy* (London: Allen and Unwin, 1976) chap. VIII.
13. In France, the number of business enterprises engaged mainly in industrial activities dropped from 642,844 in 1961, to 574,784 in 1970 (a fall of 10.58). In 130 sectors, the reduction is more than 16 %. See F. Jenny and A. P. Webber, in *Concentration et Politique des Structures Industrielles* (Paris: la Documentation Française, 1974).
14. See, for example, N. Blattner, *Industrial Policy: A Sceptical View* (Newcastle: Fourth European Conference on Industrial Structure, September 1977) who writes: 'the higher and the more uncertain the actual and the expected rate of inflation is, the greater are the individual economic agent's difficulties in judging to what extent a variation of a single price is a real instead of a merely nominal phenomenon. This induces errors in anticipation'.
15. In the Theory of Games, this view is well-established for the case of the 'prisoner's dilemma'. In the well-known two-person nonzero-sum non-cooperative game which is ubiquitous in the economy, it is shown that, contrary to the doctrines of liberal economics, the group interest is not furthered by the independent pursuit of individual interests. The 'Pareto-better' joint maximum position is forcibly repelled by the players because of the dominant character of their individual strategies. The situation is still more complex if the joint maximum position is not 'Pareto-improving' because a player would worsen his position by such a change. Then the bigger utility total must be shared out by a suitable international distribution to make the players better off than they would have been.
16. See: S. Holland, 'Europe's New Public Enterprises' in R. Vernon (ed.), *Big Business and the State, Changing Relations in Western Europe* (London: Macmillan, 1974) p. 41.
17. E. Malinvaud, Les perspectives de la croissance française, in *Colloque sur le redéploiement industriel* (Paris: La Documentation Française, 1975) p. 102.
18. See A. Jacquemin, *op. cit.*, p. 191 *et seq.*
19. See R. Toulemon and J. Flory, *op. cit.*, p. 110–13.
20. EEC Commission, *Programme of the Commission for 1977* (Brussels, February 1977).
21. EEC Commission, *Sixth Report on Competition Policy* (Brussels, April 1977).
22. EEC Commission, *Tenth General Report on the Activities of the Community* (Brussels, 1977).
23. EEC Commission, *Programme of the Commission for the Year 1977* (Brussels, 1977).
24. EEC Commission, *Fourth Medium-term Economic Programme*: concerning the period 1976–1980, COM (76) 530 Final (Brussels, 5 October 1976).
25. Official Journal of the European Communities, no. L 101, 25, April 1977.
26. E. Davignon, 'Ebauche d'une stratégie européenne pour surmonter la crise industrielle', *Revue de la Société d'Etudes et d'Expansion*, no. 273 (September 1977).
27. See in this sense, the intervention of M. Schaeffer, Director, Directorate-General III, during the course of a European Round Table, organised in Brussels by 'European Management Forum', 18 March 1976.
28. G. d'Alcantara and A. Barten, Long-run relation between public and

private expeditures in the EEC Countries, in L. Solari and J. Du Pasquier (ed.), *Private and enlarged consumption* (Amsterdam: North-Holland, 1976).

29. The international mobility of labour (notably regarding recourse to migrant workers) is diminishing whilst the mobility of European capital runs the risk of provoking political reactions.

30. For a recent statistical confirmation, see B. Balassa, Trade Creation and Trade Diversion in the European Market, in H. Glesjer, (ed.), *Quantitative Studies of International Economic Relations* (North-Holland, 1976).

31. See also A. Cairncross *et al.*, *Economic Policy for the European Community* (London: Macmillan, 1974) in which it is stated: 'Our concern for the maintenance of effective competition extends beyond purely economic considerations. Competition is one of the foundations of an open society in which all member countries of the European Community have a substantial stake' (p. 143).

3 Social policy

PETER COFFEY

THEORETICAL CONSIDERATIONS

Basically, social policy and—more specifically—social security imply either social welfare,[1] social insurance, or a mixture of both systems. Equally, social policy must take account of the four major groups in a national economy, the government, the trade unions, the employers' organisations and consumer groupings. Last, but not least, any examination of social policy automatically implies that one has to take into consideration the basic social rights of individuals and the degree of equality existing or desirable between them. In the specific case of the EEC, this last consideration involves the question of equal pay. Unfortunately, however, and this study is no exception in this respect, works on social policy usually and wrongly (the author would maintain) omit an examination of education (and the financing thereof, together with the question of scholarships) plus the fundamental question of opportunity. The author believes that, if studies included a thorough examination of these questions, then the picture of social policy concerning individual countries that one normally receives would be changed.

Many economists believe that the differences between social welfare and social insurance are becoming blurred—at least in the Common Market. Social welfare implies that the State guarantees a minimum level of welfare (pensions, medical care, unemployment benefits, and other benefits) below which no citizen should fall. The adoption of such a policy implies a transfer of resources from the richer to the poorer sections of the population through government subsidies raised from taxation. Naturally, all individuals will pay some form of social security tax, but this is not enough to cover the full expenses of the scheme; hence the government subsidies. This system was the type as conceived by Beveridge in the famous plan bearing his name in 1942.[2]

Social insurance is quite different in that it implies some form of earnings – related benefits. However, most countries normally decide to put a ceiling on the percentage of income on which social taxes are paid. A system of social insurance implies not only that the system is in financial equilibrium or surplus, but also that large funds are generated for investment purposes.

In systems covering medical care, particularly where a national system of health care applies, it is normal for the responsible bodies to make contracts for medical products with pharmaceutical companies. In recent years, a number of scandals have been brought to light as a result of the price abuses practised these companies at the expense of health organisations.

As has already been mentioned, the differences between social welfare and insurance are becoming somewhat blurred since all countries in the Common Market attempt to implement a minimum economic and social standard of living below which no citizen should fall. Whilst there is growing support for the introduction of a British/Danish type of health service throughout the Community (in the face of the understandable opposition of dentists and doctors), there is an equally growing support (especially in countries which had not previously practised such policy) for earnings-related benefits. The one element common to all these demands is a growing pressure on the State (and/or the Community) to provide greater financial resources for social ends.

THE EEC AND SOCIAL POLICY

Until the early 1970s, the Community's attitude towards social policy was extremely narrow. This narrowness of attitude had its origins in the fact that the EEC was, until the end of the 1960s, in the process of creating a customs union. The basic aims of such a union included the free movement of labour. Thus the EEC's social policy was concerned almost exclusively with the question of migration (though, it is true, this included the retraining of workers) and with the benefits which migrants should enjoy in the receiving/host country. This latter consideration naturally raised the whole question of what kind of social security system the Community should have. Originally, the French desired the implementation of an optimum system. Such a system would have entailed the provision of enormous resources, and a compromise was adopted whereby migrants who were nationals of Community Member States[3] would eventually (by the end of the transition phases) be eligible for the same social security benefits as those enjoyed by the nationals of the host/receiving country. However, the main plank of the EEC's Social Policy has been the question of migration. It is to this question that we should now direct our attention.

THE FREE MOVEMENT OF LABOUR

According to Articles 48 and 49 of the Treaty of Rome, the free movement of labour was to have been achieved in the transitional period of the customs union. In fact, this was achieved for nationals of EEC Member States by 1968. The situation is now that Community nationals may move freely within the Community and spend up to three months in any member state in the search for employment. Once having worked in a Member State, an EEC national has the right to remain there and to maintain a residence there even though, thereafter, working elsewhere within the Community.

Originally, the Community anticipated an important movement of workers between the EEC States which would bring the supply of labour into equilibrium with the demand. To this end, a number of organisations were created which were intended to provide the framework of a European Labour Exchange. Thus, under the control of the Commission, the European Coordination Bureau was created in 1961. This office, which acts as a European Vacancy Clearance System, receives offers of vacancies and unemployed workers from the Member States and attempts to match supply with demand. Similarly, a Consultative Committee (composed of representatives of governments, trade unions and employers' organisations) and a Technical Committee (composed of government representatives) were set up to advise the Commission. Ten years later, an Administrative Commission for the Social Security of Migrant Workers (made up of a representative of each Member State with a Commission representative acting as adviser) was created to settle and expedite matters concerning the social security of migrants. This commission is advised by a Consultative Committee. Finally, a Standing Committee on Employment has existed since 1970.

Although nationals of EEC states may move freely in search of employment, the Community did, even in 1968, foresee the possibility of economic upheavals and therefore implemented legislation which might discourage workers from migrating within the Common Market and which would temporarily suspend the workings of the European Vacancy Clearance System.[4] Further, while workers belonging to EEC Member States can move freely within the Community, civil servants do not enjoy a similar freedom since their positions (apart from a few exceptions) are reserved for the nationals of the individual Member States. Similarly, until recently when agreement was reached regarding the recognition of diplomas and degrees awarded by different Common Market countries, members of the liberal professions did not enjoy freedom of movement. Now, members of the liberal professions who are nationals of the Member States may work and set up in practice wherever they wish.

SOCIAL SECURITY BENEFITS AND MIGRATION FLOWS

The obvious complement to the free movement of labour is naturally the rights that a worker will enjoy when he or she moves from one country to another. Initially, France had hoped that a Community social security system might be introduced which would consist of the optimum benefits enjoyed in all the original six Member States. Here the only approximation to such a system that was accepted was the principle of the application of equal pay throughout the Community (this principle already being an integral part of the French constitution). In the case of social security, however, a compromise was agreed upon. Thus it was accepted that migrants who were nationals of Common Market countries should enjoy the same social security benefits as the nationals of host/receiving countries. Such migrants could also accumulate pension rights as they moved from one country to another.

When all this legislation had been enacted, some economists and politicians did anticipate a major movement of labour within the Community itself. Some economists suggested that workers in some countries might be tempted to move elsewhere because the wages and/or social security benefits were higher in other Common Market countries. In fact, despite differences in the levels of wages and social security benefit, workers only tended to move elsewhere if they literally could not find employment in their own region.

It appeared, therefore, that workers were more influenced by subjective local ties than by the 'moneyness' of their wages. Such may not be the case with the liberal professions—now that they can move freely—since they do seem to be more conscious of salary/earnings differentials in the different Member States, and the beginnings of a movement from low-income to high-income areas can already be observed. The observation about the reluctance of Community workers to migrate (unless they cannot find employment at home) is underlined by the figures in Table 3.1. These figures indicate that the main internal

TABLE 3.1 Number of migrant workers 1974 estimate

Sending countries	Receiving countries									TOTAL
	Germany	Switzerland	France	Belgium	Netherlands	Luxembourg	Austria	Sweden	U.K.	
Portugal	81,000	3,000	475,000	4,000	4,000	9,000*	—	1,000	10,000	588,000
Spain	160,000	75,000	265,000	34,000	19,000	2,000	—	2,000	17,000	574,000
Italy	405,000	306,000	230,000	70,000	10,000	11,000	2,000	3,000	—	1,037,000
Yugoslavia	495,000	23,000	50,000	3,000	9,000	1,000	166,000	23,000	—	770,000
Greece	223,000	5,000	5,000	6,000	2,000	—	—	8,000	—	249,000
Turkey	585,000	14,000	25,000	10,000	33,000	—	29,000	2,000	—	698,000
Finland	5,000	1,000	1,000	—	—	—	—	105,000*	—	113,000*
Morocco	14,800	—	130,000	30,000	23,000	—	—	—	1,000	197,800
Algeria	—	—	440,000	3,000	—	—	—	—	—	443,000
Tunisia	10,600	—	70,000	—	1,000	—	—	—	—	81,600
Others	415,600*	158,000	209,000*	70,000	57,500*	—	—	—	—	2,784,000
TOTAL	2,395,000	585,000*	1,900,000	230,000	158,500	18,000	32,000	53,000	1,772,000	7,535,500
						41,000	229,000	197,000	1,800,000	

* of which 10,000 Austrians

* settled and annual; excludes 152,000 seasonal and 98,000 frontier workers

* particularly Africans and citizens of EEC countries except for Italy; excludes 130,000 seasonal workers

* excludes 25,000 West Indians and Surinamese

* 15,000 according to Portugese figures

See Footnote

* 100,000 according to Swedish figures; 110,000 according to Finnish figures

* excludes 1,000 Finns in Denmark and 2,000 in Norway

Source: OECD Observer, No. 76, July–August 1975, p. 14.

The table does not claim to be definitive. It is based on original estimates prepared by the SOPEMI rapporteur Professor B. Kayser and submitted for comments to the SOPEMI correspondents. Where the latter have proposed differing corrections, either that which appeared the more recent has been preferred or a compromise figure has been given. In the case of the United Kingdom, the pattern of immigration is such as to make comparison difficult to achieve by such a procedure: however, the British correspondent has also supplied data from the 1971 census which has been reproduced alongside for indicative purposes.

UNITED KINGDOM – 1971 Census active population born outside the country:

Ireland	478,000	Spain	36,000
Australia		Poland	78,000
Canada, New Zealand	73,000	United States	49,000
Others Commonwealth	558,000	USSR	33,000
Germany	69,000	Others	330,000
Italy	75,000		
Others EEC	37,000	TOTAL	1,816,000

source of Community migrants is and has been Italy, which, before and since the beginning of the EEC, has had a persistently larger number of unemployed than other Member States. In turn, the majority of migrants nevertheless come from non-Community States. There are probably many reasons why this should be so.

The first reason must be that, during the 1960s, boom conditions existed in the Community, and that, with the exception of Italy (where the situation changed in the late 1960s), there were few unemployed workers. Also, in the early years of the Community's existence, Algeria was treated as part of France and the already traditional movement of Algerian workers into France was intensified. Another reason, which would seem to be more valid today, is that even where unemployment exists in Common Market countries, there are some jobs which unemployed Community nationals just will not take—preferring instead to enjoy social security benefits until such time as the job for which they feel themselves best fitted turns up. There exist, certainly, less positive reasons why so many migrants from non-Member States are employed. Some employers prefer to make a direct contract with workers in non-Member States – either individually or via agencies. The advantage to the employers is that such contracts need not be renewed. The employers thus protect themselves against possible poor economic conditions in the future. The position of non-Community migrants is insecure because it is only when they have worked and lived in a Community country consistently for five years that they have any claim to permanency. Frequently they are unaware of their rights and are consequently more easily influenced by employers than are their EEC colleagues.

Even where Member States and/or the Community have signed agreements with non-EEC sending countries, e.g. Turkey, Yugoslavia and Portugal, these countries and their migrants do not always get the best deal since they are negotiating from a weak position. Naturally, these observations should not imply that the sending countries are losing from the arrangement—since migrants' remittances constitute a very important balancing item in their balance-of-payments—but they do imply that non-Community migrants are inevitably in a weaker legal and economic position than are EEC nationals.

THE ECONOMIC EFFECTS OF MIGRATION

The economic effects of migration are many-sided. As has already been mentioned, the flow of remittances (see Table 3.2) back to the migrants' home states is a very important source of revenue for these countries. In fact, in most cases, the balance-of-payments of the sending countries would be in persistent deficit if these flows were to dry up. Some countries, too, which cannot provide jobs for all their nationals, actively encourage emigration. In the specific case of Turkey, successive governments have preferred emigration to inflows of foreign investment because they can control the inflow of remittances more easily than foreign investment flows. The importance of remittances can be gauged by estimates made by the OECD in 1971, which concluded that remittances were $1\frac{1}{2}$ times more important than receipts from tourism in the case of Greece, 5 times more important in the case of Yugoslavia, and 22 times more important in the case of Turkey.

TABLE 3.2 Transfer of remittances to migrants' home countries (millions of dollars)

	1973	1974	1975
Portugal	1,025	1,100	690
Spain	1,185	1,070	–
Italy	844	753	979
Yugoslavia	1,398	1,621	1,695
Greece	735	645	734
Turkey	1,183	1,426	1,300
TOTAL	6,370	6,615	5,398*

Source: OECD * excluding Spain

These benefits, however, present only one side of the picture. Migrants have made an indispensable contribution to the economic wealth of Common Market and other West European Countries. Moreover, in an increasing number of cases more migrants have had industrial training and/or experience in their home countries and hence bring these skills with them to the receiving countries. This evolution is demonstrated by estimates made by the OECD, which showed that, in the period 1971–2, the following percentages of migrants had already had industrial experience: Portugese, 46 per cent; Spanish, 67 per cent; Yugoslavs, 26 per cent; Greeks, 30 per cent; and Turks, 23 per cent.

These facts, linked with the bad social conditions which migrants frequently face in hostile and congested industrial areas, have led to calls for the Common Market to create work in the sending countries, thus reducing the need for the movement of migrants into the Community

TABLE 3.3   EEC social security benefits and contributions in 1972

	Belgium	Germany	France	Italy	Lux-embourg	Neth-erlands	U.K.	Ireland	Denmark
Social Security									
Total expenditure in % of the gross domestic product at market prices	19.8	22.4	19.3	22.5	19.2	23.2	16.8	13.7	20.9
Function of the benefits in %									
Sickness	22.5	29.3	27.1	26.4	17.6	31.1	25.9	29.1	28.9
Old age, decease, survival	37.6	45.3	40.6	35.4 }	63.3	38.2	48.1 }	36.7	34.1
Invalidity	4.5	7.4	3.6	13.3 }	1.0	9.8	4.0 }	10.4	9.8
Physical or mental disability	1.9	–	1.1	2.6		3.8	4.5		3.3
Occupational injuries, occupational sickness	4.5	4.5	4.5	3.2	6.4	–	1.3	0.5	1.4
Unemployment	4.7	0.9	1.8	1.7	0.0	4.1	4.7	5.6	2.5
Family	16.8	9.9	20.1	10.2	11.1	12.9	8.9	15.7	16.4
of which maternity	0.7	1.0	1.4	0.7	0.5	0.5	1.7	2.2	1.4
Political event, natural disaster	3.5	–	–	4.2	–	–	–	–	0.3
Miscellaneous	4.0	2.7	1.2	3.0	0.6	0.1	2.6	2.0	3.3

TABLE 3.3 *(contd)*

	Belgium	Germany	France	Italy	Lux-embourg	Nether-lands	U.K.	Ireland	Denmark
Receipts (by nature, for financing social expenditure, in % of total receipts)									
Employers' contributions	46	50	62	54	36	43	34	19	10
Households' contributions	20	24	20	15	24	36	18	14	6
Governments' contributions	30	23	16	24	31	13	40	66	81
Income from capital	4	2	1	3	8	8	8	1	3
Other receipts	0	1	1	4	1	0	0	0	0
TOTAL	100	100	100	100	100	100	100	100	100

Source: EEC Commission 1973, Social Accounts.

and the loss of skilled workers by the sending countries. To date, only two Common Market countries have actively responded to this call. But, interestingly enough, the initiative had originated among migrants and their governments in two sending countries, Turkey and Yugoslavia. In the case of Turkey, Village Development Cooperatives had been started in 1963. Later, Turkish migrants in West Germany were empowered to create workers' companies, and in 1975 a joint programme was set up with the West German Ministry of Economic Cooperation through which German/Turkish Government loans are organised on a 50:50 basis.

The other Common Market country which has responded to the call is the Kingdom of the Netherlands, which, in 1974, embarked upon a five-year research project in six sending countries and subsequently allocated 30 million guilders for regional development in these states for the period 1975–6.

SOCIAL SECURITY

As already mentioned, the European Economic Community had intended to have a harmonised social security system. In fact, Article 117 of the Treaty of Rome not only mentions the 'harmonisation of social systems', but also the 'equalisation of such conditions in an upward direction'. However, mainly because of the costs which harmonisation in an upward direction would entail, a compromise was agreed upon whereby a migrant who is an EEC national automatically enjoys the benefits enjoyed by the nationals of the host country. In the case of state pensions, as has already been mentioned, an EEC national accumulates his or her benefits according to the contributions made in the different Member States in which the migrant has worked.

Basically, the situation concerning social security in the EEC is in a full state of evolution. Thus, whilst the two fundamental philosophies relating to social security are social welfare and social insurance, the division between the two is now becoming blurred. Only in Britain, Denmark and Ireland (see Table 3.3) does the state maintain a basic social welfare philosophy in that it is responsible for financing the major part of social security. Nevertheless, in the field of pensions and unemployment benefits, the concept of earnings/contribution-related benefits is gaining ground. Paradoxically, whilst this concept is gaining ground, citizens everywhere would like (as is the case in the United Kingdom and Denmark) to see the state assume greater responsibility in the field of medicine and health. Such moves are, as might be expected, bitterly opposed by many doctors and dentists—especially by the richest ones! Despite this opposition, a national health service is in the process of being introduced in Italy.

The statistics shown in Table 3.3 indicate that different Member States allocate different amounts of resources to social security and that they have different preferences, which range from an emphasis on child/family allowances in France and Belgium to pensions in the case of West Germany and the United Kingdom. Only in Denmark do all forms of social security appear to have priority! Unfortunately, what these statistics do not show are the ever-increasing resources transferred from the Community's citizens and state national health schemes to pharmaceutical companies for purchases of drugs and medicines. The scandalously high profits made by such companies are notorious and merit a much more severe control by the Commission in Brussels. The statistics in Table 3.3 suggest, too, that the most economic use of resources is not being made in all countries. Thus, for example, whilst in the United Kingdom, through the National Health Service, the coverage of the population is complete, the resources allocated to health are among the lowest in the Community. This would suggest that either the British are not allocating enough resources to health or that in other countries doctors, dentists and pharmaceutical companies are making exorbitant profits. Again, this is an area which merits scrutiny by the Commission.

THE SOCIAL FUND AND THE SOCIAL POLICY ACTION PROGRAMME

The organ of the Community responsible for structural changes in the social field is the Social Fund. The Fund was originally only intended to supplement the work of the Member States. It pays 50 per cent of the expenses of accepted projects undertaken by EEC countries. Its operations mainly consist of the retraining and resettlement of workers. During the period 1960–72, over one and a half million workers were helped; 879 thousand being retrained and 712 thousand resettled. Unfortunately, unlike the Regional Fund, the Social Fund has never had enough financial resources to meet all the demands put upon it. In Table 3.4 this shortfall is clearly shown.

It is particularly unfortunate that this shortage of financial resources should persist just as the Community finds itself in the midst of a Social

TABLE 3.4 European Social Fund resources and requests (in million units of account)

	Resources	Requests
1973	222.95	320.0
1974	267.8	406.8
1975	355.9	500 plus
1976	441.0	700 (approx.)
1977	617.1	n.a.

Source: EEC Commission.

Policy Action Programme, and equally since the Social Fund only acquired the right to initiate its own projects two years ago.

A combination of circumstances is probably responsible for the potentially important initiative which the Community is currently undertaking in the field of social policy. The mandate for the drafting of the Social Policy Action Programme was accepted at the Paris Summit Conference in 1972 and became the object of a Council resolution in January 1974. The three over-riding criteria for this programme were the achievement of full and better employment in the Community, the improvement in living and working conditions, and an increased participation by both sides of industry in the economic and social decisions of the Community and of workers in the conduct of the firm. More specifically, the programme, which was to have been executed during the period 1974–6, consisted of seven points, as follows:

1. The provision of assistance from the European Social Fund for migrant workers and for handicapped workers.

2. The organisation of a programme for handicapped workers.

3. The setting-up of a European General Industrial Safety Committee and the extension of the competence of the Mines Safety and Health Commission.

4. The provision of a directive on equal pay for men and women.

5. The overall application of the standard 40–hour working week and 4 weeks' paid holiday.

6. The setting-up of a European Foundation for the improvement of the environment and of living and working conditions.

7. The provision of a directive on collective redundancies.

Some of the points in this programme (all of which had become the subject of regulations or directives by 1975) merit further attention.

The first one, concerning migrants and handicapped workers, has become more urgent as the economic and employment situation has worsened in the Community and since migrants tend to be the most vulnerable group.

Unfortunately, although the resources of the Social Fund—whether for these or other purposes—have been increased, they are persistently inadequate compared with the needs. The author is thus pessimistic about the implementation of this aim.

The fourth aim, concerning equal pay, has proved to be a controversial one (although it is one of the fundamental objectives of the Treaty of Rome) and the earnings gap between the sexes is showing signs of widening rather than narrowing.

That part of the fifth aim relating to the application of the 40-hour week was probably most fortunate in its timing since it coincided with a decline in economic activity and with demands made by both trade unions and management for a reduction in working hours. Similarly, the seventh aim is most timely because of the danger of the increase in redundancies in the Common Market.

The overall objective concerning participation in industry has been at least as controversial as the aim of equal pay. The reason for this controversy is the varied attitudes adopted by trade unions to this principle—and indeed towards the Common Market itself! These differing attitudes are frequently due to the very different structures of trade unions in different countries. Thus in West Germany, where the trade unions are organised on an industrial basis, they favour joint management. In both France and Italy, where unions are organised on political and/or religious lines, there is normally strong opposition to the idea of participation in industry. In the United Kingdom, where unions are organised mainly on a craft but also on an industrial basis, there exists only a modest interest in participation.

It is perhaps surprising that the Social Policy Action Programme did not include any reference to poverty, since independent organisations had, in 1973, assessed that about 25 million people in the EEC were living in or close to poverty. It is true, however, that the Commission did, at a later date, organise a number of poverty pilot study projects in a selected number of major cities.[5] This gesture did, unfortunately, leave the basic problem untouched.

THE FUTURE OF SOCIAL POLICY IN THE COMMUNITY

The Social Policy Action Programme has been translated into directives, and all Member States are in the process of putting into practice the principle of equal pay. However, grave problems and differences exist both between the Nine as well as within each individual country.

There also exist grave problems such as unemployment among young people, poverty, and the very different standards and levels of availability of medical treatment within the EEC. Unfortunately—and somewhat scandalously—the Community has done little or nothing to solve these problems. What is to be done then?

Further, these problems become more and more relevant since, as a result of the recognition of national diplomas and degrees and through the application of freedom of establishment by members of the medical profession (throughout the Community), there is likely to be an ever-increasing movement of dentists and doctors from the poorer to the richer areas of the Community.

Ideally, the solution might be to move towards the adoption of the old French welfare concept of aiming at the optimum of all the national welfare systems as the eventual Community norm. Such a policy is unlikely to be adopted in the foreseeable future—for obvious economic reasons. Thus, the best alternative would be to use the present resources most effectively whilst planning for the future. The more effective use of resources implies to some degree their re-allocation. Thus, for example, where the pharmaceutical companies are making scandalous profits from national health schemes, they should be made to reimburse the Community (the United Kingdom has set a precedent in this field). Dentists and doctors who have received a free training in a poorer area of the Community and who wish to move to a richer area might be asked to repay their training expenses. The Community might create a health council, financed through national and Community contributions—and levies from pharmaceutical companies—and could use its budget for many purposes, including the payment of financial incentives to dentists and doctors to remain or to move to under-staffed areas. But, in the long run, the Community must have a realistic plan. It should, by 1990, aim at the availability of a specific number of dentists and doctors and facilities in all equivalent population districts of the EEC. This is very important since, for example, in a city like Amsterdam it is even more difficult to have access to a dentist than it is in Southern Italy—even if one wishes to pay for the treatment oneself! In the meantime, whilst waiting for the new medical schools and their products to come on stream, the EEC might launch a Community-wide system of health education and emphasise a policy of preventive medicine.

The problems of unemployment among the young and the level of poverty among certain groups still remain to be solved. In the long run, one is almost tempted to propose a guaranteed minimum level of income throughout the Community. Such a policy would be very difficult to organise and finance and might not, after all, achieve the aim it is designed to fulfil. Instead, it would seem to be wiser to solve the unemployment problems and try to alleviate the worst poverty problems.

Regarding unemployment, a slowing-down of salaries among the top half of academics, teachers and civil servants would permit the employment of hundreds of thousands of young people.[6] Simultaneously, Community- and nationally-financed investment projects in areas such as aeronautics would create jobs, income and demand. Here, the emphasis should be placed more on quality, and, where possible, on labour-intensive projects.

Regarding the problem of poverty, national and Community aid projects for the worst-hit poverty areas should be implemented. But first—and swiftly—the Community should define its poverty standards and seek the most effective means of remedying the worst cases.

In all the fields just enumerated, just as in the areas of economic and industrial policy, never before has the need for inter-governmental cooperation and Community action been greater. In the case of social policy, with the notable exception of the excellent though always inadequately-financed work of the Social Fund, one can say that cooperation and initiatives have not been adequate to meet the Community's needs.

NOTES

1. See T. H. Marshall, *Social Policy* (London: Hutchinson University Library, 1965).
2. Beveridge, W. H., *Social Insurance and Allied Services* (London: HMSO, 1942).
3. Special protocols have been signed between individual Member States or the Commission and third parties which send migrants to the EEC. These agreements set down the social rights for which these workers are eligible.
4. *Regulation 1612/68*

   1. When a Member State undergoes or foresees disturbances on its labour market which could seriously threaten the standard of living and level of

employment in a given region or occupation, that State shall inform the Commission and the other Member States and shall supply them with all appropriate particulars.

2. The Member States and the Commission shall take all suitable informative measures so that Community workers shall not apply for employment in the said region or occupation.

3. Without prejudice to the application of the provisions of the Treaty and of the Protocols annexed thereto, the Member State refered to in para. 1 may request the Commission to state that, in order to restore to normal the situation in the said region or occupation, the operation of the balancing machinery provided for in Articles 15, 16 and 17 should be partially or totally suspended. The Commission shall decide on the suspension as such and on the duration thereof not later than 2 weeks after receiving such a request. Any Member State may, within a strict time-limit of 2 weeks, request the Council to annul or amend any such decision. The Council shall take a decision on any such request within 2 weeks.

4. Where such suspension does take place, the employment services of the other Member States which have indicated that they have workers available shall not take any action to fill vacancies communicated directly to them by employers in the Member States refered in para. 1.

Footnote

Lastly, a Member State may request the Commission to suspend the Vacancy Clearance System.

5. The concern with poverty did not materialise until somewhat later (and quite inadequately, the editor would submit). Thus, on 22 July 1975, twenty-one national (submitted by the governments of the Member States) pilot poverty study schemes and two cross-national schemes were accepted by the Commission. The aims of these study schemes were 'to test and develop new methods of helping the poor and those threatened with poverty' and 'to improve the understanding of the nature, causes, scope and mechanics of poverty in the Community'.

The basic ideas concerning these projects were that the cross-national ones would have a life of one year and would be completely financed by the Community. In the case of the national ones, they would have a life-span of between two and five years (after five years they would no longer be seen as experiments), whilst the financing would be equally shared between the Community and the host Member States.

An initial report on the work of these projects was published by the Commission in 1977 (*Study/Report*, Brussels, 13 January 1977, COM, 76, 718 FINAL), and this was followed by the publication of a working document entitled *The Perception of Poverty in Europe* (EEC Commission, March 1977). Once again, the editor would submit that such modest moves do not even begin to scratch the surface of the problem of poverty.

6. Here, one is naturally thinking of countries such as France, the Netherlands and West Germany, where the top salary levels are particularly high.

4 Fiscal policy

ALAN R. PREST

INTRODUCTION

The first clarification must be that we shall interpret 'fiscal policy' in a very wide sense, i.e. as embracing the whole corpus of public finance matters and not just macro-economic aspects such as anti-recession or anti-inflation policies. Accordingly we shall start by looking at the role of fiscal policy, as thus defined, in a single country, ignoring international aspects; then consider the consequences of allowing for international relationships; move from there to the problems of a free-trade area or customs union; then proceed to those of the EEC itself. The section following will examine the meaning and role of the harmonisation of taxes (and where relevant, other aspects of public sector policy) in the EEC, with a strong accent on the issues involved in the removal of barriers to flows of labour, capital and goods. The next section will encompass the role of the Community Budget—what it has been so far, what it is likely to be in the near and further future, and so on. Finally, we shall draw together the threads of the discussion in a brief section of conclusions.

I THE DIFFERING ROLES OF FISCAL POLICY

SINGLE COUNTRY – INTERNATIONAL ASPECTS IGNORED

Following traditional lines of thought one can distinguish between three different topics:

The size of the public sector
The division of public sector responsibilities between different tiers of government
Taxation and expenditure criteria

Taking *the size of the public sector* first, there is a whole range of questions associated with its definition and measurement.[1] If we are looking at public expenditure, we are concerned with the cost of the payments which the Community has decided to make on a collective or non-market basis; if looking at the revenue side, we are interested in the flow of income which is compulsorily diverted from individuals, corporations and the like and so is not at their direct disposal. But it is much easier to set out these propositions in general terms than to resolve many of the detailed conundrums. To illustrate, it seems reasonable to make a distinction between those public activities which are essentially of a commercial character, where the sums paid over by people directly correspond to services rendered, and those activities which do not involve any *quid pro quo*. But then one has to ask awkward questions about the treatment of contributions for social security purposes, or petrol taxes ostensibly levied for the finance of road-building, and so on. As another illustration, one would think it important *a priori* to distinguish between public receipts which stem from compulsory levies and those which do not; but this immediately leads one to ask why the 'inflation tax' or real capital gain of the public sector, which has been so important in recent years in so many countries, should not be included in any taxation total. We cannot spend more time on these points here; all we want to show is that the arguments are not by any manner of means cut and dried.

Having somehow specified the meaning of public revenue or public expenditure, one then comes to the many theories attempting to explain them. One major divergence of views has been about causation. Does the expenditure level determine the amount of revenue which it is necessary to raise, as many neo-classical economists were inclined to argue? Or is it that the ability to raise revenue is really the controlling force over expenditure as implied in the well-known work of Peacock and Wiseman?[2] Another major development during the last 25 years or so has been the emphasis on the differing cases of market failure, i.e. where the properties of some goods and services are such that the normal freely-functioning market mechanism could not be expected to work, or, at best, could only work imperfectly. This theory of social goods, as it has come to be known, is in turn closely bound up with various aspects of political theory, especially those related to voting procedures. The essential point is that, if preferences expressed through normal market processes will not produce the optimal, or indeed any, result, one has to turn to other methods and this essentially means signals from voters to political representatives and their advisers, via the ballot box. Another set of enquiries has been concerned not so much with the conditions for the optimal division of responsibility between private and public sectors, but rather with the determination of those forces chiefly responsible for comparative levels of revenue and/or expenditure in different countries at the same time or at different times in the same country. Leading examples of such econometric investigations are to be found in the work of Bahl[3] and Chelliah *et al.*[4] Yet another topic is the examination of the relationship between the total level of public expenditure and its composition. Thus it can be argued that, if public expenditure is entirely on the provision of consumption-type goods and services, the consequences of the associated taxation for incentives to work, take risks and the like will be much more marked than if public expenditure is more concentrated on subsidies.[5]

Needless to say, this kind of cataloguing is a dwarf's thumb-nail sketch only. But it may give the flavour of the sorts of debates which have been taking place in recent years among the specialists in this area.

Turning to *the division of public sector responsibilities* between different tiers, it is customary to argue[6] that, whereas action on and concern with the distribution of income and wealth or the management of the level of demand in an economy is best left to central government, there is very real scope for dividing general public spending functions and, to a lesser degree, revenue raising functions between different tiers of government. The precise basis for any such division is extremely complex depending on such considerations as the extent to which any particular type of expenditure generates benefits of a nation-wide or a purely local character, the economies of scale to be obtained from centralised provision as against the benefits of diversity of localised provision, the protection of minority interests, and so on. The answers may also differ depending on whether one has a federal or a unitary constitution, since in the former case reserved powers for State or Provincial governments are likely to have a stronger constitutional basis.

When one comes to *taxation and expenditure criteria* one is ploughing a field which has been cultivated intensively ever since the famous discussion by Adam Smith.[7] We can therefore be very brief. Suffice it to say that there is general agreement on the following criteria:

Resource allocation: i.e. taxes and/or expenditure must be judged according to whether, and to what extent, they steer resources between ends in a way more in accordance with consumer preferences than would happen in their absence. It must be understood that this heading covers such choices as those between work and leisure as well as, say, between working in a pleasant and an unpleasant occupation or between consuming butter and margarine.

Equity: i.e. taxes and/or expenditure must be judged according to their effects on relative shares of different people. This is a multidimensional concept: it may be a matter of considering the distribution of income or the distribution of wealth and it may be a matter of distribution between rich and poor people or between the inhabitants of North and South Italy—with many other possibilities too.

Demand Management: i.e. taxes and/or expenditure have to be arranged in such a way as to minimise the fluctuations in economic activity which might otherwise take place, whether looking at problems of unemployment or inflation.

Administration: i.e. whatever the merits of particular tax and expenditure arrangements from other points of view, one always has to ask about the practicability and cost, in terms of administrative resources, of adopting such measures.

SINGLE COUNTRY — IN INTERNATIONAL SETTING

Various new considerations must be taken into account once we enlarge our vista to cover international aspects.

The first one is in respect of resource allocation. Various types of taxes can affect the flow of goods and services between countries. The most obvious examples are selective tariffs on imports, but essentially the same results follow if a country levies a differential tax on its exports, e.g. a value-added tax on a selective origin basis,[8] as we shall see later in more detail. Nor should it be thought that only taxes specifically levied on selected goods and services can have distorting effects on international trade flows. A tax on corporation profits which works its way forwards into prices of products rather than backwards on to net incomes of factors employed can be thought of as a selective tax on goods and services.[9] In so far as this selectivity relates to exports or import substitutes, essentially the same consequences hold for international trade flows.

Resource allocation effects are not confined to trade flows: we must also think of factor flows between countries—primarily capital flows but also labour flows. The main problem with capital flows is whether profits are taxed in their country of source (or, synonymously, origin) or in the country of residence of the recipient. It can be shown easily enough[10] that to minimise interference with such flows, the residence principle must be the overriding one. Only in this case is one likely to secure what is often called capital export neutrality. But the word 'overriding' should be noticed in that it is perfectly possible to have a system of taxation in the country of source as well as taxation in the country of residence provided that the former can be fully credited against the latter. This is in fact more or less what is achieved by many double-taxation treaties which allow both source and residence countries to tax a particular income flow but reduce tax in the latter case by the amount levied in the former.

Analogously with the trade case, interference with factor flows may arise from taxation of goods as well as taxation of factor incomes. If taxes on goods work themselves out through reductions in factor incomes rather than increases in goods prices one could, in principle, have perverse effects on factor flows between countries.

Finally, in this catalogue of public finance resource allocation ramifications in the international setting, one must note that expenditures can have many similar effects to taxes, e.g. subsidies on import substitutes can interfere with trade flows just as much as tariffs on imports; or public purchasing policy may have a bias in favour of home-produced goods which is also exactly analogous to tax-induced effects.

When one turns to *equity* as distinct from *resource allocation* aspects, there are a number of complications. One is the division of tax revenues between countries. Obviously, this links up closely with the preceding discussion of the choice between and integration of taxation by source and by residence. But there are further ramifications in that, for instance, the precise form of corporation tax can influence the extent to which one country rather than another receives tax revenue, even though the basic choice between origin and residence principles is settled.[11]

There are also important questions relating to the taxation position of individuals who draw income from abroad relative to the position of those living on domestically generated income. The main issue is whether taxes paid abroad should be treated as a *credit* against home tax liability or as a *deduction*. From a broader international point of view, one can argue that a man with a given level of income from abroad should pay the same total of tax as another with the same level of income generated at home. From a narrower national point of view, one can argue that justice is done if the domestic tax rate is the same on all income received within that country. Obviously enough, there can be no finality in equity matters of this sort.

The final remark to make in this catalogue of international complications is that there is now a new dimension to demand management, as well as to resource allocation and equity. Fiscal measures may, for instance, spend themselves in adding to imports rather than to domestic production. But this whole subject is too well known in general and too complicated in detail for it to be elaborated here.

FREE TRADE AREA OR CUSTOMS UNION

We now introduce the further complication that a country has external economic relationships but that those with some countries are of a different nature to those with the remainder. In the free trade area case (e.g. EFTA) there are no tariffs on domestically produced goods but individual countries retain their own tariff structures and apply them to goods imported from outside the area, though not always fully so.[12] In the customs union case this process is taken further. There is then an identical tariff structure for all the countries within the union *vis-à-vis* those countries outside it but no duties whatever on intra-union trade.

The abolition of import duties on intra-union trade means that, by definition, such duties cannot be raised or lowered as is possible with countries which preserve independent trading relationships. There are also further consequences. Once import duties disappear for intra-union trade, the spotlight moves on to other taxes or subsidies which may interfere with trade flows. Thus if there are value-added taxes in the countries concerned and these are of an origin nature then it will follow that if such taxes are imposed at differing rates commodity by commodity in any one country (other countries not differentiating between commodities) trade flows will be affected.[13] So there is bound to be pressure to avoid such an arrangement, so as not to lose the benefits of freedom of trade flows resulting from the abolition of tariffs on trade between members.

Another consequence of such tariffs abolition is that there is then likely to be a demand for the abolition of fiscal frontiers. If there is no need to retain intra-union frontier inspection by customs authorities for the purpose of levying duties why not dispense with these authorities at such points? This in turn leads to the argument that if the countries concerned have value-added taxes on a destination basis they should be transformed on to an origin basis so that this end can be achieved. As there are trade-distortion objections against levying such origin taxes on a selective basis we are then apparently left with the conclusion that out of the four possibilities with value-added taxes (i.e. origin or destination; general or selective) the only acceptable one is the origin-general variety.[14]

These are the sorts of implications which follow from a customs union or (to a lesser extent) from a free trade area when we think of tax policy on goods and services. Are there any consequences for taxes bearing on factor mobility? It should be clear immediately that there is no question of a perfect correlation between freedom of labour movement and freedom of goods movement. There are plenty of historical examples of customs unions without labour mobility (e.g. the ex-British Caribbean) and of labour mobility without customs unions (e.g. the U.K. and Ireland during the last fifty years). Nor is the flow of capital between countries necessarily made easier by a customs union. At the same time, there is a general *a priori* likelihood that, if trade flows more easily, factors of production may do so too. There are then a number of further ways in which tax policies may be affected as a result of forming a customs union.

The first is that there is a strengthening of the case for the origin principle for value-added taxes. If there is a great deal of trans-frontier migration within the customs union there may be real difficulties in abolishing fiscal frontiers if the destination principle is in operation;[15] without customs posts it would be just too easy for people to carry goods from a low-tax jurisdiction to a high-tax one with consequential revenue losses to the latter. Another area where tax policy may have to be re-thought is in respect of social security contribution and benefits. Should contributions paid in one country be a basis for benefits in another? And, if this general principle be admitted, should it be possible for a man now living in country B (where high contributions and high benefits prevail) to be able to draw the same rate of benefit as native-born citizens even though he has paid many, or even all, of his contributions in country A (where low contributions and low benefits prevail)? And if the answer is that the man originating from A cannot draw the high benefits paid to B-born people, how is one to administer a social security structure with two, or more, rates of benefit for people in exactly the same situation with respect to sickness, unemployment, injury, retirement, etc.?

This social security example opens up a wider subject familiar to all students of local public finance.[16] People take into account the balance of taxes paid and public benefits received in deciding where to live and so, if there is easy mobility of labour between tax jurisdictions, migration will tend to take place from the less fiscally attractive areas to the others. This is a well-documented subject arousing much discussion in the context of migration inside individual countries as well as between the member countries of a trading union. Its relevance and importance clearly depend on th precise obstacles to migration which may be present in any particular case.

We have sketched in the role of fiscal policies in a closed economy and have also seen the consequences of admitting international economic relationships generally and those of free trade areas and customs unions in particular. So we are now in a position to look at the situation in the EEC itself.

It seems a fair appraisal to say that, in the first twenty years of its history, fiscal policy has been much more a matter of making a customs union work—at least in respect of manufactured goods—than one of setting up a Community Budget. In addition to the progressive abolition of customs duties within the Community there has been a whole series of directives aimed at 'harmonisation' of value-added taxes in accordance with Article 99 of the Treaty of Rome, culminating in the Sixth Directive of 1973 (and finally adopted in May 1977). There have also been a number of attempts to reduce disparities in the levels and coverage of excise taxes[17] within the Community. In parallel with these developments of taxes on consumer goods, attempts have been made to improve the flow of capital, notably in the original Neumark Report,[18] the later report by van den Tempel,[19] and the Draft Directive of August 1975. There have also been less important developments in the taxation of share issues and stamp duties.

The major attempt to break away from this limited role for fiscal policy was the economic and monetary union proposals of the famous Werner Report.[20] Proposals for locking parities between member countries would have increased the need for other types of adjustment mechanism, including increases in fiscal powers at the central level, e.g. for the purpose of making grants or loans to member countries in balance of payments deficit with the rest. However, these proposals did not gain general acceptance and so today we still have a situation where the Community Budget, at around 10 million budget U.A.[21] is only 0.7 per cent of the Community GNP. Agricultural expenditures, as in the past, continue to take up the overwhelming proportion of expenditure (some 70 per cent). The only substantial change in the Community Budget pattern has been on the revenue side, in that the long-argued case for replacing direct contributions by '*ressources propres*' was to come into being from January 1979 with the introduction of the contributions by member states corresponding to the proceeds of a 1 per cent VAT levy on an agreed common basis. As a result we shall have a situation where the Community Budget is financed to the tune of 12 per cent from levies on agricultural products, 45 per cent from the Common External Tariff and 43 per cent from the 1 per cent VAT contribution.

So the Community is still a very long way from having a budget in the same way as a Federal Government has a budget—both in terms of size (relatively to both member country budgets and to Community GNP) and in terms of ability to run substantial surpluses and deficits. However, there are signs of important developments in this area. One is that, since mid-1977, the budget-making machinery has changed, with the European Parliament playing a role as well as the Commission. Another is that a whole series of new or extended roles for the Community has been sketched out in an important recent report.[22] This report will be discussed more fully later, but we can say now that a number of possible developments in what is called the 'pre-federal integration stage' have been set out there with the idea of developing the Community Budget so that it amounts to $2-2\frac{1}{2}$ per cent of Community GNP (and perhaps even more) rather than the present 0.7 per cent.

What will come of such proposals remains to be seen. There have been many proposals in the past for substantial changes which have come to very little or nothing, and so it would be over-sanguine to imagine that there has been a sudden sea-change and that we are to see increased support for a much enlarged Community budget—especially in the context of the possible entry of countries (Greece, Portugal, Spain) with very different economic characteristics to those of the existing members. Nevertheless, the new horizons are sufficiently interesting to justify further discussion on their own once we have surveyed the progress towards tax harmonisation between member countries.

II MEMBER COUNTRY TAX HARMONISATION FOR TRADE AND FACTOR FLOWS

MEANING OF HARMONISATION

A great deal has been heard over the years, ever since the Treaty of Rome was signed,[23] about the need for tax harmonisation. Although value-added tax is not the only tax (or expenditure) to which the notion has been applied[24] it is the main one and so we can readily explore the general meaning or meanings of the concept in this particular context.

A low-level meaning of harmonisation would be to identify it with 'coordination'. This could in turn be interpreted to be some process of consultation between member countries or, possibly, loose agreements between them to levy tax on a similar sort of base or at similar sorts of rates. A high-level meaning would be 'standardisation' implying that both the base and rates should be identical in all member countries, the Commission having the deciding voice in the precise definition of base and rates.

It seems fair to say that in practice harmonisation has come to mean something between these limits. The system of value-added taxation operating from January 1979 implies a common base for the purpose of assessing Community contributions but not, in any immediate future, for the purpose of collecting revenue for domestic spending—though the extent to which the base differs in the latter case is limited by such general principles as common adoption of the destination principle, deductibility of capital goods expenditures, the 'tax-from-tax' method of computing liability, agreement not to extend zero-rating further, and so on.[25] But even though there is a common base for the restricted purpose of Community contributions, there is no semblance of conformity in the rate structures or in the allocation of different goods and services among the different components of rates structures.

There is another sense in which harmonisation can be said to lie between coordination and standardisation, in that the process of arriving at the 1978 structure was one in which the Commission played an active but not overwhelming role; thus it could not be said that the agreement was entirely due to either member country bargaining or to Commission *diktat*.

Another way of looking at the meaning of harmonisation is to think of two extreme cases: first, where individual country taxes and subsidies impede the free flow of trade across frontiers; and, second, where there is a single unified market inside one country. Harmonisation certainly means tax arrangements which will not impede trade flows; on the other hand, it does not mean an identical tax base and rate structure in all member countries, at any rate in practice, rather than in the eyes of some Euro-dreamers (especially when account has to be taken of such matters as the varying fortunes of different countries as economic integration proceeds). Thus harmonisation in the EEC falls short of any idealised notion of a single unified market but not very short,if at all, of the situation in some countries where competition thrives vigorously, even though tax bases and rates differ from area to area inside them.[26]

Although this discussion of harmonisation has been couched entirely in terms of value-added taxes, the same principles apply to a number of other taxes such as excises and stamp duties, as we shall see later.[27]

The history of VAT during the whole of the decade between the First Directive of 1967 and the adoption of the Sixth Directive in May 1977 has been an attempt to introduce more conformity between the practices of different countries. Initially, the pressure was to substitute VAT for existing taxes such as the German turnover tax or the U.K. (wholesale level) purchase tax; then there was a move to extend coverage of VAT to the retail sector; then to use VAT levies as a means of securing 'ressources propres' for the Community; then to secure a greater degree of uniformity of structure on the lines set out in the Sixth Draft Directive of 1973.[28]

We shall now summarise the way in which VAT operates in the member countries from January 1978 and then discuss the plans and prospects for further changes.

Let us first of all take the elements common to VAT operation in the different countries. The first is that the destination principle applies without exception, so that all member countries relieve all exports of tax, but tax all imports; some marginal problems relating to the treatment of invisible elements in the balance of payments current account were resolved following the Sixth Directive and so need not detain us. It should be clearly understood that the destination principle does not interfere in any way with the international flow of goods and services on normal comparative cost principles. Intuitively, one can think of domestically consumed goods as paying the same rate of tax whether they are produced at home or imported from abroad. Irrespective of whether the tax is thought of as being passed forward on to consumers or backwards on to producers, the relative position of home and foreign suppliers will be unchanged. And this proposition holds whether one has a single rate of tax applying to all goods and services consumed in all Member Countries or whether, in extremis, there is a different tax rate for each such good and service in each country.[29]

The second similarity between countries is that there is a wide range of coverage everywhere, stretching forward into the retail stage and no longer omitting it completely, as was once the case. There is also a general agreement on the concept of value-added and, in particular, the proposition that not only must raw materials, bought-in components and the like be regarded as deductible items when computing tax liabilities, but, in addition, expenditure on fixed capital goods and stock-building should be treated in the same way. This last point is sometimes a matter for surprise, but it is in fact logical necessity if a system of value-added taxation is to be equated to a tax on consumption rather than a tax on income.[30]

Mention of deductibility brings us to another similarity in the VAT systems in the Member Countries in that they all very largely rely on an indirect method of calculating value-added. Instead of making direct calculations of the sum of wages, profits, etc., generated in an enterprise, the value of sales is taken first and then a deduction made for the value of inputs. To use U.K. terminology, the amount of tax payable by any one firm is the output tax (i.e. the tax rate applied to total turnover) less the input tax (i.e. the tax rate applied to the total of inputs). The reason for this apparently roundabout process is the very simple one, first discovered in France, that it constitutes a self-policing operation and so helps tax collection very considerably—in that the purchasing firm will need to have an invoice from its supplier certifying that the tax has been paid before it can safely deduct input tax from its output tax, and so as a consequence each element in the chain of production and distribution will automatically police the tax paid at the preceding stage.

Admirable as is this system for the great majority of outputs, there are cases in which it would be inappropriate, primarily where transactions take place between traders inside and traders outside the VAT system. This brings us to another general similarity between Member Countries: that there are everywhere a number of exemptions from VAT whether defined in terms of particular activities or particular classes of suppliers (e.g. those with a turnover of less than a minimum amount). The precise nature of these exclusions differs very considerably from one country to another but the general principle is admitted everywhere. Inevitably, such exemptions mean that VAT does not work perfectly as a tax on consumption. Imagine, for instance, that there are three stages in the production process. If the first is exempt, this is of no real consequence; the VAT levy on the second and third stages taken together will be the same as if all three stages had been taxable. If the third is exempt, there is obviously a lower total tax take, assuming tax rates to be the same as when all stages are taxable; and in effect all the old problems emerge of wholesale stage and retail stage turnover taxes.[31] If the second stage is omitted, the total tax base is greater than where there are no exemptions, in that the first stage pays tax but there is no means by which such tax can be transmitted as an input tax to the second stage. Similarly, the third stage will not be able to claim any input tax on items bought from the second stage. So we end with a tax based on the aggregated turnover of stages one and three rather than a tax on the total value-added at all three stages.

We stated earlier that the 'tax from tax' method of assessment did not apply in some cases. We can now see why. If, for instance, a used-car dealer buys a car from a private person not registered for VAT purposes he would at the time of re-sale be liable to pay VAT on the sales value of the car without any deductions (neglecting any repairs, etc., which he might do). That would be totally inequitable and so in cases of this sort a direct computation of value-added by the supplier has to be made.

Turning to areas of VAT dissimilarity, the first is that the coverage of VAT differs very considerably from one country to another, each one having different types and levels of exemptions. There is also another feature which applies most particularly to the U.K.: the applicability of zero-rating. Whilst all countries organise VAT in such a way that exports are completely relieved of tax, the U.K. applies the same principle to a wide range of other goods and services, e.g. most foodstuffs, gas and electricity. Essentially, the difference between a zero-rated and an exempt item is that the former is relieved of the tax paid at all prior stages in the production and distribution process as well as that paid at the designated stage (so that such suppliers not only pay no VAT on their own outputs but actually receive refunds in respect of VAT paid at previous stages), whereas exempt items are only excused tax at the designated stage.

A good example of the partial nature of VAT coverage in one particular country is to be found in France. In effect there are four different categories: the normal one where VAT applies in full; the *forfait* system where it applies on a presumptive basis; the simplified system (a transitional one for those opting out of *forfait*); and the agricultural area. The overall result is that the normal system only applies to about one-sixth of the total number of VAT taxpayers.

Another major set of differences is to be found in the rate structure. Table 4.1 shows the structure that prevailed in mid-1977.

There are many other detailed ways in which the VAT system differs from country to country. Thus the U.K. has consistently refused any alleviation of value-added tax in respect of a sale to a purchaser who defaults on payment (a 'bad debt') on the grounds that any purchaser can claim such tax as an input tax in his VAT accounting and so granting relief to the supplier as well would be to allow it twice over. Other countries, such as Ireland, Holland and W. Germany, have been more generous in this respect.[32]

The Sixth Directive has done something to reduce discrepancies

TABLE 4.1   EEC value-added tax rates, 1977

| | Effective rates of value-added tax (%) | | |
	Standard	Reduced rate(s)	Increased rate(s)
Belgium	18	6–14	25
Denmark	15	–	–
France	17.6	7	33.33
Ireland	20	10	35–40
Italy	14	1–3–9	18–35
Luxembourg	10	2.5	–
Netherlands	18	4	–
U.K.	8	–	12.5
W. Germany	11	5.5	–

Source: M. Parr and J. Day, 'Value-Added Tax in the U.K.' National Westminster Bank Review, May 1977.
Notes: (1) The effective rate of tax is the rate of tax on the price excluding tax. The relationship to the nominal rate (i.e. the tax rate on the price including tax) is given by $te = tn/1 - tn$ and $tn = te/1 + te$, where te is the effective rate and tn the nominal rate. (2) The tax rate in Denmark was due to increase from 15 per cent to 18 per cent on 1 January 1978; an increase was also in prospect in W. Germany.

between value-added tax application in different countries, e.g. by tidying up the treatment of imported and exported services, by limiting zero-rating to that which is already in existence and by laying down ground rules for the structure which all Member Countries should plan to adhere to in the long run.

But the breadth of this cleaning-up operation should not be exaggerated. Much of the impact of the Sixth Directive has been to secure an agreed basis on which the 1 per cent Community VAT levy can be imposed without in any sense insisting that countries should from now on and for evermore stick to this base in levying VAT for their own domestic purposes. Thus the Sixth Directive exemption limit for small traders is lower than that now in being in the U.K., so the U.K. 1 per cent levy is calculated by reference to the amount of value which would be added if the exemption limit were at the Directive level, i.e. there is a notional rather than an actual application of the Directive exemption limit.

When looking at future developments in VAT, the most important possibility is the long-term move to a 'restricted origin' basis, i.e. one in which value-added tax would continue to be on a destination basis in respect of trade between an EEC Member and an outside country but would be changed to an origin basis for trade between EEC Members.

The case for such a change, advocated in one form or another ever since the Neumark Report,[33] is essentially that it would allow the abolition of fiscal frontiers between Member Countries and thereby approximate more closely to a true common market.

Suppose we grant this argument for the moment. What would be the implication? The crucial point, as we have seen,[34] is that the origin base would rule out the possibility of value-added tax rate-patterns differing from country to country. Although country A could levy a tax at a generalised rate of x per cent and country B at a generalised rate of y per cent without let or hindrance to trade flows, it would not be possible for country A on its own to exempt just one good from tax without upsetting trade flows—in just the same way as a differential pattern of taxation on the demand side (i.e. a tariff on a particular commodity) hinders trade flows.[35]

From the above, it follows that a move to the restricted origin base would necessitate a common tax rate pattern in each Member Country if the original trade flow intentions of the Common Market founders are not to be frustrated. But this is clearly something which cannot be achieved for many years to come, if ever. So we appear to have the dilemma that fiscal frontiers cannot be abolished without a VAT origin basis; and one cannot have an origin basis without massive re-shaping of VAT tax patterns.

The solution may well be in questioning the dogma that the disappearance of fiscal frontiers is so closely correlated with the adoption of the origin principle. First of all, even if the origin principle were in being it would be necessary to retain customs authorities at all points where trade can take place with a non-EEC country; in effect, this would mean all British and Irish ports, for instance, and a smaller but non-negligible proportion in other countries. In addition, some sorts of checks may well be needed on flows of dangerous and/or prohibited goods (drugs, etc.) crossing frontiers. The second question is whether there is a need for customs posts even if the destination principle remains in being. In so far as the tax-from-tax principle applies, it is of no great consequence whether VAT is collected at the point of entry or at a later stage in the selling process—what is missed initially will be caught later. So in the great majority of cases the absence of customs posts at the point of entry simply does not matter. There are some exceptions: goods such as used cars where the tax-from-tax principle does not operate, international mail order supplies and goods carried across frontiers by individuals would be obvious cases. But it does not seem beyond the wit of man to devise methods to ensure that VAT is not escaped in such cases; it may be that the rate to be applied will have to be that of the country of origin rather than the country of destination but, provided the relative rates are not far apart, this could be acceptable.[36] Putting the whole issue in another way, the U.S.A. has many different levels of State sales taxes operating on a destination basis; and no internal fiscal frontiers. Yet the system works reasonably well. The key may well be that rates do not diverge too much between States,[37] but whether that is correct or not the EEC should surely think rather carefully about this precedent and be willing to reconsider the long-expressed desire to move to a restricted origin basis in order to eliminate fiscal frontiers.

CORPORATION TAX

The very general principle lying behind the Community's concern with Corporation Taxes over the years has been that of improving the working of its capital markets. Such improvements have two dimensions: inside any one country there has been a good deal of emphasis on the desirability of profit distributions rather than retentions by individual firms; and between countries there has been an anxiety to see capital flowing to those outlets offering the highest before-tax rates of return. Emphasis on the latter has pointed to the principle of capital export neutrality (i.e. where an investor pays the same rate of tax, irrespective of the country of location of the investment) rather than that of capital import neutrality (i.e. where the same rate of tax is payable in a country in respect of an investment therein, irrespective of the location of the investor.[38] There are various complications in any such outlook, for example, if an investor in a Member Country has the same tax treatment in respect of investment in any Member Country but different treatment in respect of investment outside the magic circle, then the re-direction of capital flows may not increase overall efficiency; but we shall not pursue this point here.[39]

Consideration has been given over the years to various forms of Corporation Tax. The Neumark Report of 1963[40] recommended a split-rate system, analogous to that prevailing in W. Germany until very recently, whereby retained profits are taxed at one rate and distributed profits at a lower rate at the corporate level but are also subject to personal income tax. The van den Tempel Report[41] of 1970 recommended that the Community should adopt the so-called 'classical' system found in Holland, i.e. tax all corporation profits, distributed or undistributed, at one rate and then subject distributed profits to personal income tax without any allowance for the Corporation Tax which has already been paid. The Draft Directive of August 1975 argued for yet another system—the imputation system—whereby corporation profits are all taxed at the same rate, whether distributed or undistributed, but credit is given for some of the Corporation Tax at the stage when dividends are subject to personal income tax, as in France and the U.K. So all three of the major types of Corporation Tax have been considered at one time or another.

Another subject of discussion has been the method, as distinct from the basis, of harmonisation. The main question here has been the desirability of a single Community–wide Corporation Tax as against the conformity of the tax in all Member Countries to a single pattern. Although arguments can be made in favour of a single Community tax (e.g. it solves any question of companies trying to maximise profits in the least-taxed country by suitable manipulation of transfer prices) it would seem quite unrealistic to expect any such development in the foreseeable future. On the other hand, it has also become clear that there are serious disadvantages if different Member Countries choose different Corporation Tax bases or systems, and so the emphasis has come to be placed on the inevitability of different Member Country taxes, but also on the necessity for a degree of harmony between them.

For various reasons the choice has narrowed down in recent years to the separate system (a more accurate term than 'Classical') and the imputation system.[42] There are, in fact, fairly clear-cut advantages and disadvantages in both arrangements. From the viewpoint of the capital market inside a country, the separate system has the disadvantage of penalising distributions relatively to retentions, whereas the imputation system can be so arranged that the choice between distribution and retention is tax-neutral.[43] But from the viewpoint of international capital flows the boot is on the other foot. This is a complicated argument and so must be looked at in more detail.

The precise way in which an imputation system works is that when a company distributes a dividend it must also calculate a tax-credit according to some predetermined formula. This tax-credit, or 'avoir fiscale' in France, has three different functions. First, it is a basis for grossing up the dividend so as to arrive at the relevant amount to be included in the recipient's income for personal income tax. Second, it is the basis for the credit against personal income tax to compensate for the payment of corporation tax in respect of the sum distributed. Third, it is the basis for a part-payment of Corporation Tax by the company—'Advance Corporation Tax' in the U.K. The first two functions are clear; the reason for the third is that if a dividend is distributed to a resident with no personal tax liability he can normally claim for the refund of the associated tax-credit—but revenue authorities are remarkably reluctant to make such refunds unless they have already received a corresponding amount of tax revenue themselves.

Given this *modus operandi* of an imputation system, one finds that there may be a bias in favour of domestic investment. Suppose a company in country A can invest in either country A or country B; that Corporation Tax rates and personal income tax rates are the same in both countries; and also that there is a double-tax treaty crediting tax payments in one country against those due in the other. If the company invests in A it will pay Advance Corporation Tax when it makes a distribution, but such a payment will be fully taken into account in the final assessment for Corporation Tax. But if it invests in B only it will pay Corporation Tax in B, and this will be credited against liability in A; given the assumption that tax rates are the same there will be no liability to Corporation Tax in A. Yet if it declares a dividend on the basis of the profits generated in B it will be liable to Advance Corporation Tax in A. So it ends up paying both full Corporation Tax in B and partial Corporation Tax in A – a clear penalty on investment in B relatively to that in A.

In practice, the contrast between the tax rates on home and foreign investment may not be quite so stark. For instance, if a company is engaged in both home and foreign activities it may have a sufficient liability to Corporation Tax in the home country to be able to offset Advance Corporation Tax on dividends arising from operations abroad against such a liability. Nevertheless, the tendency to penalise foreign operations is embedded in an imputation system, whatever the amelioration in practice.

No such problem arises with the separate system. Taking our earlier example, the company in country A would pay Corporation Tax at the same rate whether investing in A or in B. As personal tax in country A on dividend payments is completely divorced from Corporation Tax whether it is paid in A or in B there can be no question of penalisation of foreign investment.

So the upshot is that neither the separate system nor the imputation system gets full marks. The separate system does not discriminate against foreign investment but does discriminate between distributions and retentions, and the reverse holds for the imputation system.

In formulating its Draft Directive for Corporation Tax the Commission has endeavoured to grapple with these difficulties. It has plumped for the imputation system and has suggested that Corporation Tax rates should be within the range of 45 per cent to 55 per cent. It has also been suggested that the imputation credit should be 45 per cent to 55 per cent of the Corporation Tax chargeable on the dividend distributed *plus* the underlying Corporation Tax. Designating the Corporation Tax rate as a and the imputation credit rate as b, the rate of tax credit as a percentage of the *net* dividend will be given by $[a \div (100 - a)] \times b$ (e.g. if the corporation tax rate is 50 per cent, the tax credit rate as a percentage of net dividend $= b$). To convert a tax credit rate into an imputation rate, we use the formula $[c \times (100 - a)] \div a$, where c is the tax credit rate. Thus the U.K. 35/65 tax credit rate of 1975–6 would imply an imputation rate of 49.7 per cent—derived from $(35/65) \times (100 - 52)] \div 52$. It will be noted that the actual U.K. rate for a is within the permitted range; and so is the derived rate of b.

It is further proposed that the problem of surplus Advance Corporation Tax arising out of intra-EEC investment be dealt with by a system of credits from countries of source of profits to countries of destination. In other words, the cost of meeting advance liabilities in the country of destination is to be apportioned against other EEC countries on the basis of the Corporation Tax rate they have levied in respect of a firm's activities and their rate of imputation credit. So we end up with a situation where the EEC country in which profits originate collects Corporation Tax less a tax credit; the EEC country where profits are received collects personal income tax and the tax credit.

Another feature of the 1975 proposals is that portfolio investors will be hit in one way and helped in another. It is proposed to have a general withholding tax of 25 per cent on dividends offsettable against final personal income tax liabilities inside the Community; it is also proposed that Corporation Tax credits in any one country should not be restricted to domestic shareholders but be available on a Community-wide basis.[44]

There are many points of detail which could be argued about in these proposals, but as they are still very much *sub judice* it would be pointless spending too much time on them. Perhaps the most important aspect is that they do make a very serious attempt to circumvent the anti-foreign-investment bias inherent in the imputation system. Besides this, any imperfections in the system of calculating tax credits or of withholding taxes on dividends are relatively minor.[45]

It should not be assumed that the transition to the new system will be easy. This can be deduced from two different sorts of considerations. The first is the disparities which existed in 1977 between Corporation Tax systems in the different countries, as shown in Table 4.2.

TABLE 4.2 EEC Corporation Taxes, 1977

	Corporation Tax system	Corporaton Tax Rates (%)
Belgium	Imputation	48
Denmark	Separate	37
France	Imputation	50
Ireland	Imputation	50
Italy	Separate	35
Luxembourg	Separate	40
Netherlands	Separate	48
U.K.	Imputation	52
W. Germany	Imputation	56

Source: European Taxation, various issues.
Notes: 1. Reduced rate for small companies omitted.
2. Although the new system in W. Germany introduced from 1 January 1977 is classified as an imputation system, it does in fact contain elements of the former split rate system, the rate of Corporation Tax being reduced from 56% to 36% in the case of nil profits retention.

The second set of considerations arises from asking whether some countries and some existing procedures are likely to suffer more than others from the new system. There seems to be some reason for thinking that it will work to the disadvantage of Holland which is a relatively attractive location for foreign investment at present.[46] It would also seem to be the case that the present system of double tax relief might disappear—that in effect Corporation Tax would be left to the country of source rather than the present system of crediting such liabilities against Corporation Tax in the country of destination.

OTHER TAXES, ETC.

The Community has devoted most of its energies in the tax harmonisation field to VAT and Corporation Tax, but a few other aspects of its activities should also be noted.

It has long been an aim to harmonise *excise taxes* for reasons analogous to those we have seen in the VAT case. But progress has been very slow for a variety of reasons, e.g. the enormous differences between tax rates on liquor, tobacco, etc. in the Member Countries, the complications of Länder as well as Federal interests in W. Germany, and so on. The greatest progress has been made in the tobacco field, where a new harmonised system was due to operate from 1 January 1978, the principal components being to scrap any duty on raw tobacco leaf (as heretofore in the U.K., for instance) but to have a combination of a new sales tax at manufacturer level, a specific tax per cigarette and VAT – the overall result being to increase the relative prices of the cheaper brands of cigarettes.

This seems to be a fairly small mouse to emerge from a big mountain of labour. But once again one must ask whether the present discrepancies in systems and rates of excise duties between Member Countries matter all that much. Given the destination principle, competition between countries can proceed without hindrance and so one might reasonably ask – why worry?

Another field of endeavour has been that of *stamp duties*. It has been argued that differing systems of taxing security transactions were likely to impede the free flow of capital between Member Countries, and so, after a good deal of cogitation, a draft directive came out in 1976. The proposals were essentially a compromise between existing systems, both in terms of the tax rate and the tax point, the idea being to levy taxes on both sellers and purchasers of securities (0.3 percent for bonds, 0.6 percent on other securities). Rates for bearer securities were to be one-half of the standard rates. It was recognised that some countries operated systems very different from the above (e.g. U.K. 2 per cent on purchases of equities, for anyone resident in the country), but time was to be given for adjustments to be made to the new system.

Finally, even though for reasons of space we are largely confining ourselves to the tax side, there have been a number of harmonisation moves on the expenditure side, especially in the *subsidies* field. Thus there have been attempts to classify subsidies in different categories—transparent (i.e. readily seen), assessable (i.e. calculable with an effort), and opaque (self-explanatory). There is one well-known example in which the Commission intervened to condemn the Italian reduction of social security contributions in textiles and clothing industries as being contrary to the usual competitive principles in the Community. No doubt this side of the Commission's work will gather strength, as it needs to do, given the vast range and complexity of subsidies found in every Member Country.

III THE ROLE OF THE COMMUNITY BUDGET

PRESENT POSITION

As we have seen, the budget of the Community itself has so far been a miniscule affair, totally unlike that of the Member Countries. The 1977 figure was some 10 million budget U.A.,[47] out of which some 70 per cent was devoted to the purposes of the Common Agricultural Policy (CAP) (an obligatory expenditure under the Treaty of Rome); social and regional expenditures amounted to another 10 per cent; and the rest was on a variety of small items. Altogether, as we have seen already, this expenditure was no more than 0.7 per cent of Community GNP compared with Member Country budgets amounting in several cases to something of the order of 40 per cent or more of their GNP. Although there is always scope for disagreement about the measurement or meaning of these ratios, the contrast between 0.7 per cent and 40 per cent speaks for itself.

Nor is there much to be said about the revenue constituents. The Common External Tariff produced some 45 per cent of the 1977 total and the CAP levies a further 12 per cent, the remainder coming from country contributions broadly related to ability to pay, though with a number of transitional provisions for the new members admitted in 1973. The logic of attributing the CET and CAP revenues to the Community rather than to Member Countries is clear enough; both types of revenue arise from Community-wide policies and so, to illustrate, there is no case for attributing CET revenues derived from imports through one particular port to the country in which that port happens to be situated.

Two recent changes in these arrangements have already been mentioned but now need further discussion. The first is that the long-awaited switch from direct contributions to 'ressources propres' was due to come into being from 1 January 1979. Revenue up to 1 per cent of the yield of VAT on a commonly-agreed basis was to be available to the Community from that date. Several points should be noted about this changeover. First, the length of time taken to bring it about; discussions have been going on for the better part of ten years on the subject. Second, the change is more apparent than real in that the (up to) 1 per cent levy does not represent a Community tax in the true sense but is only the basis for the contribution to be paid over by each Member Country. There is no question of a separate Community administration of VAT; nor do countries have to meet this precept by an increase in their existing VAT rates, in that they can raise the necessary revenue by any method they think appropriate. Nor does the existence of a common VAT basis for this purpose mean that Member Country VAT structures must be immediately adjusted to it for the purpose of raising their own VAT revenues. So, overall, the importance of the change is, at any rate in the present form, all too easily exaggerated.

The other major change is in budget-making machinery. Since mid–1977 the European Parliament has had a role as well as the Council of Members in budget formulation. It is too early to say exactly what difference this will make, but potentially the significance is very great, in that once direct elections take place there will, for the first time, be a representative body concerned with these matters—as distinct from them being purely a matter for Ministers. It should also be noted that no one country will have a veto in these matters (in accordance with Article 203 of the Treaty of Rome).

FUTURE POSSIBILITIES

By far the most intensive and extensive work on future Community budgetary possibilities is to be found in the work of the MacDougall study group[48] and what we have to say is largely based on their exposition.

A number of different possibilities are distinguished by the authors. A growth of Community budget expenditure to roughly 1 per cent of Community GNP is already in train; and this happens to be about the maximum amount which the existing sources of revenue (CET and CAP levies together with the 1 per cent VAT contribution) will support. Beyond that, there is the stage of what is dubbed 'pre-federal integration', associated with a Community budget amounting to some 2 per cent of GNP and necessitating a $2\frac{1}{2}\%$ VAT levy, allowing for the likely trends in the other revenue sources. The next stage is called 'small public sector federation', with Community expenditure amounting to 5 per cent or so of GNP and necessitating an 8 per cent VAT levy. Finally, a stage of 'large public sector federation' is envisaged with 20 to 25 per cent of GNP being taken in Community expenditure; but no one would think that such a change is remotely conceivable for very many years to come and so we shall not discuss this (bad?) dream here.

There are a number of ways in which one can think about the details of an enlarged Community budget. But before exploring them one point should be given the greatest possible emphasis; the intention, or at any rate the hope, of the MacDougall Report was not to advocate an extension of the public sector at the expense of the private one, but rather to enlarge the Community role at the expense of Member Country governments, whether at central or at local level. So the whole of what follows should be understood to be very specifically formulated in that context.

One way in which the enlargement of Community functions can be considered is in terms of standard economic concepts—pure public goods, spillovers between jurisdictions, regional and personal income distribution, stabilisation and demand management policies and so on. It is possible to make some mileage here in various ways. Thus it can be argued that representation of Community interests in international trade negotiations or world energy discussions is best done on a centralised rather than on a Member Country basis.[49] Income distribution is not just a matter of that between countries but also of that between regions in different countries. The figures in Table 4.3 show the nature of the problem.

TABLE 4.3   Personal income differentials in EEC countries

Country & year	Poorest Region/State		Richest Region/State		Maximum/minimum ratio
	(Average level = 100)				
W. Germany (1970)	Saar	81	Hamburg	133	1.6
France (1970)	Midi-Pyrénées	80	Paris	139	1.7
Italy (1973)	Calabria	60	Liguria	134	2.2
U.K. (1964)	N. Ireland	69	South-East	119	1.7
EEC 9 countries (1975)	Ireland	57	Belgium	123	2.2
EEC 2 regions (1970)	Calabria	41	Paris	161	4.0

Source: MacDougall Report, op. cit., Vol. I, p. 27.
Note: For the EEC comparisons (last two rows) purchasing power parity exchange rates are used.

Given disparities of this sort—and even greater ones which could emerge in the process of economic integration—there would seem to be some *prima facie* case for looking into them at Community level. However, one has to be careful here. First of all, one reason for intervention at higher than at lower levels of government which exists in some countries is not so important in the EEC in that the danger of better-off people moving from more heavily taxed Member Countries to more lightly taxed ones is less than, say, between the States of the U.S.A. Therefore the necessity for intervention at an upper level of government is accordingly less; it is difficult to argue this is not something which can be done effectively at Member Country level.[50]

In addition, one must also remember the limitation of Community expenditure-making powers in the foreseeable future. Unless and until a grants system can be levied. which can somehow be tied to helping particular people in particular regions or particular countries, Member

Countries could only too easily thwart any redistributional intentions at higher levels by diverting funds to other purposes.[51]

With respect to stabilisation policy, the main question is whether, as integration proceeds, the cycle in the different Member Countries is likely to converge so that something akin to a Community cycle would emerge. There are some grounds for suggesting that this would tend to happen.[52] If so, this in turn leads to some arguments in favour of Community remedies for Community ills; one possibility is Community financing of unemployment benefits, retraining courses and the like. It has also been suggested that the Community VAT levy could be varied in a countercyclical fashion. But this proposal is subject to the serious drawback that it is not a tax which is directly imposed by the Community on consumers and so there could be no guarantee that Community changes in VAT levies on Member Countries would be reflected in net tax burdens on residents. Such a move would also presumably carry with it the necessity for the Community to have borrowing powers, but this latter difficulty is less formidable than the former one.

There are other approaches to the discussion of enlarging Community functions, such as, for instance, what the MacDougall Study Group called 'looking from the bottom up' at specific expenditure functions like agriculture, education, health, etc.,[53] rather than, as we have done so far, 'looking from the top down'. But we have said sufficient to indicate the sort of ways in which expenditure might go; and the very real inhibitions on the growth of such expenditures. Rather than going further into this, we might ask about the likely methods of financing such expenditure increases. As we saw earlier, relatively modest increases in Community expenditures would necessitate relatively large increases in VAT levies. A particular suggestion by the Study Group was that such levies should have a progressive element in them so that a country with a high GNP per head would be subjected to a higher percentage rate of levy than one with a smaller GNP per head. This proposal brings us face to face with the central question lying behind proposals for additional Community—level expenditure. If there is no redistribution between Member Countries (i.e. if extra taxes in a country pay for its extra benefits) what is the case for Community rather than Member Country expenditure? If there is redistribution, whether via the revenue or expenditure sides, are the richer countries really prepared to make anything more than minimum contributions to poorer ones? Unless and until this latter question can be answered in the affirmative (taking account not just of the existing membership but also of the potential accession of Greece, Portugal and Spain) plans for large increases in Community expenditure are likely to exist in a dream world only. This does not in any sense mean that one cannot look forward to marginal increases in the Community budgets as a percentage of GNP over the years, but simply that more than major reversals of political attitudes will be needed before less than major increases in such expenditure are feasible.

IV. CONCLUSIONS

The overriding consideration in any discussion of fiscal policy in the EEC is that the Community is a strange and perhaps even unique animal. The links between the Member Countries in respect of trade and factor flows are certainly closer than those found between fully separate countries, most especially in respect of trade in manufactures. On the other hand, the pattern of relationships is much less close than that found in the classic federation, whether one considers the linkages between Member States or that between the States and the top tier of government. In particular, the role of the top tier in the EEC is extremely limited.

So it is not surprising that until now the major thrust of fiscal policy has been in the direction of removing impediments to trade between Member Countries, with the dismantling of tariff barriers, the introduction of and partial harmonisation of VAT, and so on. Although there is plenty more to think about on this front (e.g. the abolition of fiscal frontiers, the effects of subsidies on trade flows, and so on) it is clear that other topics are likely to come much more to the front than in the past. The 1975 Draft Directive on Corporation Tax and its implications for capital flows is one illustration. Far more radical are the proposals for greater revenue and expenditure powers at Community level. Starting from a situation where the Community's main expenditure role is in respect of CAP outgoings, there are now wide-ranging suggestions for a Community presence on matters of common interest to Member Countries, for grants directed towards regions suffering from the process of economic integration, for Community demand management, and so on. It might well appear to some that the 'ressources propres' ingredient in the Community's revenue from January 1979 is a signal for taking the cork out of the expenditure bottle with a flourish. However, it would seem more realistic to think that the rate of progress on such ambitious lines is more likely to resemble that of the tortoise than that of the hare, especially in view of the new problems likely to arise if membership expands to include Greece, Portugal and Spain.

NOTES

1. See A. R. Prest 'Government Revenue, the National Income and All That' in R. M. Bird and J. G. Head, *Modern Fiscal Issues* (Toronto: University of Toronto Press, 1972).
2. A. T. Peacock and J. Wiseman, *The Growth of Public Expenditure in the U.K.*, 2nd edn. (London: Allen and Unwin, 1967).
3. e.g. R. W. Bahl, 'A Regression Approach to Tax Effort and Tax Ratio Analysis' *I.M.F. Staff Papers*, November 1971.
4. e.g. R. J. Chelliah, H. J. Baas and M. R. Kelly, 'Tax Ratios and Tax Effort in Developing Countries 1969–71', *I.M.F. Staff Papers*, March 1975.
5. The crucial point is that raising more tax revenue must be expected to have substitution effects (anti-work) and income effects (normally pro-work). Public provision of goods will only have income effects (normally anti-work) and so the overall effect is work-adverse. But subsidisation will have both substitution and income effects, thus roughly cancelling out the revenue side-effects. Cf. C. S. Shoup, 'The Limits on the Taxation Capacity of a Country' (*unpublished paper*).
6. See for example, R. A. and P. B. Musgrave, *Public Finance in Theory and Practice*, 2nd edn. (New York: McGraw-Hill, 1976) Ch. 29.
7. *Adam Smith, The Wealth of Nations*, Book V (eds R. H. Campbell, A. S. Skinner and W. B. Todd) (Oxford: Clarendon Press, 1976).
8. An origin basis for a value-added tax indicates that exports are taxed but not imports—the reverse being the case with a *destination* basis. A *selective* value-added tax has to be contrasted with a *general* one applying to all the relevant goods and services.
9. A. R. Prest, *Public Finance in Theory and Practice*, 5th edn (London: Weidenfeld & Nicolson, 1975) Ch. 17.
10. *Ibid.* Ch. 18; and M. Sato and R. M. Bird, 'International Aspects of the Taxation of Corporations and Shareholders', *I.M.F. Staff Papers*, July 1975.
11. Thus when the split rate system of corporation tax (see above, p. 84) prevailed in W. Germany, a U. S. subsidiary operating in Germany was able to remit a larger fraction of its profits home than could a German subsidiary operating in the U.S.A. (See A. R. Prest, *op. cit.*, p. 387). Realisation of this point played a major role in persuading the U.K. government to adopt an imputation system of corporation tax rather than a split-rate system in the early 1970s.
12. Thus a commodity entering country A from outside the EFTA is taxed on the basis of A's tariff; if it is subsequently re-exported to EFTA country B, it would not be liable for any additional duty on the basis of B's tariff structure, if value-added in A is equal to 50 per cent or more of the value of the export to B.

13. Cf. R. A. Musgrave, *Fiscal Systems* (New Haven: Yale University Press, 1969) Ch. 11, for a detailed exposition.
14. We shall return to this subject in the specific context of the EEC. See below p. 83.
15. As we shall see later, the destination principle is more likely to fall down in this respect than in the case of freight movements, i.e. there is a better chance of avoiding duty losses in the latter case.
16. Much of the literature stems from well-known articles published in the 1950s, e.g. J. M. Buchanan, 'Federalism and Fiscal Equity', *American Economic Review* (September 1950) and C. M. Tiebout, 'A Pure Theory of Local Expenditure', *Journal of Political Economy* (October 1956).
17. e.g. the Commission proposals of 1972.
18. *Report of the Fiscal and Financial Committee* (EEC, Brussels, 1963).
19. A. J. van den Tempel, *Corporation Tax and Income Tax in the European Communities* (EEC, Brussels, 1970).
20. *Economic and Monetary Union* (EEC, Brussels, 1969).
21. 2.4 budget U.A. = £1 sterling.
22. *Report of the Study Group on the Role of Public Finance in European Integration*, Vols. I and II (EEC, Brussels, April 1977).
23. Article 99 provided explicitly for the harmonisation of indirect taxes.
24. Other taxes include excise duties, stamp duties and Corporation taxes. There are also many other applications of the concept (e.g. the draft directive on products liability) outside the realm of public finance.
25. We shall have more to say about these characteristics later in this chapter.
26. The U.S.A. is the obvious example. See p. 84.
27. See p. 88.
28. The elapse of four years between the issue of the Draft Directive in 1973 and its final adoption in 1977 is in itself an indication of the trials and tribulations of gaining agreement on tax harmonisation within the EEC. This argument holds *a fortiori* if one also takes into account all the discussions prior to the publication of the Draft Directive.
29. For a formal exposition, see R. A. Musgrave, *Fiscal Systems (op. cit.)* Ch. 11.
30. With a closed economy, and taking $Y = GNP$, $W =$ Wages and Salaries, $P =$ Gross Profits, $C =$ Consumption and $I =$ Gross Capital Expenditure, we then have $Y \equiv (W + P) \equiv C + I$. It therefore follows that if value-added is defined as $W + P - I$, the tax base will be consumption. If one only deducted capital consumption rather than gross investment from $(W + P)$, one would then have a base equal to net national product. The same arguments still hold once foreign trade is admitted.
31. Cf. A. R. Prest, *Public Finance in Theory and Practice*, 5th edn. (London: Weidenfeld & Nicolson) p. 410 ff.
32. A change may be in the offing in the U.K. on this matter. Cf. *Value Added Tax – Bad Debt Relief* (Discussion Paper prepared by H. M. Customs & Excise, London, 1977). Also Finance Act, 1978.
33. *op. cit.*
34. p. 74 above.
35. Cf. R. A. Musgrave, *Fiscal Systems (op. cit.,* Ch. 11), for fuller discussion.
36. Thus, for instance, a sale of a used car by a French dealer to a German non-trader for his own use would escape tax in both countries initially; but this

could be picked up at the next registration. Personal exports and mail-order supplies crossing frontiers could best be dealt with by withdrawing zero-rating privileges in such cases; they would then be taxed at the rate prevailing in the country of origin rather than in that of destination.

It should be noted that the personal export and mail-order-supply cases differ in that the origin principle (i.e. no zero-rating on exports) is more readily applied in the former than in the latter case. If the origin principle is in fact applied in the first case, it is the difference in country rates which would be at stake; but if the origin principle is not applied in the second case, VAT would be escaped in both countries.

37. Thus it is reported that highly differentiated taxes on cigarettes in New York and North Carolina have led to difficulties in recent years.
38. See H. Sato and R. M. Bird, *op. cit.*, p. 408.
39. *Ibid*, p. 448, for elaboration.
40. *Op. cit.*
41. *Op. cit.*
42. Partly because France and the U.K. had already adopted the latter form, and because W. Germany was known to be planning to move away from the split-rate system.
43. See A. R. Prest, *op. cit.*, Ch. 17.
44. The principle of non-restriction of credits already applies but depends on specific agreements between pairs of countries.
45. See J. D. R. Adams and J. Whalley, *The International Taxation of Multinational Enterprises* (London: Institute for Fiscal Studies and Associated Business Programmes, 1977) Ch. 18 for extended discussion on the whole of this subject.
46. *Ibid.*
47. 2.4 budget U.A. = £1 sterling. (As from 1978, budget expenditure was to be expressed in European U.A., with a conversion rate of 1.6 U.A. = £1 sterling.)
48. *Report of the Study Group on the Role of Public Finance in European Integration, op. cit.*
49. *Report, op. cit.*, Ch. 12.
50. Cf. W. E. Oates, 'Fiscal Federalism in Theory and Practice' in *Report, op. cit.*, Vol. II. If the plans for Economic and Monetary Union implying fixed exchange rate parities were to be revived, there would obviously be another reason for advocating transfers between Member Countries.
51. Even if the Community grant were tied to particular types of spending, Member-Country disbursements for such purposes might be correspondingly reduced, unless some matching arrangement were in being.
52. Cf. W. E. Oates, *op. cit.*
53. *Report, op. cit.*, Ch. 12.

5 Trade and monetary policy

PETER COFFEY

TRADE POLICY: THEORETICAL CONSIDERATIONS

A group of countries which form a customs union is faced with a wide choice of theoretical and practical policies which may be adopted in its trading relations with third-party countries. At the outset, it goes without saying that the Member States of the customs union will have liberalised trade between themselves, thus implying that trade is, thereafter, concerned with third parties. However, the internal economic policies adopted by a customs union will also profoundly influence its trading policies toward non-Member Countries. Nowhere is this more apparent than in the case of the European Economic Community.

To return to basic theoretical issues, a customs union faces a selection of options ranging between two extremes. On the one hand, it may opt for self-sufficiency (perhaps using the argument of security of supply—for strategic reasons) and consequently it will adopt a restrictive policy towards imports from third parties. On the other hand, the customs union may opt for internal economic policies whereby, over time,the prices of internally-produced goods will be aligned with world prices. Should the union adopt such policies, then one may assume that, once its prices are aligned with world prices, the *raison d'être* of the customs union disappears and the union might no longer exist. Whichever of these policies (or combination of policies) is adopted, the welfare of some of the inhabitants of the Member States will be increased. If the former policies are adopted, the welfare of producers in the union is most likely to be promoted since they will be protected; whereas, if the latter policy is adopted, the welfare of consumers is most likely to be increased since they will have access to supplies of goods at world prices (assuming that world prices are lower than those for goods produced within the union).

Unfortunately for the economist, many nuances and a host of non-purely-economic considerations are likely to influence both theoretical and practical trade policies. Thus, for example, some of the Member States may favour the adoption of economic policies of self-sufficiency whereas others may desire to adopt somewhat more open trading policies towards third parties. In both cases, the Member States will be seeking to maximise their economic advantages. On the other hand, when engaging in international trade negotiations, the Member States may present a united front in order to obtain concessions (in the Vinerian sense) from third parties. Some Member States may wish to maintain links with former colonies and/or associates for purely political reasons, whilst others may wish to maintain access to existing sources of supply for certain raw materials and products. In the Member States themselves, some lobbies and interest groups will have a political influence out of all proportion to their size and will doubtlessly seek to use this power in order to maximise their welfare. As a consequence of these pressures and because of other considerations, a customs union may have a public preference for some economic sectors and may seek to protect such activities from competition from third parties.

All the afore-mentioned considerations imply that the formation of a customs union and the adoption of trading policies towards third parties will seek to maximise both the economic and political welfare of certain sectors within the union itself and among some of its trading partners. Nevertheless, whilst a mixture of both trade diversion and creation is likely to occur, should the economic prosperity of the customs union increase substantially, then this may have a beneficial effect on trade with third parties. The trading policies adopted and their consequences will necessarily be dependent upon the economic structure of the Member States making up the union.

In the specific case of the European Economic Community, this basic economic structure would prove to be of overriding importance in the creation and implementation of its trading policies.

THE EEC: THE SIX

When the Treaty of Rome was signed 1957, the six Member States of the Common Market displayed the following characteristics. They were mainly industrial countries with important agricultural sectors and heavily dependent upon foreign supplies of oil and raw materials. Also, some of these states, especially France, possessed colonies for which special provisions would have to be made. Thus, specific internal economic and external trading policies were adopted.

Internally, provisions were made for the gradual removal of tariffs on industrial goods and the erection of a common external tariff. This common external tariff was to be an average of existing tariffs. Similarly, provisions were made for the creation of a common agricultural market based on the principle of 'security of supplies'. Although, at the famous Stresa meeting in 1958, the basic aims of the Agricultural Policy seemed to be the restructuring of the sector and the eventual aligning of Common Market prices with World ones, the outcome has become more a policy of self-sufficiency. However, what is most important here is that during the period in which the common agricultural market was being formed, the Community expressly refused to include agriculture in international trade negotiations. Further, it is the agricultural consideration which continues to upset trading relations with third parties.

When the Community was set up in 1958, certain clearly defined geographical areas of trading interest existed. As has been mentioned, some Members possessed colonies, and, in the special case of France, that country has already stated at the Venice meeting of 1956 that a precondition for her membership the EEC was the making of some arrangements for her African colonies. Also, since Algeria was treated as part of France, the French expected this arrangement to continue. Two countries, Germany and Italy, took a somewhat different stance, since they wished to maintain supplies of bananas and coffee from traditional sources. The outcome was that in the Treaty of Rome specific provision was made for the special trading interests of the Member States. Both theoretically and practically, the Common Market may be regarded as a strange phenomenon, since it is a customs union whose members wished to maintain their former special trading links with third parties.

Geographically then, the main areas of trading interest may be said to be Africa, the Mediterranean and Eastern Europe. A special feature concerning the last-mentioned area is the special situation of the two Germanies. Trade between these two countries is treated as being internal German trade.

The listing of only three areas of special trading interest outside the Community does not, of course, imply that the EEC did not have interests elsewhere. It naturally had an interest in trading with Western Europe, North America, Asia and other parts of the world. It had considerable interest in international trade negotiations, world monetary questions, energy problems and in the dialogue with the Third World countries in general; but the three afore-mentioned areas were clearly defined geographical parts of the world for which policies were laid down. It is to these individual areas to which we should now turn our attention.

AFRICA

The special consideration of the emerging agricultural market influenced the relations between the Community and Africa—as it did relations with all other trading partners. Thus in the initial preferential trading arrangements which were made for the African partners, temperate agricultural products were excluded. Also, special arrangements were made which allowed Italy and Germany to import bananas and coffee from traditional sources.

These two considerations simply meant that the initial arrangements made for these African countries gave them a secure and bigger market in Western Europe for their tropical products at guaranteed prices, and that they received aid which supplemented the aid already being granted by the mother colonial powers. In turn, their own markets were opened up to the manufactured products of the Six, and in fact, most of these African Associated Territories gave reverse preferences to the countries of the Common Market.

When these initial agreements expired, many of the African Associates had attained, or were in the process of attaining, independence, which meant that a new agreement with an institutional framework had to be drawn up. There were two such new agreements which were known as the Yaoundé Agreements.[1]

Both Yaoundé I and II were notable for a number of features. These were: the exclusion of temperate agricultural produce; the application (with the exception of some of the Associates) of the principle of reciprocity; duty-free entry for raw materials from the African states; guaranteed prices—at a lower level than formerly—for African tropical products; and an increase in the amount of aid provided by the Six. There was also, it is true, a small but potentially important gesture which was part of Yaoundé II and which took the form of interest-free loans which were intended to help cushion fluctuations in world prices for the products of the African Associates.

Analytically, the results of the two Yaoundé Agreements are of particular interest to economists studying both developed and developing countries. As was to be expected, a diversion of African Associate trade is noticed from France to the other five Members of the Common Market. However, although there is an increase in the trade of the African Associates with the Community, it nevertheless falls as a percentage of total EEC trade during the period 1961–71.[2] This fall implies that the terms of trade of the African Associates have tended to fall for traditional exports, which, despite diversification, remain the mainstay of most of the economies concerned. Indeed, although the African Associates did increase their industrialisation during the period just mentioned, it does not seem to have been enough to make good the general loss in terms of trade. Also, further research might even show that part of the industrial enterprises are under some form of foreign control, implying that some of the earnings will have been transferred abroad.

These observations tend to underline a belief that the Common Market wished, in making the Yaoundé Agreements, to maintain and secure its traditional sources of supplies of raw materials and tropical foodstuffs whilst carefully protecting its infant Common Agricultural Market. In turn, it would also be true to say that some of the African Associates are among the poorest countries in the world. In such cases, it would be difficult to see how they could survive unless they could count on assured markets at guaranteed prices for their products and substantial French and Community financial aid. Naturally, for such countries, the EEC did not demand reciprocity in the framework of the Yaoundé Agreements.

It was natural that when the Yaoundé Agreements came up for re-negotiation—and in view of Britain's impending membership of the Common Market— some arrangements would have to be made to widen trading relations between the Community and the Third World. The outcome has been the much-discussed Lomé Convention.

The Lomé Convention, whilst evolving logically along the basic lines of the Yaoundé Agreements, is nevertheless a major leap forward as far as the African, Caribbean and Pacific (ACP) States are concerned and contains important innovations. Basically speaking, although presenting a list of demands,[3] the aspirations of the ACP countries can be said to have been the removal of the principle of reciprocity between the two sides, the obtaining of the best financial and commercial deal from the Common Market, price guarantees for some basic products and regional development (through regional groupings) and industrialisation of ACP States.

Most of these demands were met. To economists, the two significant advances were the three trade agreements (at guaranteed prices) for sugar, rum, and bananas; and the STABEX system which is aimed at giving financial assistance if the revenue from the earnings of certain products falls below agreed levels. The STABEX scheme has not been received without some dissension, because the EEC has made the proposal that those countries able to do so should make repayments so as to reconstitute the reserves of the fund five years after receipt of financial aid.

Despite criticisms of the reconstitution proposal for STABEX and reservations made by some observers about the real amount of aid being given to the ACP States, present and future, the Lomé Agreement does mark an improvement on the Yaoundé Agreements. It is much more a dialogue between equals, it is an 'open' treaty, and it does contain two important developments in the commodity trading agreements and the STABEX scheme. Also, the Community maintains that 94.2 per cent of the ACP States' exports to EEC Countries will now enter the Community free of duty. It is too early, as yet, to see whether this claim is completely realistic. If it does prove to be true, it will be an important opening in the agricultural policy of the EEC.

THE MEDITERRANEAN

The Community has had economic, cultural and political links with Mediterranean countries since before its inception. In fact, policies towards both African and Mediterranean countries began simultaneously, since both France and Italy asked for special arrangements to be made for countries in both areas with which they had special connections. In the special case of France, Algeria was treated as part of France and special arrangements were made for Morocco and Tunisia. However, here any similarity between policies towards the two areas ends. Further, it was not until 1972 that the adoption of a 'global' Mediterranean policy (i.e. the creation of a free trade area) was being clearly discussed.

Between the dates of the special agreements made for the Magreb countries and the 1972 proposals, a whole host of agreements of many kinds were made, of which the two most important ones were association agreements made with Greece and Turkey. The Greek one was rather generous—particularly in the field of agriculture. It is perhaps this somewhat irresponsible act of generosity which has prompted Greece and other Mediterranean countries to ask for full membership of the EEC—which is their basic right since most of them are European democracies. However, most of them present one problem to the Community, which is their production of a number of agricultural goods which will compete with French and Italian products. This is a serious situation since the EEC is already self-sufficient in some agricultural products.

The request for membership by Greece, Portugal, Spain—and eventually Turkey—does, nevertheless, present a varied picture. In fact, Greece would probably present the least economic problems to the Community. The Greek economy is at present a strong one and her equally strong currency is an obvious candidate for the European 'Snake', the arrangement whereby national currencies of Common Market (and some other) countries fluctuate within a narrow band of 2.25 per cent. With the possible exception of tobacco, her agriculture does not present too great a threat to that of France and Italy. Further, she has ceased to be a sending country of migrants, and, by contrast, welcomes foreign capital. Greece also has a balance between weak and strong industries: the former would probably disappear and the latter improve their position if Greece became a Full Member of the Community. Nevertheless, as in the case of Portugal and Spain, Greece's overriding reason for wishing to join the Community is political.

Whilst sharing Greek political motivations in their desire to join the Community, the economies of Spain and Portugal present quite a different picture vis-à-vis the EEC. The two countries have one thing in common, they are important migrant-sending states which wish to maintain the right for freedom of movement for their nationals within the Common Market. However, the Spanish economy presents the more important industrial and agricultural competitive challenge to the Community. Spain is an important industrial power, producing goods at competitive prices. Some agricultural products, too, especially wine, compete with similar French and Italian products.

The case of Portugal is very different. Indeed, with the exception of textiles and quality wines, Portuguese agriculture and industry do not present a competitive threat to the EEC. Rather, the situation is one where Portugal would require considerable help from the Community. Regarding agriculture, Portugal, like the United Kingdom, imports half her food. Further, whilst the south, with its large-sized holdings, could eventually be geared to the Common Agricultural Policy, the north could not, since it is composed of multitudes of smallholdings. Furthermore, if Portugal were forced to accept the Community's agricultural policy, it would mean an unacceptable rise in the cost of living for the inhabitants of a country with the lowest income levels in Western Europe.

Portuguese industry, with the exceptions of textiles and ship-repairing, would need massive aid and a breathing-space of at least ten years before being in a position to accept the full rigours of Common Market competition. The only possible solution for Portugal, if it is not to become an American colony, is for the EEC to give the country massive European Marshall Aid.

Although Turkey has not yet made formal request for full membership of the EEC, this country has the same right as has Greece since both countries are Associate Members of the Community and it was always understood that they would, one day, become Full Members. Turkey does, however, present potentially more competitive problems for the Common Market than do the other candidates. Turkey's economy is heavily dependent on agriculture and flows of migrants' remittances. Thus, the Turks actively desire the Common Market to be open to their agricultural exports and migrants. In recent years, there have been conflicts due to the growing reluctance of the EEC to accept any further liberalisation in these fields. Turkey, also, is not keen (for historical reasons) to receive foreign capital and would prefer to protect its weaker industries.

The basic problem common to EEC relations with Mediterranean countries is agriculture. It is difficult to envisage the creation of a Mediterranean Free Trade Area embracing both sides unless there is some change in the Common Agricultural Policy and a more open attitude on the part of the Community regarding imports of industrial goods—especially textiles. In the immediate future, there is no sign of such a change: rather one sees a move in the opposite direction.

EASTERN EUROPE

In contrast with the Community's Mediterranean policy, the EEC's attitude towards Eastern Europe can be said to display consistency. The origins of this policy are found in Common Market fears of possible 'dumping' in any one or several Community Countries by East European states. Thus, in 1960, the Council of Ministers decided to request the insertion of a 'Community Clause' into all trade agreements, thus allowing for the renegotiation of clauses not conforming with the Community's common policy. Further, this clause was intended to counter the policy of the Soviet Union, which favoured 'long-term' bilateral trade agreements, whilst the Community favoured arrangements of a more 'short-term' nature. Also—and this is of some importance in international legal relations—the Soviet Union has always refused to recognise the Common Market as a juridical entity. Hence this clause has tended to counter Soviet policy in that it has given the EEC an international legal personality.

The situation is now one where the Commission negotiates on behalf of the Community. Official contacts have been made (including exchanges of visits) between COMECON and EEC Commission officials. However, the relations between the two bodies move up and down with a boring regularity. In 1975, for example, when the two sides met in Moscow, little was achieved due to lack of enthusiasm on the part of the COMECON. More recently, at a meeting in Brussels, one noted the same lack of success—but due, on this occasion, to the lack of enthusiasm by the Community!

During the late sixties trade did increase between both sides, but it still accounts for only a small percentage of EEC trade. As with the Mediterranean policy—and so many of the Community's trading policies—the obstacle has been the Common Agricultural Policy. Thus, in the case of the East European countries, the Community's beef 'mountain' led to a curtailment of EEC imports of this product from Eastern Europe. This was a grievous below for these countries and it is hard to see how trade can increase between the two sides unless agricultural trade is liberalised. Also, any increase in trade in other products will depend very much on the degree to which the Common Market can offer credits to East European countries.

OTHER TRADING POLICIES AND RELATIONS

Although clear trading policies can only be discerned in the case of the three groups of countries just examined, these groups are not, in fact, major trading partners of the Community. During the period 1961–71, in descending order of importance, the major trading areas of the Community were the EEC itself, the rest of the world (which included Eastern Europe, Asia, the Middle East, Commonwealth Countries, Latin America and European countries which were not members of EFTA or COMECON), EFTA and the USA. But, among these groupings, in percentage terms, trade only increased between the members of the EEC themselves and between the Community and the USA. In global financial terms, however, Community trade increased threefold!

Different studies have observed different reasons for these phenomena. Most observers are in agreement about the trade 'diversion' effects of the Community's agricultural policy. The excellent EFTA study of 1972 was also clear about the trade 'diversion' effects between the EEC and EFTA.[4] However, these observations have played down somewhat three important considerations. These considerations were the effects of the Kennedy Round Negotiations, the 'Community effect' on third parties due to the persistently high level of investment and income creation in the 1960s, and the trade phenomenon of the period lasting from the late 1950s to the early 1970s when the greatest trade increases were between highly industrialised countries trading in similar products. Here it should not be forgotten that this also happened to be a period in which the terms-of-trade were more favourable to the industrialised countries and that energy supplies were cheap.

The Kennedy Round Negotiations were important mainly for two reasons. First, they did lead to a major decrease in world tariffs. Second, they marked the high point of the Community's common personality and negotiating strength in international negotiations, whether trade or monetary ones. The essential factor here is that, whilst the Community had at the outset agreed in principle to the American suggestion that tariff negotiations up to a level of fifty per cent across-the-board be contracted, it stipulated, as a pre-condition, prior negotiations leading to reductions in the highest tariffs (practised mainly by the USA) before negotiating on an across-the-board basis. Since these negotiations were concluded, and since the enlargement of the Community, the unity of the EEC has declined.

When Britain, Denmark and Ireland joined the Community, it was agreed that some form of free-trading agreement would have to be offered to the other members of EFTA. These agreements were signed with each individual country on 1 April 1973 and allowed for a short transitional period lasting until 1 July 1977. With some exceptions, all the agreements are the same. During the transitional period, the partners removed tariffs on industrial products (Chapters 25–99 of the Brussels Tariff Nomenclature), thus creating a vast industrial free trade area in Western Europe.

Unfortunately, the rules of origin are not liberal since the effective value-added is about 60 per cent of the ex-factory price of the finished products. According to Madame Victoria Curzon, 'A manufactured product will thus qualify for preferential treatment in the EEC and its individual EFTA partners if it is "wholly produced" within the area of association . . . or if it has undergone "sufficient" transformation within the area'.[5]

PRESENT AND FUTURE POLICIES

Apart from the Lomé Agreement, the enlarged Community is engaged in a number of important negotiations and is crystallising a general policy towards trade.

On the positive side, the EEC associated itself with a major commodity agreement (for sugar) in the first week of October 1977. This agreement, which covers 14 per cent of world production but which excludes the Lomé countries, will run for a period of five years as from 1 January 1978. It is an important agreement because it could become a model for other commodity agreements. It provides for floor and ceiling prices as well as the use of quotas and stocks. The latter will be financed from levies from exporters and importers but special help is provided for the poorer countries.

On the negative side, not only has the Community dragged its feet in the Geneva negotiations about the setting-up of a Common Fund intended to stabilise the prices of the products of Third World countries, but also has adopted a negative and authoritarian attitude in the renewal of the Multi-Fibre Textile Agreement with over thirty countries which was concluded in Brussels in November 1977. This latter agreement is of most negative portent for the future since it implies that the Community still wishes to protect its home producers of goods such as T-shirts as well as other textiles.

It is quite ridiculous for a group of sophisticated industrial countries like the Nine to wish to produce very basic textiles instead of specialising in the production of quality goods. Further, if the Common Market allowed Third World countries to specialise in producing basic textiles, the welfare of both sides would be increased. However, the main international trade negotiations in which the Community is presently engaged are the Tokyo Round negotiations, being held at Geneva in the framework of the GATT. Once again, as with the Kennedy Round negotiations, the main protagonists are the EEC and the United States. On one point both sides seem to be in agreement—they both desire to examine and attempt to remove non-tariff barries. This is a not unimportant basis for agreement. However, there the agreement ends, since the policies of the two sides are at such variance that one can only describe the negotiations as being at a stalemate. Basically speaking, the USA wishes to remove tariffs over a period of between 5 and 10 years, they wish to attack non-tariff barriers, and they desire concessions in the agricultural field—though preferably outside the GATT framework and taking the form of commodity agreements between producer countries.

TABLE 5.1. Total imports of EEC Member Countries by area of origin in 1961 and 1971 ($m)

| | Area of origin | | | | | | | | | | | | |
| | Total imports | | EEC | | EFTA[c] | | USA | | African associated countries[a] | | European associated countries[b] | | Rest of the world | |
	1961	1971	1961	1971	1961	1971	1961	1971	1961	1971	1961	1971	1961	1971
Germany	10,944	34,341	3,432	16,088	2,112	4,786	1,512	3,544	144	707	128	357	3,616	8,859
France	6,672	21,057	2,100	10,539	684	2,243	732	1,798	1,236	1,420	31	136	1,889	4,921
Italy	5,220	15,830	1,536	6,716	792	1,624	864	1,425	84	367	55	135	1,889	5,563
Netherlands	5,112	14,684	2,508	7,997	732	1,612	564	1,413	48	192	12	57	1,248	3,413
Belgium-Lux	4,224	12,334	2,136	7,776	588	1,366	372	797	252	420	15	52	861	1,923
EEC 6 total	32,172	98,246	11,712	49,116	4,908	11,631	4,044	8,977	1,764	3,106	241	737	9,503	24,679
EEC 6 in %	100	100	36.4	50.0	15.3	11.8	12.6	9.1	5.5	3.2	0.7	0.7	29.5	25.1

Source: Basic Statistics of the Community, 1972, 12th edn., Statistical Office of the European Community, Luxembourg (Brussels, 1972); *Trade by commodities, market summaries: imports*, (Table 5.2: *exports*) Vol. I (Jan – Dec 1971) OECD (Paris, 1973); *Trade by commodities, market summaries: imports* (Table 5.2: *exports*), Vol. I (Jan – Dec 1961) OECD (Paris, 1963). Table reprinted by permission from P. Coffey, *The External Economic Relations of the EEC* (Macmillan, 1976)

[a] This item covers the following countries: Mauritania, Mali, Senegal, Upper Volta, Ivory Coast, Togo, Dahomey, Niger, Chad, Cameroon, Gabon, Central African Republic, Congo, Zaire, Rwanda, Burundi, Somalia, Mauritius, Madagascar, Kenya, Uganda, Tanzania.
[b] This item covers the following countries: Turkey, Greece, Malta, Cyprus.
[c] The European Free Trade Area.

TABLE 5.2. Total exports of EEC Member Countries by area of destination in 1961 and 1971 ($m)

	Area of destination												
	Total exports		EEC		EFTA[c]		USA		African associated countries[a]		European associated countries[b]		Rest of the world	
	1961	1971	1961	1971	1961	1971	1961	1971	1961	1971	1961	1971	1961	1971
Germany	12,684	39,040	4,020	15,647	3,588	8,740	864	3,770	72	441	229	727	3,911	9,715
France	7,224	20,344	2,424	10,059	1,080	2,722	420	1,098	1,536	2,117	88	267	1,676	4,081
Italy	4,188	14,974	1,308	6,688	888	2,030	384	1,469	48	342	119	398	1,441	4,047
Netherlands	4,308	13,534	2,052	8,616	984	1,989	192	541	48	224	30	119	1,002	2,045
Belgium-Lux.	3,924	11,969	2,088	8,207	636	1,218	372	815	60	228	42	103	726	1,398
EEC 6 total	32,328	99,861	11,892	49,217	7,176	16,699	2,232	7,693	1,764	3,352	508	1,614	8,756	21,286
EEC 6 in %	100	100	36.8	49.3	22.2	16.7	6.9	7.7	5.5	3.4	1.6	1.6	27.0	21.3

Source: *Basic Statistics of the Community*, 1972, 12th edn., Statistical Office of the European Community, Luxembourg (Brussels, 1972); *Trade by commodities, market summaries: imports*, (Table 5.2: *exports*) Vol. I (Jan – Dec 1971) OECD (Paris, 1973); *Trade by commodities, market summaries: imports* (Table 5.2: *exports*), Vol. I (Jan – Dec 1961) OECD (Paris, 1963). Table reprinted by permission from P. Coffey, *The External Economic Relations of the EEC* (Macmillan, 1976)

  [a] This item covers the following countries: Mauritania, Mali, Senegal, Upper Volta, Ivory Coast, Togo, Dahomey, Niger, Chad, Cameroon, Gabon, Central African Republic, Congo, Zaire, Rwanda, Burundi, Somalia, Mauritius, Madagascar, Kenya, Uganda, Tanzania.
  [b] This item covers the following countries: Turkey, Greece, Malta, Cyprus.
  [c] The European Free Trade Area.

TABLE 5.3 Total imports of EEC Member Countries by area of origin in 1973 and 1975
(in millions of European units of Account)

| Importing country | Total imports | | Area of origin | | | | | | | | among which | |
| | | | EEC 9 | | U.S.A. | | Japan | | Rest of the world | | AOM^a | ACP^b |
	1973	1975	1973	1975	1973	1975	1973	1975	1973	1975	1973	1975
Germany	43,421	57,244	22,675	28,339	3,667	4,418	1,081	1,334	15,998	23,153	604	1,646
France	29,574	40,429	16,398	19,945	2,477	3,078	434	754	10,265	16,652	1,537	2,010
Italy	22,259	29,089	10,877	12,489	1,842	2,542	296	354	9,244	13,713	474	683
Netherlands	19,539	26,520	11,923	15,088	1,709	2,614	256	383	5,651	8,435	271	921
Belgium-Luxemb.	17,492	23,166	12,358	15,555	986	1,472	214	317	3,934	5,822	603	603
U.K.	31,026	40,248	10,164	13,051	3,174	4,532	868	1,185	16,820	21,478	501	1,921
Ireland	2,225	2,850	1,596	1,971	153	206	31	50	445	623	18	41
Denmark	6,161	7,850	2,826	3,601	413	474	163	164	2,759	3,611	38	117
EEC 9 total	171,698	227,396	88,817	110,038	14,422	19,338	3,342	4,532	65,117	93,488	4,044	7,941
EEC 9 in %	100	100	51.7	48.4	8.4	8.5	1.9	2.0	38.0	41.1	2.4	3.5

Sources: *Basic Statistics of the Community*, 1977, 1973–4.
Note: The figures for the individual Member States have been rounded off and therefore do not exactly correspond with the grand totals.
a This item covers the following countries: Mauritania, Mali, Senegal, Upper Volta, Ivory Coast, Togo, Dahomey, Niger, Chad, Cameroon, Gabon, Central African Republic, Congo, Zaïre, Rwanda, Burundi, Somalia, Mauritius, Madagascar, Kenya, Uganda, Tanzania.
b This item covers the following countries: Turkey, Greece, Malta, Cyprus.

TABLE 5.4. Total exports of EEC Member Countries by area of destination in 1973 and 1975
(in millions of European Units of Account)

| Exporting Country | Total exports | | Area of destination | | | | | | | | among which | | Total exports of EEC Member Countries by area of destination in 1973 and 1975 (in US $m) | | Total imports of EEC Member Countries by area of origin in 1973 and 1975 (in $m) | |
| | | | EEC 9 | | USA | | Japan | | Rest of the world | | AOM ACP | | EFTA (cif) | | EFTA (fob) | |
	1973	1975	1973	1975	1973	1975	1973	1975	1973	1975	1973	1975	1973	1975	1973	1975
Germany	53,552	68,821	25,235	29,984	4,533	4,083	824	730	22,960	34,024	476	1,334	10,496.5	14,021.3	4,710.4	6,672.9
France	28,453	38,858	15,964	19,276	1,350	1,540	337	285	10,802	17,757	2,112	2,280	2,974.9	3,969.2	1,975.6	2,758.0
Italy	17,794	26,354	8,918	11,881	1,525	1,724	223	226	7,128	12,523	313	616	2,190.7	3,064.4	1,937.1	2,217.6
Netherlands	19,255	26,650	13,968	18,927	683	727	114	114	4,490	6,882	307	643	1,762.1	2,476.3	1,254.1	1,731.3
Belgium-Luxemb.	17,854	21,724	13,043	15,322	1,003	887	161	115	3,647	5,400	250	415	1,316.7	1,826.0	839.1	1,210.7
U. K.	24,374	33,103	7,884	10,693	2,975	2,956	535	517	12,980	18,937	439	2,046	3,810.4	5,151.2	4,915.0	6,074.3
Ireland	1,697	2,415	1,292	1,918	166	147	14	15	225	335	6	45	62.8	84.1	138.5	171.2
Denmark	4,951	6,605	2,261	2,973	356	348	63	93	2,271	3,11	99	120	1,628.5	2,373.6	2,098.7	2,616.4
EEC 9 total	167,931	224,530	88,565	110,975	12,591	13,288	2,270	2,095	64,505	99,047	4,001	7,499	24,242.5	32,966.0	17,868.4	23,452.3
EEC 9 in %	100	100	52.7	49.4	7.5	5.5	1.4	1.0	38.4	44.1	2.4	3.31	14.44	14.68	10.40	10.30

Sources: Basic Statistics of the Community, 1977, 1973–4. EFTA Trade 1973, 1975.

TABLE 5.5.   List of ACP States (in February 1978)

1. Bahamas	19. Guinea	37. Senegal
2. Barbados	20. Guinea – Bissau	38. Seychelles
3. Benin	21. Guyana	39. Sierra Leone
4. Botswana	22. Ivory Coast	40. Somalia
5. Burundi	23. Jamaica	41. Sudan
6. Cameroon	24. Kenya	42. Surinam
7. Cape Verde	25. Lesotho	43. Swaziland
8. Central African Empire	26. Liberia	44. Tanzania
9. Chad	27. Madagascar	45. Togo
10. Comoros	28. Malawi	46. Tonga
11. Congo	29. Mali	47. Trinidad and Tobago
12. Equatorial Guinea	30. Mauritania	48. Uganda
13. Ethiopia	31. Maritius	49. Upper Volta
14. Fiji	32. Niger	50. Western Samoa
15. Gabon	33. Nigeria	51. Zaïre
16. Gambia	34. Papua – New Guinea	52. Zambia
17. Ghana	35. Rwanda	
18. Grenada	36. Sao Tomé Principe	

In contrast, the EEC prefers a harmonisation of tariffs rather than their complete removal, suggests an examination of non-tariff barriers between producers and consumers, and suggests a series of special agreements for agricultural products—again, frequently between producers and consumers.

However, what is in fact really happening, at least on the side of the Community, is the gradual adoption of a policy of 'organised free trade' which takes the form of 'orderly marketing agreements' (OMA)—in steel, for example—and which really imply voluntary restrictions of exports on both sides. In turn, this implies that the Community is adopting a more protectionist attitude to trade with third parties.

In conclusion, we may say that the enlargement of the Community has not been a unifying factor in its international trading policies. The positive side, however, has been the conclusion of the Lomé Agreement and the association of the Community with the international sugar agreement. In general, however, the EEC's attitude to other third parties is becoming increasingly restrictive. It is doubtful whether the relatively 'open' policy adopted towards the ACP countries through the Lomé Agreement will compensate in global terms for the increasingly restrictionist attitude being adopted to other third-party countries.

The author must, with regard to the long run, repeat that the future of both the Common Market and of third parties lies to an ever-increasing degree in what our friend Alexis Jacquemin describes as 'product differentiation', that is, the EEC will increasingly produce quality articles (corresponding more with its level of education, training and technical development). In adopting such a policy, a more sophisticated type of international division of labour is likely to develop and both sides will be economically active. Thus, through this type of specialisation, with nuances, a new kind of international complementarity may develop. If the Community does not adopt internal economic policies more fitted to its intellectual and technical development, then it and its trading partners may well be foredoomed to a form of economic stagnation.

MONETARY POLICY[6]

Many, many schools of economic and monetary thought have offered many different suggestions for economic and monetary unions during the past ten years.[7] Unfortunately, in reality, the only blueprint which has been accepted to date is the Werner Report,[8] and, despite symbolic achievements such as the creation of the European Monetary and Regional Funds, we still seem to be in the first phase of the application of the aforementioned report. Some economists may point out that the only real achievement is in fact the 'Snake'. Alas, this reptile, which does symbolise a zone of monetary stability and a unified front *vis-à-vis* the dollar, is composed both of Common Market and non-Community countries! Thus, one might come to the conclusion that we are further away from the achievement of an economic and monetary union than ever before.

In view of such a disappointing record, it is perhaps wise to cast our minds back to the end of the 1960s, at which time the initial plans for such a union first saw the light of day. The Community was composed of six countries which had created a customs union, whose economies had grown together and whose trade was mainly conducted among themselves. Further, with the exception of the South of Italy, one may say that the economies of the 'Six' had reached a similar level of economic development. Economists would be correct in therefore assuming that most of the preconditions had been met for embarking upon the road to union.

The economic and monetary conditions which existed at the end of the 1960s were unique and are unlikely to be repeated this century. Thus one may say that the Werner Report was unrealistic (certainly in view of the enlargement of the Community) and therefore inapplicable. Hence, at this stage, our problem is to find out what should have been done, and what should be done in the future. But, first, what does an economic and monetary union imply? Basically it implies common economic, fiscal, and monetary policies (very probably with centralised control), the free mobility of the factors of production, irrevocably fixed exchange rates and a common external monetary policy. To democratically elected governments such a list of conditions implies a similar level of economic development among participants and/or a generous regional policy towards the disfavoured regions. To most economists any move towards the fixing of exchange-rates presupposes a similar level of inflation (though some talk of a 'natural level of unemployment').

From the beginning, we may say that the Commission was more concerned with the implementation of an institutional 'crawling peg' system (the 'Snake') than with structural reforms among the economies of the Member States. Perhaps, in view of the international moves towards floating exchange-rates and the energy crisis, the introduction of the 'Snake' was something of a non-starter, so what should be done now? From the beginning, the author (and, happily, the EEC Commission) has always stressed the inadequacy of the resources placed at the disposal of the Monetary Fund. Also, once a European currency has been launched, the author would prefer a 'permissive' system of monetary support for national currencies as proposed by Mundell.[9] However, such magnanimous support implies responsibilities on the part of the Member States. The author would maintain that it is here where the whole exercise has gone and may still go wrong. In exchange for financial aid for internal economic and industrial structural reforms, the Member States should have and will have to accept certain anti-inflation and other policies related to economic and monetary stability. Such policies might even include a more equitable sharing of the defence burden, for example.

At this stage, what should be done? The author would suggest that three tasks are important and that two are of more immediate urgency. However, in view of past experience, it would perhaps be wiser not to lay down too strict a timetable (if, in fact, any at all) for the implementation of economic and monetary union.[10] The first two tasks concern the creation of a European currency and the implementation of the aforementioned structural policies. The third task concerns the irrevocable fixing of exchange-rates or the general usage of a European currency. This final task would naturally be accompanied by the creation of the Community economic and monetary organs necessary for the supervision of a complete economic and monetary union.

The introduction of a European currency for official and limited usage is to be recommended because the Community is conducting most of its trade internally and therefore needs an effective term of reference (especially in the case of the Agricultural Policy).

Also, since the dollar has, as far as Europe is concerned (not to speak of the rest of the world), become a currency of questionable credibility, the EEC needs a currency of its own. Here the real problem is the composition of such a currency. There would appear to be two schools of thought, that of the Group of Louvain[11], and that composed of economists such as the author and Professor Rijnvos. The former group would prefer the use of an inflation-proof 'Europa', whilst the latter group would prefer a currency consisting of a basket or *'panier'* of national currencies. The former considers that an inflation-proof 'Europa' would be attractive, whilst the latter believe that their version is closer to reality (it would reflect the real economic conditions and the composition thereof could be changed as the necessity arose) and would be less likely to encourage a manifestation of Gresham's Law. Whichever scheme is adopted, the fundamental problem is that the politicians fear that the use of the 'Europa' would make it too attractive *vis-à-vis* their own national currencies. Such fears reinforce the necessity of the second task: structural reforms.

The Community finds itself on the threshold of at last having the means (and even the will) for implementing structural reforms. As Professor Prest has indicated, the EEC has from 1978 had important means at its disposal through the constitution and use of the Community Budget. To these means should be added the great acceptibility of Community-backed loans on the international money markets. It is, however, essential that the enlarged budget should not be used to give additional price support to farmers. Where used in agriculture it should be used more for qualitative structural reforms in the field of 'product differentiation'. An optimistic note along these lines was struck by the EEC Commissioner for Agriculture in December 1977.[12] Thus financial aid should also be earmarked for modernisation of services and industries and Community projects in pace-making sectors. Such policies would be more likely to conserve our scarce resources through the removal of duplication, to create employment among young people, to improve the competitive strength of the EEC internationally, and to permit the achievement of similar levels of economic development.

As an intermediate measure and with the aim of introducing a degree of monetary stability among the currencies of the EEC Member States, Professor Rijnvos and the author [13] have proposed that a version of the old European Payments Union be resuscitated. In view of the improvement in the balance-of-payments position of Italy and the United Kingdom and a reduction in the inflation rates of these two countries, such a suggestion could be applied with relative ease. Such a possibility is reinforced by the growing alignment of the monetary policies of some Member States.

Hitherto we have been concerned with the achievement of an economic and monetary union as a purely internal Community matter. The author would insist that there is an equal need for the EEC to adopt and present a common international monetary policy. In the 1960s, despite the unified front presented at international trade negotiations and despite the consolation success of obtaining a right of veto concerning future major reforms in the Statutes of the IMF and regarding any new creation and allocations of SDRs, the author is forced to conclude that in the field of international monetary relations the Community has been divided, brow-beaten and pushed around by the United States. Such a record is astonishing when one considers the economic and trading strength of the EEC, and that, in most recent years, the IMF (traditional fief of the Americans) has tended to be replaced to an increasing degree by the international money markets and the commercial banks.

The present European and international dissatisfaction with the dollar, linked with the paramount trading position of the Common Market, automatically call for the creation of a 'Europa' for restricted official use. In this desire the author finds himself in complete agreement with the Group of Louvain.

Further, one may conclude that the 'Snake' (which is the only technical achievement, to date, of a monetary union) does create a zone of monetary stability in the world, even it cannot survive unless fundamental structural reforms are carried out. Also, even this technical achievement has led neither to the creation nor to the introduction of the 'Europa'. This achievement has also blinded the Community to the very basic truth that, in the intermediate phases of an economic and monetary union, at a strict inter-Community as well as at an international level, we are essentially concerned with balance-of-payments problems and adjustments. However, once exchange-rates are fixed or a common currency is introduced, we are faced with regional problems and adjustments (the problems will, of course, already have manifested themselves). Thus, in the intermediate phases, we are really concerned with aid for balance-of-payments problems and structural reforms which should, over time, remove such problems. The Community should, therefore, devote most of its energies to these tasks. None of these problems and their solutions prevent the introduction for restricted use at an official level of the 'Europa' during the prolonged intermediate phases. The successful (and necessary) achievement of an economic and monetary union is essentially linked with the dynamic application of internal industrial and other economic reforms (as applied, for example, by the Coal and Steel Community) and trading policies. All these policies must be applied together. The alternative is economic and social stagnation and the collapse of economic and monetary union before it has even got off the ground.

More recently, in the spring and early summer of 1978, and more immediately associated with the meetings of the heads of governments at Copenhagen and Bremen, interest has been revived in an economic and monetary union. More specifically, apart from an apparent West German willingness (under certain conditions) to share its reserves of foreign exchange with other Member States of the EEC, the main attention has centred on ways and means of bringing the 'Four' (Britain, France, Ireland and Italy) back into the 'Snake'. The plan which has so far received most support is that whereby the margin of fluctuation for EEC currencies would be widened, thus creating a form of 'Boa' rather than a 'Snake'. Here, the author does not believe that the Community has got its priorities right, and believes that the essentials for the future of an economic and monetary union are as follows.[14]

An economic and monetary union is very difficult to achieve for a number of reasons. The two fundamental problems are implicitly linked with the transitional phase and the full union. During the transitional phase, the member states of the customs union are basically concerned with balance-of-payments problems between themselves and with other countries. This concern partly prevents them from adapting their economic structures to the levels demanded by a full union. When a full economic and monetary union has been established, the member states no longer face balance-of-payments problems between themselves, since these problems then become questions of regional disequilibria. Thus, a prerequisite for such a union would seem to be a similarity of economic structure among member states . . . . or the existence of other compensating factors (discussed below). These facts are most important since a full economic and monetary union not only implies fixed exchange rates (plus convertibility) or a common currency, but also the completely free movement of factors of production. Equally, it does presuppose a degree of fiscal harmonisation together with some centralisation of economic and monetary policies. However, it is the free movement of the factors of production, especially capital, which is so important for regions in an economic and monetary union.

Thus, in the specific case of the European Economic Community, the author maintains that a full economic and monetary union should only be contemplated when the following conditions have been met:

(i) At the monetary level, a similar degree of inflation must exist, since without this speculation would destroy any linking of exchange rates.

(ii) A similar level of economic development should exist throughout the Community.

(iii) All regions should have access to basically similar economic, social and cultural facilities.

(iv) Where the criteria (ii) and (iii) are not satisfied, some form of compensation from rich to poor areas must be seriously considered.

(v) In advance of full economic and monetary union, a progressive system of direct taxation and welfare benefits must be set up which could act as an internal 'inbuilt stabiliser'.

(vi) The structure for a type of federal banking/monetary system should be set up, shortly before the full economic and monetary union is implemented, which would ensure the satisfactory movement of funds within the Community.

Unless these conditions are fulfilled in advance of the complete implementation of the Union, the author does not think that the Union would work since no region and no national government could accept economic suicide.

Finally, well before a full economic and monetary union is achieved, a well-endowed monetary fund would have to be set up. In this connection, many proposals have been made during the past decade. However, the author would strongly propose that during the intermediate phase of economic and monetary union at least a percentage of the reserves of foreign currencies of the member states should be placed at the Fund's disposal—together with a quota of the national currency of each Member State.

Initially, intervention should take place, as at the present time, between the national currencies in order to keep them within the agreed margins of fluctuation. There should, however, be a difference from present practices. This difference would be that in contrast with the current situation whereby accounts between central banks are, in principle, settled at the end of each month, the Fund should, under certain specific conditions, be willing to give unlimited support to the currency of a member state facing speculation—without any necessity of reimbursement by that state.

As soon as the 'Europa' was relatively widely used in the Community, the Fund would also be required to intervene between the 'Europa', currencies of member states and currencies of third parties. Lastly, if and when a common currency were to be adopted, the Fund would intervene in the international monetary markets to maintain the value of the 'Europa' in relation to the currencies of non-member states.

In conclusion, the author stresses that if, in the field of economic and monetary union, the main concern of the Community is the 'Snake' and a wider participation therein, then a well-endowed European Monetary Fund with flexible rules of operation is a minimum pre-condition for a participation by most or all Member States.

NOTES

1. For a more detailed examination of these agreements, see P. Coffey, *The External Economic Relations of the EEC* (London: Macmillan, 1976).
2. As a percentage of total EEC imports, products from the African Associated Countries fell, between 1961 and 1971, from 5.5 to 3.2, whilst EEC exports to these countries fell from 5.5 to 3.4.
3. The full list of demands and the main items of the Lomé Convention are set down in P. Coffey, *The External Economic Relations of the EEC*, Part 4, *op. cit.*
4. EFTA Secretariat, *The Trade Effects of EFTA and the EEC 1959–1967* (Geneva, 1972).
5. Victoria Curzon, *The Essentials of Economic Integration: Lessons of the EFTA Experience* (Macmillan, 1974) pp. 234–9.
6. In this section, the author is mainly (though not exclusively) concerned with policies related to the moves towards the implementation of an economic and monetary union.
7. A fairly comprehensive account of the different proposals may be found by consulting the following works, all published by Macmillan, London.
    P. Coffey and J. R. Presley, *European Monetary Integration* (1971).
    G. Magnifico, *European Monetary Unification* (1973).
    P. Coffey, *Europe and Money* (1977).
8. Council – Commission of the European Communities, *Report to the Council and to the Commission on the Realisation by Stages of Economic and Monetary Union in the Community (The 'Werner Report')* (Luxembourg: October 1970).
9. See *European Economic Integration and Monetary Unification* (EEC Commission, 1973).

10. P. Coffey, 'Practical Steps towards the Achievement of a Monetary Union', *Quaderni di Economia e Finanza dell'Istituto Bancario San Paolo di Torino* (Turin, 1977) No. 2.
11. See All Saints' Day Manifesto, *The Economist* (1 November 1975).
12. "£650 m EEC Plan for Mediterranean Farms", *The Times* (10 December 1977).
13. P. Coffey and C. J. Rijnvos, *Versterking van het Slangarrangement*, (*E.S.B.*, 15 June 1977).
14. See P. Coffey, 'Europe, EMU and the World Monetary Crisis', *Revista Internazionale Di Storia Della Banca* (Naples, 1978).

6 Transport policy

PETER A. BROMHEAD

THE TREATY OF ROME

A common policy in the field of transport was one of the fundamental objects named in the Treaty of Rome, though the Treaty itself reflected the lack of common vision of the purpose and dimensions of any such common policy. The Treaty explicitly covered only transport by rail, road and inland waterway. For transport by air and sea there was merely a provision enabling the Council to decide on 'appropriate provisions'; there was no indication of the purposes which such provisions might serve, and any decision must be unanimous. As the basis of a constructive transport policy must include a common view of the roles of rail and air transport in relation to one another, as a basis for decisions on investment in these modes, the failure explicitly to include air transport restricted the scope for any action programme; and the exclusion of sea transport did not help any plans for integrated means of access to the ports.

Articles 2, 3 and 74 are vague, having the quality of a preamble to guide the Commission and its staff in preparing proposals for consideration and possible action by the Council. They merely demand a common transport policy, leaving its fundamental objectives to be determined by subsequent decisions.

The more specific transport sections of the Treaty laid down some preconditions for the formulation of a positive policy, rather than any guide to the policy's direction. They were concerned with the removal of existing obstacles to free movement, and of distortions to trade caused by old-established national practices, for example to favour exports as against imports.

Article 75 required he Council eventually to 'lay down . . . (*a*) common rules applicable to international transport to or from the territory of a Member State or passing across the territory of one or more Member States; (b) the conditions under which non-resident carriers may operate services within a Member State; (c) any other appropriate conditions'.

These rules were to be prepared by the Council on proposal from the Commission and after consulting the Economic and Social Committee and the Assembly.

Article 79 stipulated that all discrimination by carriers on grounds of country of origin or destination of goods must end by 1970. The article was intended to put an end to the charging of different rates or the imposition of different conditions for the carriage of goods for export as distinct from imported goods, or any similar discrimination. As a step towards effective implementation, the Council adoption of Regulation No. 11 in 1960 was a positive achievement; but the discrimination aimed at was in any case not substantial.

Article 80 prohibited any Member State from imposing rates or conditions involving any element of support or protection in the interest of any particular industry or undertaking; though specially favourable rates might nevertheless be charged for the support of underdeveloped regions. Such reduced rates were in fact allowed to be applied to southern Italy, Sicily and Sardinia, and for transport of agricultural produce from some regions of western and central France.

One instance of difficulty in the application of this article was a long battle occasioned by a German 'support tariff'. In order to relieve the Saar region of the damage caused, and soon to be extended, by closure of coal mines, and to foster other industries, the German Government in 1964–5 wished to charge subsidised low tariffs for movement of goods by rail from the Saar to the North Sea ports and south Germany. The Saar suffered from the lack of good water transport, and there was a plan to provide a canal to the Rhine. So the railway-rates were set at a level equal to what the rates by barge might have been if such a canal had already been in use. A German claim that this 'as-if' tariff was not discriminatory was examined by the Court of Justice in 1968, without a clear conclusion. Eventually in 1969 the Commission accepted an alternative German plea to treat these tariffs as discriminatory but for the purpose of regional aid, permissible under the terms of Article 80.

These articles reflect the objectives of the older Coal and Steel Community Treaty of 1951, which was avowedly not concerned with transport as an activity in itself. Its Article 70 had sought to prevent the use of transport services in such a way as to discriminate between users.

The Rome Treaty pointed the way to regulated competition between transport operators, with transport regarded primarily as an economic activity like any other, subject to interference only for declared social purposes. It made no prescriptions concerning infrastructure. The Commission and the Council each had a member concerned with transport, the Parliament a committee. When the directorate was set up its members addressed themselves at first to the conditions of the transport market. Soon some basic patterns were established, leading to continuing work on points of detail. The problems associated with infrastructure presented themselves later.

An illustration of the weakness of the Community in the face of national whims is to be seen in the recently-introduced divergent national practices with clock changes between summer and winter.

EARLY ACTION TOWARDS A COMMON POLICY FOR THE MARKET

The first statement of intent to emerge from the Commission, the document of 1961 which came to be known as the Schaus Memorandum (after Commissioner Schaus), had as its key word 'an integrated system'. The implied aim, then, seemed to be the identification of the actual and potential merits of the different transport modes, the development of each mode's infrastructure so that it could perform well the tasks for which its merits were best adapted or adaptable, and to secure effective intermodal links wherever they might be useful for journeys most effectively performed partly by one mode and partly by another.

A more specific 'Action Programme' followed in 1962. In its avowed pursuit of three great aims—'liberalisation, harmonisation, organisation'—it was concerned with access to the transport market, with the eventual creation of equal conditions of competition, and with coordination of services and—most noteworthy, but vaguely— infrastructure investment. Its proposals scarcely constituted a common transport policy, but they turned out to be the foundation of community action for the next fifteen years.

First, where national laws had the effect of creating conditions favourable to some carriers those laws should be brought into harmony. Second, the number of lorries allowed to cross frontiers, which was currently determined by bilateral quota agreements, should be increased, and a Community quota should be established. Third, a system of 'bracket tariffs' should be introduced, under which compulsory minimum and maximum rates should be charged by all freight carriers.

The purpose of this was to establish a regulated competition so as to preclude both cut-throat competition and exploitation of high demand or monopoly. A necessary corollary was that all users of transport infrastructure should pay for the share which they used: a principle involving enormous difficulties.

Action by the Council to implement the programme was slow. The first directive came on 23 July 1962. It allowed lorries to penetrate across a frontier up to 25 km (as the crow flies) without limit and without regard to any quota. It also made special exemption by which transport of certain specified types of goods was to be allowed without any limit at all, and outside any quota arrangements. The rather bizarre list of the types of exempted goods reflected, in a common-sense way, the demands of some small types of economic activity: fried food, bees, dead animals, damaged vehicles and refuse were named.

On some aspects of the Action Programme the Commission produced proposals on which the Council of Ministers took decisions (embodying their own modifications) in 1965;[1] these decisions laid down a timetable for measures aimed at harmonisation of conditions of competition on the inland surface modes. Most of them were followed by further supplementary provisions, through a flow of directives which was still continuing in 1977, when there were still further Commission proposals awaiting Council action.

First, taxation systems should be altered so that they might become 'neutral' in their effects, avoiding effective discrimination between elements of transport. A common turnover tax system, when adopted by the Council and introduced by Member States, should apply to freight transport. Higher taxes on own-account transport than on public transport, such as those levied in Germany, should cease. (These provisions came into effect in 1972–3, affecting principally Italy and Germany).

Double taxation on motor vehicles used for transport operations in a Member State other than that in which they were registered was to be brought to an end by 1967, but in fact the further detailed provisions proposed by the Commission in implementation of the plan were not adopted by the Council. Instead, reciprocal agreements between States had effectively achieved the objective completely by 1972.

The trifling matter of the charging of duty on fuel contained in the tanks of frontier-crossing lorries was dealt with in 1968 by Directive No. 68/297, which required at least fifty litres of tank fuel to be admitted free of duty. In practice only the French and Germans continued to impose charges on tank fuel exceeding fifty litres.[2] Rules concerning drivers' working conditions were to be standardised by 1969.

The public service obligations of the railways were to be ended by 1967 except that they might be obliged to maintain services considered essential in the public interest, and would have the right to compensation for losses incurred through any such provision. During the period 1968–72 railway accounts were to be normalised, so that they might operate and charge commercially. Any losses (or profits) arising from obligations imposed by governments were to be clearly identified, together with compensations paid in respect of such losses. A series of later decisions brought further refinements, the most important being Regulation 1192 of 1969.[3]

The proposal concerning bracket tariffs came up against an effective Dutch veto in the Council. Dutch barge-operators had a major share of the vast Rhine traffic. They objected to a scheme which might prevent them from offering transport at rates which they could profitably charge. In response to their pressure the Dutch government resisted this proposal. Its resistance could well be supported by rational argument. If 'organisation' had the effect of damaging, by artificial means, the ability of one mode to perform a function which it could perform well and cheaply, the effects of that 'organisation' seemed likely to be negative in relation to its ultimate and proper purpose. As water transport did not harm the environment and used energy economically, it seemed absurd to damage its economic competitiveness. Apart from these arguments, there was a legal problem, arising from long-standing agreements which laid down the principle of freedom of navigation on the Rhine for all vessels and cargoes irrespective of nationality, and excluding any regulation of inter-national freight rates by any state or states. The Central Rhine Commission had been created in the nineteenth century, under agreements extended by the Treaty of Versailles, to make such regulations as it might think fit in accordance with the general principle. The Treaty of Rome could not create any new authority superseding the old, and the bracket tariff plan could not easily be applied to Rhine shipping unless these long-standing arrangements were abrogated by a new Rhine treaty.

However laudable the bracket tariff scheme might be in helping to prevent (probably in the wrong way) the continuance of the spiral of transfer of freight from rail to road, there was little objective ground for promoting a transfer from water to rail. An independent report by five academics was unfavourable to the device of a single bracket tariff system.[4]

In 1965 a Dutch veto was effective under the unanimity rule, but it was and might still be upheld against a qualified majority. Rhine traffic accounted for around five per cent of the total freight-carrying by all transport modes in the Community as then established; Dutch operators were carrying 53 per cent of it. A consideration such as this might well justify an eventual Dutch attempt to invoke the special safeguard in Article 75(3) by which, even after the impending general validation of a qualified majority in the Council of Ministers in 1966, a unanimous decision of the Council could still be demanded when vital national interests were threatened. (Such an argument was used in 1977 to justify an effective government subsidy to Dutch lorries.)

Eventually, on 22 June 1965, the Council agreed on a system of bracket tariffs for road and rail, and non-mandatory 'reference' tariffs for internal shipping. A timetable was laid down for this 'common organisation' of the market. In 1967–70 it would apply only to international movements. Member States could either maintain any existing scheme for their internal transport or adopt the Community system. In 1970–3 the Community system would be extended to all transport, but the system of 'reference' tariffs (as distinct from mandatory maximum and minimum rates) would apply not only to water transport but to the carriage of all bulk goods—coal, iron and steel, petroleum, building materials, and grain. For these markets the 'reference' tariff allowed a carrier to charge less than the minimum (which was in general expected to be set at 10 per cent below a norm) but must give publicity to his action; the term 'transparency' was used, and became an essential element in Community transport law.[5]

The proposal for a 'Community quota,' allowing a stipulated number of lorries to cross frontiers in addition to those allowed under bilateral quota agreements, was not brought into operation until 1968, when Regulation No. 1018/68 provided for 1,200 licences to be apportioned between the six Member States, each of which then issued its licences to selected carriers who were then allowed to engage in road haulage on all traffic links between states (but still not to carry loads between points within any national boundary). The regulation providing for the Community quotas was effective only until the end of 1971, but further Council regulations greatly increased the number to 3402 in 1979.[6]

In a decision of 4 November 1976 the Council decided to make the Community quota system permanent, and to keep the number and apportionment of licences unchanged. At the same time the bracket tariff system for road transport was extended for a further year.[7] Both the brackets and the quotas have been subjects of long and repeated negotiations, and occasionally used as counters in the battle over lorry-weights. Further agreements were reached at the Council meeting of October 1977.

PAYMENT FOR INFRASTRUCTURE

Work on the method of calculating the social marginal cost of infrastructure was taken in hand in 1965, when the Council entrusted the Commission with the task of undertaking a survey of the problem in depth.[8]

> 'The purpose of this survey, which was carried out with the help of experts from different Member States, was to assess various possible different systems of charging for the use of traffic infrastructures and the corresponding methods of calculation.'[9]

At this stage a detailed survey of the Paris – le Havre transport route was carried out in 1965–9, so as to provide a 'practical example.'[10]

This was followed by further surveys on particular aspects of the question in 1970–1.[11] However, there was little in the findings to serve as a guide to choices between new major investment in one mode rather than another. For the case of railways, 'in the sample survey, the calculation of the marginal cost of use of railway infrastructure took into account only the renewal cost for main lines and catenaries'.

In 1971 the Commission made a detailed proposal for a Council decision on the introduction of a common system of rates to be charged for the use of infrastructure[12] for the purposes of transport by rail, road, and inland waterway.

The proposal recognised that the introduction of a system of charging for infrastructure would involve difficulties, both in establishing criteria and in adapting existing practices to whatever new criteria might be produced. The process should therefore not be hurried and should move by stages. The Memorandum (para. 12) suggested fifteen years as the appropriate period of delay; however, 'the guide-lines and general principles for such a system should be laid down now'.

By a letter of 10 May 1971 the President of the Council requested the Parliament, pursuant to Article 75 of the EEC Treaty, to deliver an opinion on the Commission's proposal. Parliament referred the proposal to its Transport Committee and to the Economic Affairs Committee, as well as the Committee on Energy, Research and Atomic Problems.

The Transport Committee discussed the proposal and the attached memorandum at seven meetings up to the end of 1972, and the newly-created Committee, with Regional Policy added to Transport, continued the work until October 1973. Both it and the other committees involved made important proposals for change and other observations.

The proposal's preamble, which set out some fundamental aims, deserves quotation in part:

> . . . the introduction of a common transport policy entails the establishment of a common system of charging for the use of infrastructure (which) must apply to rail, road and inland waterway infrastructure in such a way as to ensure fair conditions of competition in transport . . .[13]
>
> . . . the system of charging must satisfy the dual aim of promoting optimum utilisation of existing infrastructure and of ensuring that all expenditure involved in the construction and use of infrastructure is borne by users of that infrastructure[14] . . . .this objective will be attained if the charges for various categories of traffic are fixed according to the relevant marginal social cost, with the addition, where necessary, of an amount sufficient to ensure that the total expenditure in respect of the infrastructure in question is covered by the revenue from the use thereof.

The Commission's proposal of 1971 read:

> The aim of such a system of charging shall be to promote optimum utilisation of infrastructure,[15] while generating sufficient revenue to cover all expenditure relating to such infrastructure attributable to its transport function.

The Committee on Regional Policy and Transport amended this as follows:

> The aim of such a system of charging shall be to generate sufficient revenue to cover all related expenditure chargeable to the transport sector *for the construction and maintenance of infrastructure. At the same time, these charges should help to promote a satisfactory spread between the various categories of infrastructure and result in a socially satisfactory traffic volume.*

The method, as agreed, was set out in seven articles, of which the first two included the following:

1. To this end, the charges applicable to the various categories of traffic must be so fixed as to be equal to the marginal social cost of the use of infrastructure by those categories. Should the revenue produced by such charges be less than the corresponding expenditure, there shall be added to the marginal social cost an equalising charge, the amount of which shall be such as to ensure that the said expenditure is covered.

2. The Council, acting by a qualified majority on a proposal from the Commission, shall lay down rules for calculating marginal social costs and equalising charges.

The system was to be introduced by stages over a fifteen-year period, with the railways, in the meantime, receiving compensation to cover any shortfall of payment by other modes.

One problem seemed not to be provided for. The road motorway network was already in general adequate, except near cities. There had as yet been virtually no investment in new railway-infrastructure. If in the future large investments should be made in new railway-building (even only up to a mere 4,000 km), while road users continued to enjoy the use of the more than 20,000 km of motorway already recently completed, without any payment, some new imbalance could be foreseen.

During 1972 the Committee on Finance and Budgets, in preparation of its *Opinion* on the Commission's plan, attempted an analysis of the charging systems currently in use.[16] They varied greatly, though in the case of motor transport the fuel taxes, though raised theoretically for revenue purposes and not specifically designed as charges for the use of infrastructure, could properly be treated as though they served that purpose.

The analysis was based on figures for 1966, produced under the procedure of the 1964 Decision and 1965 Regulation; by 1971 it was already rather out of date. There were some salient points.

In every one of the Six the subsidies paid to railways in 1965 were less than the railways' infrastructure costs of 1966.[17] (The first two-yearly report of the Commission, which was produced in 1977 and applied the 'transparency' rule to railway accounts for 1973–5, showed the difficulties involved in obtaining any coherent picture because 'historical' debt and the interest it attracts varies from one system to another.)[18]

In the case of roads, the Committee concluded that in 1966 tax receipts covered only about 85 per cent of road expenditure in Germany and the Netherlands, but covered 180 per cent in France and Italy.[19] However, increased fuel taxes in subsequent years may have removed the shortfalls.[20] In Britain, where in 1976 it was calculated that charges on heavy lorries fell short of their real costs, a big increase in their annual payments attempted a partial rectification.[21]

For inland water transport Mr Gerlach's document found that in every country with significant movement of this kind the contribution of the users failed to cover more than one-tenth of the expenditure on infrastructure incurred on their behalf. In the case of the Netherlands the users paid only 2.7 per cent of the infrastructure costs.[22]

The proposal was considered also by the Committee on Energy, Research and Atomic Problems. In its Opinion (delivered in October 1971), two years before the 'energy crisis') it made the most important point that the implications of the proposed system were 'neutral' in their effect upon energy use. It pointed to the reliance of road transport on oil, an essentially unreliable energy-source; and it noted that at present only railways, trams and trolley-buses use electricity. Hence, in its conclusion, it proposed: 'The Community should promote research into the development of means of transport which use *reliable* sources of energy'.[23]

By 1978 nothing positive had emerged from the search for a common system of payment for infrastructure, except a recognition that a serious policy in this direction was an essential part of a market/competition transport policy. There were hints that the drift from rail to road was partly a consequence of the failure to find a solution; and that this drift was not only promoted by distortion but was also contrary to the public interest. If air transport too had been included, with an examination of the costs of airports and their means of access, a similar conclusion might well have emerged.

While the search for a policy in this field went on there was a parallel search for a common policy for decisions on new investment in infrastructure. This is the subject of the ensuing section.

NEW INFRASTRUCTURES

The conditions of competition are affected even more by decisions to build, or not to build, new roads, railways, canals or airports, or to improve existing ones, than by payment of the costs of infrastructures by those who use them. But it is not only competition that is affected by the quality of infrastructure: the whole economic life of the Community is involved. This was recognised as long ago as 1955, when the Messina Conference aimed at 'a common study of the plans of development based on the establishment of a European network of canals, of motorways and electrified railways and the coordination of air transport'.

In 1961 the Commission put forward a plan for a network of trunk routes to be examined in relation both to the needs of the Common Market and to proper economic criteria.[24] Regional-development considerations might be allowed to modify the conclusions of economic tests, or, to put it in another way, might be legitimately introduced as variables in the economic models which might be built for the purpose of assessing projects. The proposal for a Eurepean network was soon dropped. It did not correspond with the priorities which Member States were already establishing.

Next, the Commission made a proposal which began at the other end. Any project under consideration by a Member State should, if of Community importance, be subject to consideration by Community institutions, which should have the right to be consulted about the form, priority and financing of such projects; and the Council should have power to enforce cooperation between Member States in transport investment programmes where such cooperation was not forthcoming voluntarily. The Council acted on the first proposal, but not on the second.

ROADS

In 1966 a Council decision (66/161)[25] instituted a procedure for Consultation between Member States on infrastructure plans of Community interest. There was also scope for Community funds to help with selected projects, and this was extended in 1976. Meanwhile, apart from railway electrification, investment was in fact concentrated mainly on waterways and airports and, above all, on new roads.

The spread of ownership and use of private cars, as a result of people's choices at a given stage of economic growth, has been a dominant feature of the environment of transport decision-making. Neither any national government nor the Community's institutions played any role in the process of rapid growth. In 1958 the number of cars per 100 population varied in the Six between 5 and 10; by 1974 it had risen to between 20 and 30. In each of the Nine (except Ireland) between 60 and 80 per cent of all households had the use of a car.[26] The national governments responded by improving their road systems, each in its own way and at its own pace—though some new works, notably in the Italian South, received assistance.

Each national government collected from motorists through taxes an annual contribution fixed largely on the basis of budgetary policy. In France and Italy the taxes exceeded the cost of the capital and current cost of the work on the roads by about 80 per cent in 1966; in Germany and the Netherlands they fell short by about 15 per cent. The tax on fuel was crudely related to each vehicle's use of infrastructure, though its application was relatively beneficial to heavy-freight carriers. The fixed annual charge, like the tax at the point of purchase, was unrelated to road use, but in the case of private cars could be accepted as a revenue device;[27] and the big increase in the annual tax on lorries in Britain in 1977 (as explained in the 1977 White Paper) could reasonably be regarded as a crudely effective charge on road-use on the assumption that a lorry-owner does not leave it idle.

While cars and lorries were served by motorways on all main routes, the railways, still with their ancient tracks, could not exploit the new high-speed technology which had been applied in Japan, with great success, since 1965.

NEW OPTIONS

By 1970 not only the key sectors of the railway but also those of the motorway were at saturation or approaching it.[28] Some of the airports serving links in the 300–600 km range would need expensive extensions to their equipment and to their means of surface access to deal with expected traffic increase; but their traffic within the corridor and within these distance limits was a significant part of their total current traffic and of the increase which they would need to accommodate in future in the absence of the diversion to rail which new rail-construction could promote.

There was thus a concrete problem for Europe to tackle, and it presented itself for urgent decision about 1970: which mode—rail, road or air—should have priority for expansion to cope with expected traffic growth, in preference to other modes.

Environmental and social considerations clearly favoured rail rather than air or road. By 1970 a new factor pointing in the same direction was added: rail's greater economy in energy consumption, further supported by its ability to use electric power; unlike road and air, rail was not wholly dependent on oil, and by 1970 the approach of oil-shortage was already recognised.

The Commission's Communication to the Council of 25 October 1973 raised the issues, but only in general terms, in relation to a vague programme for the future. Paragraph 12 notes the need to avoid waste of resources through a wrong choice between transport techniques designed to serve the same ends; paragraphs 14 and 41 abjure unnecessary multiplication of modes and choices for transport users; paragraph 36 refers to the importance of the energy factor; paragraph 50 envisages a *master plan*. This important communication led to yet more expensive studies of the problem. On 15 November 1974 the Transport Advisory Committee issued an Opinion putting forward criteria for notification to the Commission by Member States of infrastructure projects, and criteria for assessing those projects.[29] In 1975, terms of reference were agreed for a committee of experts to examine the long-term needs of freight haulage in 1985–2000.[30]

ACTION AND INACTION AFTER 1970

Around 1970–5 some of the nations of the Community took uncoordinated decisions to build new railways to serve a few sectors of the major corridors—all well within their own national boundaries, though of great importance to Community transport. No such decisions were taken for frontier-crossing routes. In 1968 a German plan envisaged that the whole of the routes from Cologne to Munich and Hamburg, and from Hamburg to Munich, would be provided with tracks for high-speed trains by 1985, including 800 km, in some separate sections, built on new alignments, motorway-style. Italy began work on the Rome–Florence *direttissima* line. In 1975, after much delay, the French Government approved the start of such a new line, to provide a frequent service from Paris to Lyon (470 km) in 2 hours (later $1\frac{3}{4}$) instead of 4. In England, the main route north from London already had four tracks and spare capacity. With a few exceptions its curves would allow a proposed fleet of 'Advanced Passenger Trains', helped by a tilting device, eventually to maintain 250 km/h with little interruption.

These plans together provided the nucleus of a high speed railway system, continuous with the existing system, on several key sections of the main European transport corridors.

There remained the most important, most European, section of all, linking Europe's biggest conurbations and through them the other sections just mentioned: Paris to London, and Paris *and* London to Cologne–Ruhr and Holland. The indispensable element in this interrelated complex of links, a two-track Channel Tunnel, was formally approved in 1973, together with a Shinkansen-type railway for the English section—which was to be financed by the British, through separate arrangements between the Government and British Rail.

But for the continental section of the rail-link French and Belgian government approval was still awaited in 1973. A team of railway experts was at work on the details of 'Project TGV Europolitain', as the whole concept was called, but only desultory work was being done on plans for continuation from Belgium to Cologne,[31] although the UIC map showed the existing railway on that sector to be already saturated. The link from Paris and London into Belgium was planned only as far as Brussels, thus excluding the possibility of an alternative route (probably preferable) passing north of Brussels, using existing moribund but straight railway routes, from which Brussels could be reached by the existing under-utilised dead-straight line from Ghent. That option could cut the non-stop railway travel time from Paris or London to Amsterdam or Düsseldorf/Cologne (under 620 km in every case) to effective door-to-door equivalence with the air journey-time.[32]

A British Green Paper of March 1973 described the Tunnel scheme, but the Commission was notified only in November. The planned mainland rail links were not included, so the Tunnel at this stage would serve mainly to transport cars and road-borne freight. The Regional Committee's Report of November 1974 (319/74) failed to discuss the rail links. In January 1975 the British Government unilaterally cancelled the whole project. The Commission's officers learned of this decision from the newspapers.

THE CHANNEL TUNNEL: AN ALTERNATIVE

After the Tunnel had been abandoned, an unsuccessful attempt was made, through a parliamentary question in 1975, to suggest that the Commission might offer finance. In 1977 an attempt to revive the project was made. A delegation from the British National Union of Railwaymen went to Brussels to present a case, envisaging a cheaper scheme without the transport of cars or lorries. On 4 July, in the course of a debate on new procedures for Community financing of transport infrastructure, Mr Berkhouwer (Netherlands, Liberal) raised the specific question of the Tunnel, which was being taken up by the Transport and Regional Committee. He and others advocated revival. Commissioner Burke agreed in principle; the proposed committee on transport infrastructure would have power to initiate a project.

It is important to recognise that it is not only a Channel Tunnel which should be considered, but the shape of the whole transport system linking London with Paris and London and Paris with Germany and possibly the Netherlands. A Tunnel as part of a fully-developed high-speed railway system, leaving the existing routes much freer than they are now for massive freight traffic, would be a very different concept from the isolated Tunnel which was presented in 1973–4. One concept would make full use of the new potential of the railways, divert much long-haul freight to rail and greatly reduce short-haul air transport, thus preserving aviation fuel for aviation's essential long-haul tasks. The other concept (the 1973 form) would merely reduce the journey-times of road-vehicles by about an hour, and for the rest have little effect on the shape of transport.

The handling of the Tunnel, and of the associated transport links on land, suggests that there are grounds for more forceful intervention by the Community. The Commission's proposal of 1976 for the creation of a European airspace, and for rationalisation of air routes,[33] did not explicitly envisage the rationalisation of modal infrastructures, but it laid a framework for it. Nevertheless, by 1976 Europe was just twenty years behind Japan in the process of developing a rational transport infrastructure, putting technology to effective use. Paragraph 25 of the 1977 manifesto of the Union of European Federalists reads:

> The Community's transport policy should go beyond the search for common rules of competition to the promotion of common projects such as the Channel Tunnel and a high-speed train network throughout Europe.

Such Community action would not merely be symbolic. It would give a justification for the Community's very existence such as its achievements to date have failed to provide.

LONG-TERM INFRASTRUCTURE PLANNING

The question whether Europe's transport network would benefit from a coordinated system of new motorway-type double railway tracks on parts of the primary trunk routes is not yet settled. This has still been a matter for academic examination, for report after report by groups of experts. No European study was made of any selected corridor to determine the optimum balance of road, air and rail for its future needs.

The Community's work was complicated, at least until about 1974, by the claim that, if new high-speed surface transport tracks were to be built, they should take the form not of conventional railways but of one or another of the rival levitating systems to which, from the 1960s onwards, much research was devoted. Among the obvious disadvantages of all these schemes was that no new levitating guided-surface transport system would be continuous with the existing railways.

A complete system of guided-surface transport for the main trunk corridors must manifestly be far more remote in time than an equivalent development of high-speed conventional railways: far too remote to stop the wasteful drain on oil resources still being made by the aircraft which gobble oil on the busy links of 300 to 600 km between major cities, performing tasks for which they are ill-suited. By 1974 national governments were losing interest in these systems.

Nevertheless, the Commission and its officers received and examined the guided-transport arguments. One is worth quoting because it makes positive proposals for a particular route. In the 1970s the Community's institutions gave particular attention to a link of obvious 'European' character: Brussels–Luxembourg–Strasbourg–Geneva. It was given the name of 'Europole'. This corridor was familiar to people involved in the working of the Community's institutions, though in terms of traffic it is a minor corridor.

On 1 January 1971, by Resolution 471, the Consultative Assembly of the Council of Europe unanimously approved in principle the proposal for an air-cushion link along this corridor. Serious study of the project was undertaken, and the 'Europole Working Party' adopted a document setting out details of the plan in October 1973. At the high and low passenger-projections it was estimated that a break-even fare would be below the equivalent air fare, for a service which should be more eligible than air. The increased unit-costs of the existing railways serving the route, due to loss of passenger-traffic, were not mentioned; and these railways have spare capacity. This Council of Europe document was discussed by the European Parliament's Committee on Regional Policy, Planning and Transport at a public hearing on 19 and 20 May 1976.

This corridor may be of parochial interest for those who work in the Community's institutions, but if *it* is worth consideration, it would seem at least as valuable to study routes with greater potential traffic.

In 1976 the whole 'Europole' route was covered by only five rather slow passenger-trains a day: not enough to impede freight traffic. In contrast, more than 60 long-haul passenger-trains a day left Cologne towards Mainz in each 24—hour period, fanning out towards Nürnberg, Munich and Basel-Italy, using tracks already overloaded in some important sections. Thus, the scope for serious specific common action in relation to investment in a particular corridor is more obvious, and is illustrated by one set of statistics covering part of the traffic.

By 1971 national authorities had completed the motorway system from all of Germany, the Netherlands and Belgium to Milan and the toe of Italy, except for a section through the Alps, and for the Alpine crossing the road included a new tunnel under the St. Bernard Pass—a short distance from the French Mont Blanc road tunnel, longer and at lower altitude. Work was proceeding with a St. Gotthard road tunnel to give an alternative road route a little to the East.

In 1971 a million tons of freight (all long-haul) moved by road between Italy and Belgium/Holland, and a further 3 million tons between West Germany and Italy—all using these new roads, including the Brenner route, with a continuous motorway. The roads were carrying nearly 30 per cent of this transalpine long-haul traffic on a major corridor and thus apparently suitable for rail transport. But the railway had not the capacity to carry vastly growing traffic, either in part of Germany or through the Alps; and a new low-level Alpine railway tunnel was still left for a remote future. But little progress had been made towards decision on even one new Alpine railway base-tunnel to relieve the existing overloaded rail-tunnels; there was still no coordinated plan for the best means of handling growing passenger and freight movement along Europe's two principal north—south traffic-routes.

On 2 July 1975, in preparation for a hearing on future inter-city transport, the Committee on Regional Policy and Transport sent out a questionnaire[34] to experts who were invited to submit written replies. Part I asked ten questions concerning the organisation, coordination and financing of research; Part II contained seven questions on the problem of medium-haul inter-city transport, notably:

1. In your view, what are the main difficulties facing medium-haul inter-city transport and what is the best way of remedying them?

2. Do you feel that the existing road and rail network in Europe can be considered satisfactory?

3. Do you consider that the new infrastructures planned in the various Community Member States are sufficient, or do you consider that the setting up of an integrated modern rapid transport network

linking the major European conurbations is an urgent necessity?

4. Do you consider that it would suffice initially merely to improve as far as possible existing means of transport, or do you consider it desirable for thought to be given at the same time to the introduction of new and unconventional transport techniques?

5. In this light, what are the factors determining your choice?

6. What can be done to avoid the introduction of differing transport techniques which would make an integrated rapid transport system impossible?

7. Do you not consider it desirable, within the framework of the Community, to fix common objectives and work out decision-making mechanisms as soon as possible with a view to avoiding unfavourable developments?'

Short replies to the questions were given by or on behalf of: (*a*) Cost Project 33, a forward study currently being carried out on behalf of the EEC, the ECMT and 12 European governments, (*b*) Professor T. E. H. Williams, Chairman of the Civil Engineering Economic Development Committee; (*c*) Professor Klaassen, of the Netherlands Economic Institute, Rotterdam; (*d*) the Group of Nine Railways of the European Committees; (*e*) the Association of European Airlines; (*f*)–(*i*) researchers concerned with non-conventional surface transport.[35]

The replies to Part I did not indicate any fundamental dissatisfaction with the organisation or financing of research, but some observed that unnecessary duplication should be avoided, and that information should be exchanged (though none indicated whether or not there was currently a lack of coordination or exchange).

The replies to Part II indicated some disagreement over the balance of priorities being given to development of conventional railways as distinct from 'unconventional' as yet untried new technologies of guided-surface transport. Professor Williams observed that:

'at the present juncture there seems nothing to be gained, in economic terms, from speeds in excess of 300 km/h. Railway engineering is sufficiently well advanced to cope with speeds of this order, and recent projects have demonstrated a high level of economic viability.' Hence . . . ' the economic advantage (of unconventional transport techniques) over the use of railways is still wholly hypothetical'.[36]

Except for his reference to high-speed railway projects which had demonstrated a high level of economic viability, Professor Williams gave no specific instance; nor did he mention that, in relation to the primary European link (London–Paris–Holland–Cologne) the official governmental and company papers regarding the Channel Tunnel (an essential part of the project) not only omitted any assessment of the potential associated railway development but also presented the whole assessment of the Tunnel in 1990 on the assumption that there would be then, be no such railway-system in operation on the Continent.

In general the replies were little more than the expressions of the opinions of various experts, each based on considerable experience of activity, but with no information based on examples, evidence or actual problems, capable of helping in a concrete way with the choice or rejection of any particular project or group of projects, and in particular with no reference to the problems mentioned earlier.

The reply on behalf of COST 33 deserves mention for its anodyne lack of substance. It observed that, though there is a case for a basic motorway network, it was at that time incomplete, and its 'desirable capacity' was 'another question'; and that the railway network was 'technically far below what could be achieved'; one of the most important policy issues was 'whether a similar degree of improvement should be made to the railways' (i.e. similar to the road developments already completed).[37]

This unexceptionable but trite contribution to the discussion was made, it may be noted, three years after the publication of the UIC Master Plan for European railways, not, as might appear, five years before it.

It would perhaps be unfair to blame the respondents to this questionnaire for the generality of their replies, which was after all invited by the questions, though the form of the questions did not preclude reference to the real difficulties involved in making investment-decisions. But a reader of the answers, taken all together, might well be surprised to observe an exercise taking place in 1975 which might well have happened ten years before. During the ten years 1965–75 there had been a vast amount of activity, technical and commercial research, funded in part directly by public funds and in part by commercial organisations out of commercial surpluses. It seems legitimate to be disappointed at the complete absence of any sign of any return on all this work in any of the answers given.

It was suggested that all investment-projects of community interest should be submitted to the Commission in a form agreed on the basis of the principles set out in the previous chapter.

CONCLUSION

The community has numerous minor achievements to its credit in the transport field, but it seemed no nearer to achieving a common policy in 1978 than twenty years before—and further still from the objectives which a policy might set.[38]

The Commission cannot be blamed for failing to initiate studies of the problems: how best to secure in practice the principle of payment for infrastructure, how to plan investment, and how to promote safety. The *Communication* of October 1973 stated a whole series of principles and objectives. Every aspect was included: regional, social, fiscal, industrial and environmental, and the need to save energy was not forgotten. But the document lacked confidence; it put forward no specific plans, only plans of how to plan to make plans, and then in general terms.

There are solid achievements to report in the matter of safety standards and in a limited opening and regulation of the market. On the major aspects of infrastructure there is still scope for positive and specific action, necessarily including air transport, putting new technology to effective use and taking account of the likely supplies of energy in the future; and the need is urgent.

One obstacle to the development of a vigorous market-competition policy has been the series of distortions of the transport market for the sake of particular regions or vital national interests. It is very tempting to interpret these distortions as permitting discriminatory treatment to protect particular groups of producers of transport services or vehicles. Significantly, the attempts to develop a policy towards aviation have in practice been directed to the search for outlets for the efforts of the workers in the aircraft-manufacturing industry, rather than to any attempt to define a role for civil aviation as part of the European transport system.

There has been no overt recognition of those aspects of the current work of each transport mode which could usefully be developed, or of those aspects which do not deserve support. The railway is, in today's conditions, not very useful for many of the small-scale jobs which it is still performing; yet the fear of staff redundancies has tended to prevail against a vigorous policy of pruning. The railway could be better than the aeroplane for much of the medium-haul inter-city work now being done by air, but the railways have not been given the tools with which they could become an effective substitute for air. A better equipped railway could become preferable to road for long-haul freight; but the railway-managements have not been inspired to accept that practical redefinition of their role which would enable them to exploit adequately their potential merit as a long-haul carrier of freight; and on the few biggest corridors they lack the necessary tracks.

The whole world of aviation is still full of serious distortions, ignored by the embryonic aviation policy. The vast government grants already paid for development of types of civil aircraft should somehow be accounted for in any long-term charging system; but a recovery of these expenditures from air-travellers seems beyond any possibility of achievement. Again, there can be no aviation plicy without a coherent and rational system of airport charges, along with a proper accounting and payment by air-travellers for their share of the means of surface-access to the airports. Of all modes of transport—indeed of all forms of activity in the economy—air travel (except perhaps for connections with Scottish islands and the like) must surely be among those least deserving of public subsidy on social grounds.

The objective of an open market (subject to the exceptions already mentioned) demands payment for infrastructure. But the attempt to achieve a fair system for such payment may be doomed to failure. A heavy lorry employed mainly on motorways imposed little immediate cost on the other users of those motorways, but benefits immensely from the expenditure incurred in building the motorway, with a foundation strong enough to carry heavy loads. A similar lorry employed on old-fashioned roads, crawling up curving hills and fouling the narrow streets of towns and villages *en route*, imposes huge costs on those whom it delays or otherwise disturbs or threatens, and only part of these costs can be recovered satisfactorily.

In some other cases the effective imposition of charges for the use of infrastructure might seriously damage an obvious public interest. Barges on the waterways may now be receiving vast unrequited benefts; but water transport is altogether desirable in the public interest. It does not use much energy; it is relatively unpolluting and even aesthetically pleasing. The creation of the waterways may have been environmentally damaging—and on the Rhine the resource cost of curing some of the damage will now be very high. But the public interest would surely suffer if an increased price of water transport, through fairer infrastructure charges, diverted freight from water to road.

For parts of the transport market, competition between modes, even if 'fair', may well have negative effects. Because a railway's fixed costs are a high proportion of its total costs, any addition to a railway line's load within its capacity tends to reduce the average resource-cost per unit carried, at the same time as it improves the quality of service. Conversely, any successful competition against the railway tends to increase the unit-cost and impair the quality of service. Thus at some points competition may be dysfunctional.

It may be that a future European transport policy will need to plan the modal split more positively, taking into account special factors such as the desirability of saving oil. Common prudence suggests a need for caution in the planning of the use of energy at every point; and transport is one of the fields in which such caution may suggest a plan more deliberate than any yet approached.

NOTES

1. Council Decision of 13 May 1965.
2. In 1974 the Commission proposed to increase this to 100 litres; but this had already been done by national action. Cf. *Bulletin*, 6–1974, point 2278.
3. e.g. Council Resolution of 27 June 1974, under which railway accounts were to be separated from state accounts, and railways were to seek to optimise their financial performance. A working party of the Group of Nine railways worked on the principles of the calculation of railway costs. (Cf. *Bulletin*, 9–1975, point 2255). Late in 1977 the Council was actively considering a proposal.
4. Cf. D. L. McLachlan and D. Swann, *Competition Policy in the European Community*, (London: Oxford University Press, 1967).
5. The transparency rule gave rise to needs for interpretation, not yet exhausted. British Railways were in the habit of making commercial and confidential freight contracts. They were eventually allowed to maintain confidentiality, subject to a duty to disclose the terms of a contract, in confidence, to inquirers.
6. For 1979: Belgium 378, Netherlands 549, Germany 621, France 573, Italy 480, Luxembourg 98, Ireland 69, U.K. 383, Denmark 251. For 1979 the total was thus nearly three times that of 1965.
7. E.C. *Bulletin*, 11–1976, No. 2277ff.
8. Cf. Council Decision of 22 June 1964 (64/389: O. J. No. 102 of 29 June 1964, p. 1598); Decision of 13 May 1965 (65/389: O. J. No. 88 of 24 May 1965, p. 1473).
9. This description is taken from the Commission's explanatory document included as an annex to *Document* 195/73.
10. Cf. Report on sample survey pursuant to Article 3 of Council Decision No. 65/270/EEC of 13 May 1975, *Doc. SEC* (69) 700 final of 12 March 1969.
11. Council Decision of 27 January 1970 (O. J. L.23 of 30 January 1970, p. 24); Regulation 1108/70 of 4 June 1970 (O.J. No. 1.278 of 23 December 1970, p. 1).
12. *Document* 39/71.
13. The Transport Committee proposed an amendment to provide for extension to other means of transport.

14. The Committee's amendment referred also to 'the favourable distribution of traffic between the different transport infrastructures and types, from the point of view of the economy as a whole'.

15. At this point the committee on Finance and Budgets proposed the insertion of 'by creating equal conditions of competition between competitors on the transport market'. (*Document* 195/73, page 56).

16. The *Opinion* (PE 32, 719/fin) is printed in the Parliament's *Document* 195/73. It was drafted by Mr H. Gerlach and adopted unanimously by the Committee on 6 December 1972.

17. *Opinion, op. cit.,* para. 17.

18. In 1973–5 total state payments to railways varied between 47 per cent (Netherlands and about 180 per cent (Italy and Belgium) of total railway receipts, though for Germany the initial excess figure of 100 per cent was later amended to 70 per cent, to correct an error in the Commission's calculations. Cf. *Railway Gazette International* (September 1977) p. 325 and (November 1977) p. 442.

19. *Opinion, op. cit.,* para. 34. (*Document* 195/73, p. 51).

20. By 1975, according to *World Road Statistics* (quoted in British Road Federation, *Basic Road Statistics,* 1977) road taxation exceeded road expenditure by amounts varying between 0 per cent (Belgium) and 240 per cent (Italy) and for the whole of the Nine the excess was 50 per cent.

21. Cf. U.K. Ministry of Transport, *Transport Policy Consultation Document,* 1976, and *Transport Policy,* White Paper, 1977.

22. *Opinion* (Gerlach), *op. cit.,* para. 36. (*Document* 195/73, p. 2).

23. *Opinion of the Committee on Energy* (drafted by Mr H. Schwörer), para 17 (*Document* 195/73, p. 3).

24. *Recommendations of the Commission,* 21 June 1960 and 25 July 1961.

25. *Official Journal,* 8 March 1966, p. 583.

26. Cf. *Opinion of the Committee on Finance and Budgets on the Commission's proposal for a decision on a common system of payment for the use of transport infrastructure* (*Document* 195/73, p. 50f, para. 31–4).

27. The Commission's Proposal (*op. cit.*), Article 6.2, accepted 'additional charges on ownership of private vehicles or on their consumption of fuel'.

28. Cf. Union Internationale des Chemins de Fer, *Master Plan for the European Railway* (1973); and maps showing traffic densities on main routes, German Transport Ministry (*Ausbau der Bundesfernstrassen,* 1968) maps.

29. *Bulletin,* 11–1974, point 2287.

30. *Bulletin,* 6–1975, point 2290.

31. For a progress report, cf. *Modern Railways* August 1974, p. 297. The whole alignment of the route from Paris and Calais to Brussels was settled in 1975—too late, because the Channel Tunnel had then been abandoned by the British.

32. A parochial argument suggested that Belgium's capital and the Community would be slighted if the new railway route by-passed Brussels. But the Brussels traffic, with natural growth, maximum diversion from air and road, and generation of further traffic growth by the new facility, seemed likely to justify half-hourly services for Brussels alone, with some London and Paris trains serving Liège by the existing route. The position is similar to that of Birmingham, which is by-passed by the main London–North-West route; a

half-hourly service leaves that route to serve Birmingham.
33. *O.J.C.* 178, 2 August 1976; *C.* 265, 11 November 176.
34. *Documents* PE 42. 776 (Luxembourg, 28 November 1975) and PE 44.161 (22 March 1976).
35. *Document* PE 44.161.
36. *Document* PE 44.161/Amd. p. 10.
37. The COST 33 report was issued by the OECD late in 1977, under the title *The Future of European Passenger Transport*. This was a forward study of European inter-city passenger transport requirements, involving twelve countries participating in the EEC programme of Co-Operation for Scientific and Technical Research (COST). The report, of 600 pages with 300 pages of appendices, projects long-haul passenger transport demand to the year 2000, and compares the possible effects of four possible main strategies for meeting the demand.

   Two of the strategies involve new types of governmental interference with commercial and leisure choices, and both bring advantages to the transport sector—though only after these major interventions have been decided upon and implemented. A more modest strategy of meeting demand for transport by new rail-investment, where appropriate, appears no less workable, on economic grounds, than indefinite expansion of road and air facilities to meet the demands expected to arise on the basis of conventional forecasting.

   Two corridors are studied in detail. On one, Genoa-Barcelona, the prospects for rail-investment are (not surprisingly) discouraging. On the other, Rotterdam-Frankfurt, a rail strategy would appear viable, although this is a route with little air-traffic and little scope for diversion from air to rail. It is estimated that continuation with indefinite road-expansion to meet demand would require a 76 per cent increase in motorway lane-kilometres. Such a level of road-building might in any case be impracticable—even though the Report merely implies that it might also be foolish, in the light of current uncertainty about the future availability of oil. There is no detailed examination of the effects of a high-speed rail system linking London-Paris-Holland-Frankfurt, which would obviously give much greater scope for diversion from air to rail than the Rotterdam-Frankfurt corridor, and would presumably have better prospects of success.

   On the whole, the report's findings were not discouraging to the conventional high-speed rail strategy, even before allowing for its omission of some major factors (notably oil supplies) from its calculations. But these calculations, involving speculative elements, could usefully be supplemented by an examination of the Japanese experience, where the 500-km high-speed railway completed in 1965 brought an internal return of 70 per cent on the investment in the sixth year of use, even without allowing for any external benefits or oil-savings.
38. By 1978 there was extreme dissatisfaction in Parliament with the Council's inaction. On 31 July the Regional Committee (Rapporteur, Mr H. Seefield) issued a Draft Report on the present state and progress of the common transport policy (PE 54-492). It was strongly critical; sixteen members tabled a proposal for an action against the Council before the Court of Justice.

7 Regional policy

WILLEM MOLLE and JEAN PAELINCK

INTRODUCTION

The regional policy of the European Community has some characteristics that merit detailed discussion. But first the question should be asked why a European regional policy is needed (section I). Next, to make it easier to understand a specific European regional policy, regional development and regional policy are discussed in general in section II. In the next section (III) the regional problems of the European Community will be analysed; a short description of regional policy as it had developed until recently follows in IV. In 1975 there were drastic changes, and thus a separate section (V) is devoted to the policy in force at this moment. One of the novelties in this policy is the Regional Fund, which is analysed in some detail in section VI. The descriptions given in sections I to VI (inclusive), will then be put in the light of analytical developments that could help improve the efficiency of regional policy in the European Community, in section VII. Finally, some of the problems that are likely to confront the European Community in the future, as well as methods to deal with them, will be touched upon in the concluding section, VIII.

I JUSTIFICATION OF A EUROPEAN REGIONAL POLICY

The general aim of regional policy is to reduce the imbalances between parts of a territory. Such imbalances may be differences in income levels, but also unequal access to jobs, culture, etc. Inequalities and imbalances are felt as a political problem; a specific policy is needed to cope with them; self-correcting mechanisms are either absent or ineffective.

Regional inequalities are felt as a political problem mainly because large categories of the population feel that unequal access to wealth and opportunities is morally unjust as well as socially unacceptable. The literature has called the moral and social arguments for regional policy 'the call for equity'. But there are also purely economic reasons for regional policy, reasons founded in the observation that regional structural maladaptation prevents an economy from making optimum use of scarce resources and thus keeps total wealth below par. The economic argument for regional policy is generally called 'the efficiency argument'.

But why cannot the spatial socio-economic system do away with imbalances by autonomous adjustment mechanisms? One reason why it cannot is geographical: different regions are differently endowed with natural resources. Then there is the historical factor: military, administrative, and political developments have, together with economics and fate, shaped the spatial configuration of economic, social, and cultural activities that are familiar to us now. The failure of the system to adjust itself is painfully apparent, for instance, from the occurrence of unemployment in one region alongside shortage of labour in others. One would expect two movements to remedy the situation: (1) migration of people to the region where their brains and hands are in demand, and (2) migration of economic activities to the region where labour is available. However, many people do not want to move just for a job: cultural and family ties bind them to their present location. Establishments are not always keen to move towards the place where the workers are; labour is, after all, not the only factor governing industrial location, and proximity to markets for inputs and outputs, access to energy, etc., may indeed exert stronger locational pulls than labour availability.

Moreover, migration, if and when it occurs, may well have adverse effects. One need only think of the social capital embodied in housing and infrastructure that would be left under-utilised, while at the same time additional pressure is put on resources for the provision of more houses as well as social and technical infrastructure in already congested areas. Because the extra houses and infrastructure will, in most cases, be built at higher cost than those left to fate, inflation will be stimulated too.

Now the efficiency argument is that money spent on regional policy is well spent as it creates more welfare; under-utilised resources are put back to use, the cost of additional infrastructure is saved, and growth rates are boosted because monetary 'stop' policies to relieve the strained situation in congested areas will not be necessary. Economic efficiency may further benefit from the social stability that hopefully ensues from measures designed to correct regional imbalances.

Once it has become evident that it is right to pursue a regional policy, the next question to be asked is: by what authority? The national state, being the most complete expression of sovereignty, has naturally developed into the authority responsible for the equilibrium between the different parts of its territory. However, national states are themselves regions, macro-regions, of a larger territory. Until recently, equilibrium between these macro-regions was striven for only by the national states themselves; their instruments were economic growth, international trade, and monetary policy (and sometimes military intervention). Actually, the measures introduced were often used to counteract regional problems within the states; e.g. tariffs established to protect industries that are concentrated in one region, and constituting that region's sole economic base.

The European Community has greatly reduced the possibility of using the above-mentioned policy instruments for national and regional growth, for the Community is responsible solely for trade policy, and only partly influences the economic and monetary policies of its members. It was, therefore, only logical that the European Community's regional policy would be complementary to its other policies. Basically a European Regional Policy is wanted for the same reasons as a national one. The same arguments serve to justify it: the care for efficiency and equity.

The European Community being first and foremost an economic organisation, the economic argument of efficiency will be the first to be discussed here. The aim of the Community is to foster economic welfare and growth in the Member Countries by integrating the separate economies to provide a large consumer market to their producers, so that economies of scale and specialisation can be used to the full. To that end, goods, capital, labour, and products are free to move among the Member States. Indeed, the Community tries to optimise the workings of the market mechanism on the European level by cutting down all tariff and other barriers to international trade. Until the time the Community was created, however, economic activities had developed in their national context, trade barriers being used to protect certain activities in certain regions from international competition. When trade barriers were abolished, each nation had to adapt its regional economies to the new situation. While the adaptations were carried through quite smoothly in many cases, in others intervention was called for to prevent whole regional economies from collapsing completely. To safeguard economies and smoothing adaptations, the creation of the Common Market had to be accompanied by the pursuit of a regional policy. Nor was such a policy needed only in the first stages of the Common Market, for its very functioning requires the constant application of adequate measures of regional policy. Structural changes due to economic, technological, environmental, and social developments continue to occur, demanding progressive adaptation. However, under the rules of the game accepted within the European Community, national states can no longer resort to trade regulations to ease the adaptation process; trade within the Community being essentially free. The only instruments available are, then, those of regional policy.

The case for a regional policy on the Community level is greatly corroborated by the wish to create an economic and monetary union. With a Common Market it is still possible for a country to try and help production in one or all of its regions with the general instrument of exchange rates, making its own products relatively cheaper than those of other countries. Such a policy is notably effective for export-oriented production in (aided) regions. In an economic and monetary union, however, even this instrument will be taken away from the Member States, because either fixed parities between the various European currencies or one European currency will be in use.

The economic arguments set forth here merely plead the pursuit of a regional policy in the area of the European Community, but do not explain why such a policy should be conducted by the European Community's Authority itself. Nor are they the most important arguments for a regional policy to be designed and carried out on the European instead of the national level; the most important grounds are rather the socio-political and equity ones. It is indeed the solidarity of people in the better-off regions with those in more backward areas within the European Community that calls for a regional policy focused not on the parts but on the whole of the Community. That *raison d'être* of regional policy has recently been boosted by the emphasis the Community is placing on social and human aspects of life.

So far, the limited authority granted to EC institutions has not permitted regional policy to be conducted entirely on the level of the Community; in fact, it has merely been complementary to the regional policy of national states.

II REGIONAL DEVELOPMENT AND POLICY

Regional imbalances are due to the differential endowment of regions with natural and human resources, and to many technological, demographic, economic, social, and political factors that have shaped the

pattern of economic growth through history. It is these factors that
have led agriculture to concentrate in areas where the climatic and
geological conditions were favourable, basic steel industries to develop
in areas where coal and iron could be found, and so on. What with
changes in technology, economics, and the like, new industries need not
follow the same locational patterns as old ones; demographic trends
may change as such social factors as the quality of life become more
dominant. The regional configuration is, therefore, changing con-
stantly; recent changes are the decline of agriculture, the rise of modern
industries, and, the latest development, the expansion of services.
Generalising, one may say that modern industry and services tend to
locate in their market areas, which mostly coincide with large con-
glomerations of people.

The factors referred to have caused three types of problem regions to
develop:

development areas: these are mainly agricultural and have hardly
shared in the growth of industry and services;
restructuring areas: these are characterised by their heavy dependence on declining industrial sectors, such as coal and steel, and
textiles;
congested areas: these are the areas where industry and services are
largely concentrated and which, being a good breeding area for new
activities, are subject to such heavy pressures that the external costs of
further developent may outweighs the benefits.

Demographic tendencies are apt to aggravate problems of an
economic nature; people in development and restructuring areas, not
finding enough opportunities at home, are inclined to migrate to
congested areas. While easing the labour situation there, they thus erode
the labour market and undermine the basis for infrastructure development in their region of origin, making it even less likely for new activities
to be attracted there. The mechanisms involved have an unfortunate
built-in tendency to reinforce themselves.

To counteract the growing imbalances, some countries resorted to
regional policy as early as during the inter-war depression; others
followed later, and since the Second World War all the countries now
making up the European Community have known some type of regional
policy. In its early days, regional policy used to be confined to specific
aids to so-called backward, depressed, or development areas. With the
years experience has taught, however, that it was a mistake to isolate the

developments in such regions from those in normal and congested regions. In almost all countries, attention has recently shifted towards the harmonious development of all regions; a growing awareness of the problems congested areas had to face has greatly stimulated the shift in emphasis.

So nowadays regional policy has come to pursue much more comprehensive and ambitious objectives than it used to. Present aims of regional policy could be described as:[1]

planning economic development and investment in accordance not only with the need to promote the overall progress of the national economy, but also with the diverse needs and potentialities of the different regions and with the geographical distribution of the population and manpower;

reducing the imbalance between regions in the distribution of economic activity and in the levels of income, prosperity and welfare;

maintaining and encouraging the social and cultural basis of the life of the regional populations including the preservation and best use of natural, cultural and amenity resources;

planning the physical environment and infrastructure including housing, communication, and other forms of fixed capital in accordance with consistent and coherent national, inter-regional and regional aims and with the economic resources available.

To realise these objectives a number of instruments are used; they may be grouped in two categories:

incentives and restraints on expansion of economic activity in certain regions, to influence directly the regional pattern of economic activity;

elements conditional to balanced regional development, such as infrastructure and manpower;

Of course, both types of measures may be used in various degrees and in different combinations in each case. It will be clear that the above measures may also be taken in the framework of other policies, for example, sectoral policy and transport policy; indeed, a policy using these instruments can be called regional if and only if it pursues specific regional objectives.

Within each of the two categories mentioned above a number of more specific instruments can be distinguished. As far as the *incentives to industry* are concerned such instruments are:

grants for equipment, plant, and machinery;
provision of factory buildings and development sites at low cost;
loans at favourable rates of interest;
reduced taxation of profits during a certain period;
favourable tax treatment of amortisation of capital, and of revenue;
reduction or elimination of state charges, local taxes, licence fees, etc.;
alleviation of certain costs, e.g. social-security contributions, transport charges, electricity, etc.;
grants towards the cost of labour.

The purpose of all such measures is to induce companies to settle in less-favoured regions instead of in developed ones, by reducing the unattractive cost/profit ratio in the former.

Restraints on expansion mostly take the form of licences for industrial and office buildings and of special taxes in the central areas.

Sometimes governments can influence the location of activities more directly: they can relocate government services in as much as they are themselves the decision makers; when, as with nationalised industries, they are in control of activities, they can exert pressure to make them comply with regional objectives. A variant is the steering power that governments can exercise by granting procurement contracts to industries in regions in need of promotion.

Among the policies aimed at creating the *conditions for balanced development*, the first to be cited is infrastructure policy. Indeed, for economic activities to be viable they depend on the availability of energy, water, roads, communications, ports, housing, and recreation and education facilities; creating such elements of infrastructure is, therefore, tantamount to fulfilling a necessary condition for development.

Manpower policy is another case in point. Raising the level of education and training of people who, for lack of opportunity, have not acquired the skills required for modern industry and services, may fulfil another necessary condition for development. On the other hand, manpower policy may be used to make people migrate from regions whose topography, climate, or other factors make them inherently unfit for development, to regions where the conditions for development are, or may be, fulfilled.

Further essential elements of modern regional policy are the systematic analysis and identification of problems, the setting-up of strategies for improvement, the planning of development, and the creation of organisations and procedures capable of carrying out the plans in harmony with the policies pursued in other fields. Such analysis and planning is the more necessary because the problems are complicated and the resources scarce.

One of the better-known strategies for coordinated development was the growth-pole strategy of concentrating efforts to stimulate, and to improve conditions for, development in towns that show promise of self-sustained growth. To that end an attempt was made to create complexes of industry likely to generate new activities in the area. The growth-pole approach was notably followed in the period when regional policy was mainly concerned with backward areas; now its basic ideas have been integrated in a more comprehensive planning for all areas, in which all the available instruments are used in a balanced way.

III REGIONAL DEVELOPMENT IN THE COMMUNITY

When the European Community was created, nobody had a systematic picture of the regional imbalances in Europe, let alone an idea of the way the various regions were developing, though several national efforts had been made to acquire both. To remedy the situation, the Commission of the European Community called upon a conference of experts to make an inventory of regional development in their respective countries and regions.[2] Some of the problems raised during this conference were treated in more detail a few years later.[3] Unfortunately, all the Member Countries had their own special method of analysis, their own indicators of regional development and of disparities between regions, and defined their areas in different ways, so that still no systematic picture of the whole of the Community could be obtained. An attempt to set up a standard regional division for Europe was made, however, while a certain consensus on the most important indicators of development can be distilled from the reports.

The services of the Community then tried to improve the situation. In 1969 the Commission submitted a preliminary analysis of regional development in the Community.[4] The first major systematic analysis was published as late as 1971, and covered the six initial Member States.[5] Soon after the EC was enlarged, a complementary analysis was carried out for the EC including the three new Member States;[6] the present analysis is based on the two studies just mentioned and some extra information that has since become available from the Statistical Office.[7]

Three aspects were examined in the analytical survey: population, employment, and regional product. The regions considered were: the 'Regierungsbezirke' in Germany, the '*Régions de programme*' in France, the '*regioniamministrativi*' in Italy, the provinces of Belgium and the Netherlands, the 'new standard regions' in the United Kingdom, the 'planning regions' in Ireland, and in Denmark two groups of islands and the continental part of the country. Luxembourg was considered as one region. As near as possible the periods considered were those between 1950 and 1960 and between 1960 and 1970. As far as population was concerned particular attention was given to density and migration. Employment was divided into primary, secondary, and tertiary activities; income was represented mainly by Gross Regional Product per head. Levels of the diverse variables were compared to analyse disparities, and growth rates to analyse differential development. The conclusions of the analysis are of limited value, because the statistical material was not fully comparable; as far as unemployment was concerned, the basic statistics were so deficient that the material could not be analysed as an indicator. The analysis of population density brought to light a slight tendency towards further concentration in the period between 1950 and 1960, followed by greater stability in the next period. By 1970 deficiencies in the statistical material made it impossible to tell whether the evolutions observed were due to changes in migration or to differences in natural growth.

The distribution of total employment is closely related to that of population, and reveals the same trends. An analysis of the shares each region had in total Community employment, in each of the three sectors of activity considered, showed marked differences between regions, but no pattern emerged that would make it possible to attribute the development to one single factor or to distil one single tendency. One point can be made, however: regions that are predominantly agricultural are almost without exception located on the outskirts of the Community, and tend to merge with sparsely populated regions. Once more the share of each sector in total regional employment will serve to illustrate the evolution up to 1970. Evidently, industry is most developed in the central areas of the Community, while tertiary activities tend to concentrate in those areas that have administrative centres within their boundaries.

No analysis of Gross Regional Product per head was possible at all for the period 1950–60, owing to the gaps in the statistical material. Between 1960 and 1970, the regional differences in the Community of the Six seem to have decreased somewhat, mainly thanks to high growth rates in Italy as a whole and emigration from its southern regions. It was not possible to analyse development for the whole Community of the Six, but a tentative idea could be formed of the differences existing in 1970. A later statistical contribution of Eurostat's greatly improved the situation. The Eurostat statistics show that the poorest region had a GRP per head of only 37 per cent of the average, whilst the richest region boasted a figure of twice the average—more than five times as much.[8]

As is clear from the above, deficiencies in the statistical material made a full description of regional development in the European Community impossible, and invalidated many possibilities of analysis. A new study, also treating population, GDP, and employment by sector, will do away with the statistical gaps and dig much further into the questions of regional disparity and structural features of regional development in the European Community over the last two decades. (Willem Molle with Bas van Holst and Hans Smit, *Regional Economic Development in the European Community* (Teakfield, 1979).

Only recently has comparable information on regional unemployment become available from the Community Labour-force Survey of 1975. In general, regions with high unemployment figures coincide with those showing a low income per head, and, to a lesser extent, with agricultural regions. In view of the objectives of regional policy it is evident that these are also the regions to which regional aid is to be given. Other factors may influence the choice, however, such as out-migration, obsolete infrastructure, etc. No standard criteria have yet been put forward for identifying such problem areas; the final selections have so far been made by the national states, if after discussion with the Commission. We shall not go into the detailed reasons why some regions have been selected.

IV A SHORT HISTORY OF COMMUNITY REGIONAL POLICY[9]

The first attempt at Community regional policy was made under the rule of the Coal and Steel Community as far back as 1952. Article 56 of the Coal and Steel Treaty provides for aid to be given to regions that have difficulties in reconverting to other activities. Admittedly, the field of application was very limited, as it covered only regions liable to suffer from redundancy in the coal and steel industries. With the creation of the European Economic Community, the more general idea emerged of conducting a regional policy at the level of the Six. This idea was already apparent at the the Messina Conference, which envisaged a Fund to aid the least-favoured regions. Still, the Treaty of Rome did not in so many words count the pursuit of regional policy among the tasks of the European Economic Community created by it (1958), though it did pay attention to regional aspects in its preamble and in its second Article. In the more concrete Articles it becomes plain that the regional aspect is to be taken into account only as far as the implementation of competition, transport, social, and agricultural policy is concerned (Art. 39, section 2a; Art. 49, section d; and Art. 75, section 3). The three articles of the Treaty of Rome concerned with regional aspects are, in fact:

Article 80 section 2, which stipulates that, in assessing prices and conditions of transportation with a view to authorising support or protection, the Commission has to take account of a suitable regional policy, and especially of the needs of underdeveloped regions;

Article 92 section 3a, which authorises the Commission to check if help, given by national states to stimulate the economic development of regions where the standard of life is abnormally low or where there is serious underemployment, is compatible with the Common Market rules on competition;

Article 130, section a, enabling the European Investment Bank to facilitate the making of loans and to guarantee the financing of projects aimed at upgrading the less-developed regions of the Community.

These three Articles of the Treaty of Rome (and Article 56 of the Treaty CECA dealing with conversion), insufficient though they may be, are at the origin of the regional actions of the Community that took shape in the course of the sixties, to culminate in the early seventies in the conception of a genuine regional policy. From a regional aspect taken into account in elaborating other Community policies, the concept of a regional policy had become that of a policy in its own right.

The Commission of the European Communities may have acted as a motor, but essentially the development just described was an institutional one, proceeding slowly and step by step. In the framework of this short historical review, the following steps may be recalled:

1. The conference on regional economies, held in 1961 on the initiative of the Commission. Apart from the exchange of information and experience, this conference aimed at identifying the Community

problems of the regional economies and policies of the Member States. The conference clearly underlined the principal regional disparities existing in the Community as well as the necessity of carrying out regional studies.

2. Reports by groups of experts on regional policy in the EEC, submitted to the Commission in 1964. There were three of them, dealing with, respectively:

(i) objectives of regional action in the Community: to give to all Community regions the possibility of contributing more effectively to the prosperity of the national and Community wholes in particular by creating growth poles;

(ii) adaptation of ancient industrialised regions by an active policy of restructure to prevent maladjustment phenomena: and

(iii) means (infrastructure, financial advantages, administrative organisation).

3. First publication of the Commission on regional policy in the EEC, submitted to the Council on 11 May 1965. Starting from the conclusions contained in the experts' reports, the Commission underlined in its first communication the necessity of concerted action by the national and European regional authorities by elaborating regional development programmes defining the objectives to be reached and the means (Community, national, and regional) to be put to use.

4. The first medium-term economic-policy programme, 1966–70; this first programme, approved by the Council on 11 April 1967, devoted, as announced in the 1965 communication, a whole chapter to regional policy. Its primary objective was to be to place the various regions in equivalent starting conditions. It was specified that one of the principal means for ensuring development and adjustment of problem regions was the improvement of their infrastructure. The programme suggests working out priorities among the actions to be taken and phasing the whole process according to the financial possibilities.

5. Proposal for a decision in respect of the organisation of instruments for the use of the Community in matters of regional development, presented by the Commission to the Council in October 1969. In this proposal the Commission provides for:

(i) general co-ordination of the regional policies of the member states on the level of the Community;

(ii) elaborating development programmes for the problem regions of the Community;

(iii) creation of an interest-rebate fund and a system of guarantees managed by the Commission;

(iv) installation of a permanent Committee of regional development; and

(v) participation, in particular by better information, of private and public investors in the realisation of development programmes.

6. The third medium-term programme of economic policy, established by the Council in February 1971, specifies that:

(i) the policies of planning and regional development pursued by the Member States, which so far had been essentially inspired by national considerations, were in future to take account more than before of the Community dimension; to that end, national policies in certain fields (infrastructural policy, sectoral policy, regional-aid policy) would have to be better harmonised;

(ii) apart from harmonisation and coordination, a balanced development of the Community calls for the responsibility of the Community to be added to that of the Member States as regards certain regional problems of common interest; below, four priorities will be enumerated which are essentially to be granted to—in economic terms—backward agricultural regions and declining industrial regions, as well as to peripheral regions. These priorities are to guide the actions of the Member States as well as the interventions to which the Community commits itself by means of financial instruments already at its disposal (European Investment Bank, Social Fund, 'Orientation Section' of the Agricultural Fund).

7. Proposals for the Agricultural Fund arrangements, presented to the Council by the Commission in May 1971. The arrangement proposals aim at organising the economic conversion of agricultural priority regions in the Community along with the modernisation of the agricultural structures.

8. An important decision was taken in October 1971, namely, to co-ordinate the general schemes of regional aid; it took the form of a first resolution adopted by representatives of governments of Member States. Four aspects were involved:

(i) there was to be one aid-intensity ceiling, fixed for the central regions of the Community at 20 per cent in subsidy equivalent;

(ii) aid must be transparent, that is to say, 'obscure' aid must be suppressed and all kinds of aid should be taken into account for the calculation of the ceiling for a given investment;

(iii) aid should be region-specific, which means that regional aids must not cover the entire national territory, that the schemes are to define clearly the regions or zones benefiting from the aid, and that the aid must be adapted to the nature, intensity, and urgency of the problems to be solved;

(iv) regional and sectoral aids may not be aggregated until a procedure has been set up for appreciating the sectoral effects of regional aid.

9. At the beginning of 1973, the Commission published a report on the regional problems in the enlarged Community (doc. COM(73) 550 final 3–5–1973) in which the regional disparities were analysed and some guidelines drawn for a regional policy of the Community.

10. This short historical description would not be complete without quoting the Resolutions of the Council concerning the creation of the Economic and Monetary Union 22 March 1971[10] and 21 March 1972[11], resolutions by which the Member States firmly committed themselves to design a veritable Community Regional Policy, asking the Commission to submit proposals. The Heads of State and Governments, meeting at the Summit Conference in Paris in October 1972, gave high priority to the correction of regional imbalances, and invited EC institutions to set up a Regional Development Fund. In July 1973 the Commission presented its proposals to the Council of Ministers; they took up again a number of its previous proposals (notably those of October 1969); they concerned in particular:

(i) the creation of a Committee of Regional Policy (doc. COM(73) 1171 final 25–7–1973);

(ii) the creation of a European Fund for regional development (doc. COM(73) 1170 – final 25–7–1973).

Detailed operational rules were proposed, too (doc. COM(73) 1278, 25–7–1973).

After prolonged negotiations in the Council, especially about the size of the Fund and the distribution of resources among Member States, legal deeds were passed by which the two institutions were created;[12] they form at present the essential basis of the Regional Policy of the European Community.

In conclusion it may be said that, until the end of 1974, the European Community's policy was just to coordinate and regulate the actions of national states. Coordination was mostly done by the systematic study of regional development and by contributing to the setting-up of regional programmes. Regulation generally took the form of a scheme to prevent the abuse of financial incentives. The

Community's financial resources could only be used by the Commission in specific and limited fields to support national regional policies. These resources were not inconsiderable: up to the end of 1974 they consisted of:

loans from the ECSC for the conversion of coal-mining and steel-producing regions, amounting to 372 million u.a. (units of account);
loans from the European Investment Bank to less prosperous regions, totalling 3,965 million u.a.;
grants from the 'Agricultural Fund' for modernisation of agricultural areas, totalling 1,030 million u.a.;
grants from the 'Social Fund' for the retraining and resettlement of workers, totalling 1,217 million u.a.

The Community tried through its Regional policy to coordinate the various financial efforts amongst Members and their efforts made in other fields of policy, such as energy, transportation, and trade, and to direct them to the regions, most in need of Community aid.

V THE PRESENT SITUATION[13]

Community decisions adopted in 1975 on the change that was needed in the Community's regional policy were essentially the reflection of two facts. First, the progressive establishment of the Common Market had not achieved the positive results expected in terms of a better distribution of economic activity throughout Community territory. On the contrary, the prosperity of the richer regions increased while regions with less advanced economies encountered increasing difficulty in penetrating the growing market. The sustained growth of the Community economy over this period clearly had positive results, even in the less-favoured regions, but it also helped to hide the persistent imbalances which had existed before the Common Market was established.

Economic and social trends in recent years have made the situation even more complicated and worrying. Since 1973, the effects of the economic crisis and the increased cost of raw materials, as well as the new international division of labour, have led to a slower growth rate and less inclination to invest.

In an economy where growth rates have declined, the development of the weaker regions is seriously affected, and the persistence of regional imbalances even threatens the proper functioning of the Common

Market itself. Indeed, not only do the less-developed regions fail to integrate fully within the Community, but the problems to which they give rise become an increasingly heavy burden on national economies and thus increase the pressure on the public authorities concerned to refuse the constraints inherent in the mechanism of Community integration. It is, moreover, an illusion to hope for the convergence of Member States' economies so long as regional problems continue to weigh so heavily on certain economies.

In the light of this situation, Community regional policy must become more ambitious than in the past. This is not only desirable; it is now one of the conditions of continuing European economic integration.

Community regional policy has two main aims: first, to reduce existing regional problems which appear both in regions traditionally less developed and in those involved in a process of industrial or agricultural reconversion; second, to prevent new regional imbalances arising from the change in world economic structures or from measures adopted by the Community within the framework of its own policies. The achievement of these aims implies close cooperation between the Community and each Member State, and the performance of a variety of tasks.

First, these tasks involve the permanent analysis and assessment of trends in regional economies throughout the Community territory, principally, though not only, in the field of employment, to estimate the range and nature of the regional imbalances affecting the integration process on the Community level.

Second, they require that Community policies and financial instruments, structural and other, are used in a coherent and convergent way if their consequences may, at one time or another, have a regional impact.

Third, there must be coordination of the regional policies of Member States, both mutually and in relation to Community aims.

Fourth and last, there is the question of a policy of financial assistance (Regional Fund); on the one hand this takes the form of support to national regional policies, and on the other it must be a catalyst in working out and applying specific development and conversion measures on the Community level.

These aims and their achievement fall within the framework of an active employment policy. In the present economic situation of the Community, the creation of new jobs in regions where structural unemployment is greatest must be a priority task.

Its comprehensive approach also places Community regional policy in the perspective of Community land-use planning. In implementing the policy, the Commission will, particularly by means of the regional development programmes, make an effort to promote a rational use of space, a balanced distribution of activities across the whole Community territory, and effective protection of the environment and living conditions. Each of the means of action will be discussed briefly hereafter.

A comprehensive approach to regional policy involves *strengthening the system of analysis and assessment of the regional economies* of the Community as a whole and of their respective development. This analysis should include all regions and be as exhaustive as possible. Indeed, detailed knowledge of the development of all regions, including the relatively prosperous regions which supply a large portion of the resources required, will assist in diagnosing and remedying regional problems. With that intention, the tasks to be undertaken are:

to analyse regional trends and, in particular, to consider how regional disparities have developed;

to pinpoint regions facing or likely to face problems of Community size;

to work out a joint method for assessing the results of national and Community regional policies;

to provide the statistical and methodological basis needed to assess the regional effects of Community policies.

A number of key regional indicators are to be worked out on a Community basis, such as activity rates, employment by sector, unemployment, employment-shortfall forecasts, net migration, GDP and income per head of population and per employed person, fiscal capacity and effort, and data on the level of provision and needs for infrastructure. The forecasting of regional employment balances is of special importance here to indicate the regions needing Community help. The examination and assessment of the situation in each region should be undertaken within the framework of a comprehensive analysis of the Community's economic situation and of the general economic policy measures which it requires. This analytical and conceptual work should be extended to cover also the the effectiveness of the means and instruments used so as to build up a coherent system for assessing results.

On the basis of the above-indicated work as whole, the Commission will present to the Council a draft report on the social and economic development of the regions of the Community every two years, starting in

1979. This report is intended to indicate the principal regional problems on the Community level, to assess the results achieved by the joint actions of the Member States and the Community against these problems, and show the conditions for an effective coordination of the regional policies of the Member States.

The Council would approve the report and fix the priority objectives of regional development to be pursued on the Community level and, following from that, guidelines for national and Community regional policies.

It is indispensable that the *spatial dimension be assessed and taken into account in the formulation and implementation of the major Community policies*; this will permit the framing of the policies with proper regard to their regional impact and, if need be, the adoption of any measures required to ensure that these policies take full effect and that any adverse regional effects are corrected.

To that end, the establishment of a comprehensive system of analysis and assessment of regional economies should be supplemented by the systematic assessment of the regional consequences of Community policies, whenever significant new measures are contemplated.

The harmonious development of economic activity throughout the Community requires not only the *coordination of the various Community policies and financial instruments*, but also the *corresponding coordination of the policies of Member States*.

The two-yearly report on Community regional development, and the aims and guidelines fixed by the Council, will form the basis for periodic comparison of regional problems in the different Member States and of national regional policies. This comparison, which is also the first stage of a coordination process, must cover national regional policies and take account of the various structural measures with regional impact, infrastructure projects with direct or indirect regional consequences, and financial transfers between regions within a State.

In this connection, *regional development programmes* are a particularly important instrument; they should specify the requirements, aims, and priorities of each region and the means necessary and available to achieve them. Their examination on the Community level will make it possible to take into account the guidelines and priority aims set by the Council, after considering the two-yearly report, and the other Community policies. It is clear that coordination can be successful only to the extent that the guidelines and aims have themselves been laid down with some precision.

Member States will specify the use of resources received from the

Regional Fund, but it is on the level of these programmes that the complementary nature of Community action and Member-State action will be ensured, thus guaranteeing the speeding-up of the overall regional development effort.

One of the means by which coordination is to be assured is the consultation of the *Regional Policy Committee*, notably on the draft two-yearly report prepared by the Commission before its presentation to the Council. The Regional Policy Committee will further be informed of the conclusions of the main reports analysing the regional impact of Community policies: that will enable it to make a more detailed study of the implications of the geographical dimension of these policies. Moreover, the Committee will study the various development programmes presented by the Member States, and fix aims and priorities.

The *European Development Fund* is intended as a source of grants to industrial, handicraft, and service activity, and to infrastructure. The Fund is fed by contributions of the Member States; the Council of Ministers fixes the contribution of each Member State and the total volume of the Fund, as well as the share each Member State gets out of the Fund. As the Fund is the major exponent of the new regional policy, a separate section will be devoted to it.

VI THE REGIONAL DEVELOPMENT FUND[14]

The operations of the Fund were first regulated by the Council of Ministers for a three-year period. The volume was fixed at 300 million u.a. for 1975, 500 million u.a. for 1976, and 500 million u.a. for 1977. In order to take account of the respective regional problems of Member States, the resources of the Fund were to be distributed as follows: Italy 40 per cent, United Kingdom 28 per cent, France 15 per cent, Federal Republic of Germany 6.4 per cent, Ireland 6 per cent, Netherlands 1.7 per cent, Belgium 1.5 per cent, Denmark 1.3 per cent and Luxembourg 0.1 per cent. Regions that receive funds on the basis of national regional policies are eligible for assistance from the Regional Fund. However, since the Fund's resources are limited, priority is given to investment in activities in Community priority areas. In practice, therefore, aid from the Fund goes primarily to the following regions: Southern Italy, Ireland, Northern Ireland, and the special development and development areas in Great Britain, the West and the South West of France, the regions on the eastern frontier of the Federal Republic of Germany, the mining areas and some farming areas of Belgium and Luxembourg, the North of the Netherlands, and Greenland.

Investment in the French overseas departments (Martinique, Guadeloupe, French Guyana, and Réunion) is also eligible for the Fund's assistance.

Requests for contributions from the Fund are made not by investors themselves but by the governments of Member Countries on their behalf. This procedure has been decided on in order to make national regional policies and the policy of the Community consistent.

The Fund is designed to act as an incentive to investment in both economic activity and infrastructure. Each investment it contributes to must exceed 50,000 u.a.

In the first instance, the Fund may contribute to investments in industrial, handicraft, or service activities. For investments to qualify for assistance, they must benefit from state regional aids and contribute to creating at least ten new jobs or maintaining as many existing jobs. Service activities qualifying for aid must either be concerned with tourism or have chosen to set up a main activity centre in the region in question. Investments may receive a contribution from the Fund of 20 per cent of the investment cost, or 50 per cent of the aid from public authorities under national regional policy, whichever is the less. In calculating the 20 per cent figure, only the first 100,000 u.a. of investment per job created or 50,000 u.a. of investment per job maintained will be taken into account. In calculating the 50 per cent figure, the national aids taken into consideration are grants and interest rebates or their equivalents. The Fund's contribution may, according to a decision of the government concerned, either supplement or substitute aid granted to the relevant investment by public authorities.

Infrastructure is the second field of activity qualifying for a contribution from the Fund. The eligible categories of infrastructure are:

items directly linked with the development of industrial, handicraft, or service activity and totally or partially financed by public authorities. Industrial estates, for example, fall within this category; certain items required for mountain and hill farming and also farming in certain less favoured areas.

In both cases, the contribution from the Fund may be:

30 per cent of the expenditure incurred if the investment is less than 10,000,000 u.a.;

10 to 30 per cent for investments of 10,000,000 u.a. or more.

The contribution from the Fund may consist wholly or in part in an interest rebate of three percentage points on loans made by the European Investment Bank.

Applications for a contribution from the Fund made to the Commission are assessed on their merits. Applications have to contain indications of the consistency of the investment with the range of actions undertaken by the Member State, the contribution of the investment to the economic development of the region, its impact on employment, and the situation of the economic sector concerned. Among the criteria for consideration of a request, an investment's falling within a frontier area and therefore reflecting some form of collaboration between Member States is given special attention. Applications are also decided in the light of any other financial contribution to investments in the region by either the public authorities concerned or the Community through its various agencies (Coal and Steel Funds, Agricultural Fund, Social Fund, the European Investment Bank). The effective coordination of the different kinds of assistance is a key element in the conduct of the Community's regional policy.

Projects have to fit into a regional development programme to qualify for assistance from the Fund; a regional programme consists of precise indications of the planning objectives in the region and the means available or required to further them.

In the first two years of its existence, the Fund received applications for subsidy that, but for Belgium and Germany, exceeded the quota of all Member Countries. In 1975, 40 per cent of total aid went to industrial projects and 60 per cent to infrastructure projects, although, of the amounts applied for, approximately 60 per cent were meant for industry and only 40 per cent for infrastructure.[15] In 1976 the ratio had shifted towards infrastructure; indeed, in that year, 75 per cent of all grants fell in that category. That industrial projects account for so small a share is partly due to the regulations of the Fund: grants to industrial investment may not exceed 20 per cent of investment cost as compared to 30 per cent or 50 per cent of the relevant national aid, to infrastructure. Grants are also subject to a ceiling linked to the number of jobs created or maintained. The bias towards infrastructure can be explained by the bad economic conditions prevailing in 1975 and 1976, which led to less investment in industry in general. Up to April 1977, the following amounts had been received by the various Member States (in millions of u.a.): Belgium 17, Denmark 14, Germany 42, France 122, Ireland 72, Italy 390, Luxembourg 1, Netherlands 16, United Kingdom 272.

From the detailed statistics in the annual reports it is obvious that the regions that profited most from the Fund were indeed the priority regions of the Community, namely Southern Italy and Ireland. Recently the Commission asked for an increase in the Fund's resources to 750 million u.a. for 1978, and proposed a number of changes in the Fund's operational rules.[16] Specifically, it was proposed to split up the ERDF resources into two sections, a larger quota section and a smaller non-quota section. The quota section, amounting to 650 million u.a., is intended to finance support to the regional development measures of the Member States, support that is given to speed up the development in the European Community's priority regions. The non-quota section of 100 million u.a. is to be used by the Commission for specific actions. In such actions the Community wants to express its own responsibility for correcting regional imbalances. Specific actions are foreseen for those regions that bear the regional effects of Community policies and the negative effects of changes in the world economic structure. Specific actions are further intended to give incidental aid to regions that no longer qualify as Community priority regions.

It will be clear that the problems calling for specific actions may occur in regions that already benefit from the quota section. Such regions may indeed qualify for aid from both the quota and the non-quota sections.

The Commission will, of course, base the use of non-quota funds on a constant evaluation, on the Community level, of the gravity, scale, and urgency of the regional problems.

At the Council's meeting of 5 and 6 December 1977, the proposals were discussed, but no decision could be made. The Council did decide, however, on the size of the Fund and the allocation of its resources. The Regional Fund will have some 1,850 million u.a., divided as follows: 1978, 580 million u.a.; 1979, 620 million u.a.; and 1980, 650 million u.a. The French share in total resource allocation is to be increased to 17 per cent.

VII SUGGESTIONS FOR ANALYTICAL STUDIES TO IMPROVE THE EFFICIENCY OF REGIONAL POLICY

The aim of regional policy is to change the behaviour of economic agents so as to make them comply with social objectives. For that reason it is necessary to look more closely at their behaviour and at the factors that determine it. Let us consider for a moment the behaviour of two economic agents; one a firm, the other a family.

A firm in search of a site will use some form of checklist of the various location factors it considers relevant. After contemplating the 'location profile' of each site, made up of the relevant factors, the firm will choose the one with the highest potentials. There will be a threshold for the firm to jump in moving to a new location; and, to overcome that threshold, the absolute advantage of a new location over the present one, emerging from a comparison of cost and revenue elements of both and from the analysis of the risk factors, should be sufficiently high.

A family, a household, is apt to 'take stock' from time to time, comparing its present situation with the alternative situations available to it. If the potential of a new situation seems sufficiently higher than that of the present situation to overcome the threshold formed by the monetary and psychological costs always involved in a move, the family will either move house or change its jobs, or perhaps both.

The thresholds indicated above are not the only ones as far as the behaviour of economic agents is concerned. Some economic units have a potential so low that there is hardly a chance of their being the object of a well-considered choice; why, indeed, should anyone choose a miserable site so long as there are obviously better alternatives available? True, the optimum is not always chosen but that can easily be explained, the choice criteria differ from one agent to another, as does the range of their information.

For European regions, a dynamic evolution pattern emerges when an analytical model of thresholds is applied. At any moment, each of these regions shows a certain regional profile, which is very complex, composed as it is of a great variety of elements. Some of these components will be relevant to certain types of establishments, others to family decisions, others again stir the public authorities (local, regional, national, and international) into action. Let us give an example.

The analytical description of a region—that is, its profile—will include elements that are related to the accessibility of markets, labour markets, housing markets and to the action of public authorities; entrepreneurs will make their location decisions or formation decisions in consideration of these elements.

And that same labour market, that same housing market—but this time other elements of it—will feature in the decision-making process of households; while an establishment will consider the qualitative and quantitative aspects of the supply of labour, households will contemplate the qualitative and quantitative aspects of the demand for labour.

The public authorities, indeed, consider the one as well as the other; they try to correct imbalances on the labour market, imbalances that, under certain conditions, are in danger of growing. As it has been indicated above; left to itself, the system activated by individual agents risks a drift towards an explosive situation or, on the contrary, in the very long run towards zero potential.

Thus the dynamism of regions begins to show; any decision, once carried out, will modify a region's profile, and also inflect the decisions to be made in future. If the modification tends to increase the potential, so much the better; if the potential deteriorates, the region risks drifting cumulatively towards a very low potential, a situation that will be frowned upon by enlightened public authorities. Indeed, these positive and negative dynamics exist, and the entire regional policy can be defined as efforts to keep the regional potentials under permanent control. Subsidies, infrastructure policy, measures for stimulating the location of industry, creation of industrial zones, all pursue that one objective; the same is true of policies that tend to slow down the concentration of activities in certain regions.

It is evident, then, how important the threshold notion is; let us summarise its aspects:

above what threshold will a region support its own development? the loss of what elements will cause the crossing of the threshold towards downfall?
what manner and level of instruments are required to cross the threshold in the opposite direction?

It seems an exciting task for an analyst to find clear and quantified answers to these questions. Such experimental approaches are essential to any science; they must be based, however, on a central theory like the one we have just described, and which we propose to call a generalised bottle-neck theory.

Negative judgements have sometimes been passed on regional policies aimed at suppressing bottle-necks, at 'warding off the worst'. In the light of the above one may wonder if that is not, indeed, the right way, provided that one realises the significance of the concept utilised. To that end, one should begin by drawing the profile of the regions to be studied; that was the idea motivating us when we proposed, five years ago, to the Commission of the European Communities to undertake the FLEUR project, comprising a study of the location profiles of the European regions, the results of which would one day enable us to spot the most strangulating bottle-necks.[17]

That would be a necessary, but not in itself sufficient, precondition.

For identifying a bottle-neck implies the evaluation of the various elements of a profile, an evaluation that will differ according to the type of economic activity involved: consumption, industrial, tertiary, or quaternary activity, environment, or recreation. And so it is essential to recruit econometric techniques, models, a veritable discipline of spatial econometrics, which in fact has not yet advanced beyond its first stammerings.[18]

An essential element that tends to change the profile is that of the various policies: regional, sectoral, infrastructural, national with regional components, and many others. These policies must be 'evaluated' in the sense indicated above, but also on the level of their mutual consistency themselves; hence the need to evaluate the bottle-necks in the action of the public authorities, and in their contacts with the macro-economic and macro-social agents, the strategic action groups.

We do not, in fact, recommend anything revolutionary; just a new reflection on the tools that we have been using for many years, tools which, properly applied, would enable us better to settle the problems for which we have designed them. More particularly, the information on potentialities and attraction factors of the European regions could compensate for the positive and negative inertia due to externalities of information, and to the pictures too bright or too loaded that have been drawn of these regions.

VIII OUTLOOK

The regional policy of the European Community is likely to gain momentum in the coming years. One reason is the difficult economic situation that will probably persist, putting a continuous strain on the working of the Common Market. Keeping to the rules of the game as far as the free movement of goods, people, and capital is concerned may only be possible by increasing efforts in the field of regional policy.

Another reason lies in the possible enlargement of the European Community. The membership of such countries as Spain, Portugal and Greece, with their levels of development much lower than the average of the present Community, can only become effective if quite a massive amount of aid is channelled to the regions of these countries, the more so because their economies are not yet adapted to the competition within a large Common Market.

However, apart from such new factors, a well-known old factor may well push the Community towards a more vigorous regional policy, namely the increasing awareness that regional discrepancies are socially unacceptable in our modern world.

In Section V, it has been said that the Community should avail itself of a set of analytical concepts and tools to act efficiently along those lines. Some thoughts on the topic have been presented to round off our views on EEC regional policies.

NOTES

1. OECD, *The regional factor in economic development; Policies in fifteen industrialized OECD countries* (Paris, 1970) p. 24.
2. *Documenten van de Conferentie voor regionale economie*, Deel I en II (Brussels, 1961).
3. *Verslagen van de groepen van deskundigen over de regionale politiek in de Europese Economische Gemeenschap* (Brussels, 1964).
4. *A regional policy for the Community* (Brussels, 1969).
5. *Regional Development in the European Community, An Analytical Survey* (Brussels, 1971).
6. *Report on the Regional Problems in the Enlarged Community* (Com. 73 550 final) (Brussels, 1973) (*Thompson Report*).
7. Eurostat, *Regional Statistics*, various issues.
8. Eurostat, *Regional Accounts. Economic Aggregates, 1970* (Luxembourg, 1976) p. 138.
9. This section is partly based on J. van Ginderachter, 'La politique régionale de la Communauté, justification, modalités et propositions', *Revue du Marché Commun* (1973) pp. 468–86.
10. *Official Journal*, No. C 28, 17 March 1971.
11. *Official Journal*, No. C 38, 18 April 1972.
12. Council regulations (EC) No. 724/75, 18 March 1975 (Fund), and Council Decision of 18 March 1975 (committee).
13. This section is essentially based on the publication *Community Regional Policy, New Guidelines, Bulletin of the European Communities*, Supplement.
14. The first part of this section is taken from 'A new regional policy for Europe', *European Documentation Periodical*, 1975/3.
15. European Regional Development Fund, *First Annual Report (1975): Bulletin of the European Communities*, Supplement 7/76. European Regional Development Fund, *Second Annual Report* (1976), Com 77 260 final, mimeographed.
16. 'Community Regional Policy; New Guidelines', *Bulletin of the European Communities*, Supplement 2/77.
17. On its state of advancement, see W. Molle and B. van Holst, The FLEUR project, a progress report (Series: Foundations of Empirical Economic Research, 1976/15).
18. Klaassen, L. and Paelinck, J. H. P., *A Preface to Empirical Econometrics* (Forthcoming, 1978).

8 Energy policy[1]

GEORGES BRONDEL and NOEL MORTON

INTRODUCTION

In attempting an energy perspective for the European Community we base our view on the year 1973, but we do, of course, look backward to 1973, a milestone in modern energy history, and forward into the 1980s, to speculate on where the Community's energy policy, in cooperation with the energy policies of the Member States, may be headed. We look at the political as well as the economic realities, at the interaction of economic constraints with policy decisions, and at how a still developing Community energy policy is being formed.

First of all, however, it is necessary to explain the institutional constraints that fashion and control a Community energy policy. It is commonly said that the Commission proposes and the Council disposes. That is to say, the Commission has the duty to initiate policy in the energy field as in other fields, but it must also, after consulting the European Parliament and the Economic and Social Committee, seek the approval of the Council of Ministers of the nine Member States before that policy can be implemented.

It is also important to know that even when the broad lines of Community energy are approved by the Council of Ministers and enshrined in a Council Resolution, they are, for the most part, exhortatory rather than binding on the Member States. The objectives of the energy policy are achieved not by Community fiat but by requesting the cooperation of the Member States. Generally speaking, it is at a later stage that the Commission submits specific proposals to assist in the implementation of such broad policy resolutions, and those proposals then go through the process, as described above, of advocacy by the Commission and acceptance—or sometimes rejection—by the Council.

Finally, it should be noted that energy policy is sometimes discussed in the highest forum of all, the European Council or meeting of Heads of Government. Broad policy guidelines can be handed down from such meetings and, again, it is the Commission's duty and prerogative to frame resolutions for approval by the Council of Ministers in further-ance of the policies that are consistent with the guidelines.

THE DEVELOPMENT OF COMMUNITY ENERGY POLICIES

EARLY MOVES TOWARD A COMMUNITY ENERGY POLICY

'A cheap and secure supply of energy' has been the touchstone of Community energy policy since it was first announced in the 1962 Protocol of the High Authority of the European Coal and Steel Community. It was developed and elaborated upon in successive documents: 'First Guidelines for a Community Energy Policy' (De-cember 1968); 'Necessary Progress in Community Energy Policy' (October 1972); and 'Guidelines and Priority Actions under the Community Energy Policy' (April 1973)[2], in which one of the early paragraphs repeated the aim: 'the underlying problem besetting energy policy is to guarantee long-term security of supplies under satisfactory economic conditions'. Many of the problems that still concern us are mentioned in this series of policy statements—for example, relations with energy-importing and energy-exporting countries; organisation of the Community oil market; the proper place of nuclear power, coal, and gas; and protection of the environment.

THE COMMUNITY ENERGY SITUATION 1969−1972

Table 8.1 shows the Community's total primary energy consumption for the years 1969 to 1972. The steady trend away from coal can be seen, down almost 10 per cent over the four years; the 10 per cent decline is almost exactly matched by the gain in hydrocarbons (oil and gas). Oil, in fact, moved modestly ahead from 57.9 per cent to 62.3 per cent, whereas gas more than doubled its share, from 5.2 per cent to 10.7 per cent. Oil was becoming established ever more firmly as the Community's main source of energy. According to forecasts made in late 1972 and updated after the three new Member States joined in January 1973, the share of oil in primary energy demand would rise to 64 per cent in 1985, while the share of solid fuels would fall to 10 per cent. The Community's energy

TABLE 8.1   European Community—total primary energy needs,[a] 1969–1972

Fuel	1969 (Mtoe)	(%)	1970 (Mtoe)	(%)	1971 (Mtoe)	(%)	1972 (Mtoe)	(%)
Solid fuels	277	32.1	264	28.7	239	25.6	217	22.5
Oil	500	57.9	550	59.8	573	61.5	601	62.3
Natural gas	45	5.2	62	6.7	80	8.6	103	10.7
Hydroelectric power and others	30	3.5	33	3.6	28	3.0	29	3.0
Nuclear energy	11	1.3	11	1.2	12	1.3	14	1.5
Total	863	100.0	920	100.0	932	100.0	964	100.0

Note: [a] Internal consumption + exports + bunkers.

mix, with plentiful oil in prospect and with only a modest rate of price increase if the OPEC Teheran/Tripoli/Geneva agreements were implemented, was based largely on economic factors, and under those circumstances, oil was bound to emerge as the favoured fuel. Only in the very long term, it was argued, would the gradually improving economics of electricity generated from nuclear energy displace oil from its dominant position.

THE CHANGED CIRCUMSTANCES OF 1973–1974

In October 1973 the Gulf members of the Organization of Petroleum Exporting Countries (OPEC) unilaterally raised the posted price of crude oil by 70 per cent, to $5.11 per barrel for the marker crude, and on 1 January 1974 by a further 128 per cent to $11.65 per barrel. Almost simultaneously, and as a demonstration of political strength, the ten members of the Organization of Arab Petroleum Exporting Countries (OAPEC) announced progressive cutbacks in their rates of production, which had reached a peak in September 1973, and also announced embargoes on loadings of crude oil destined for the United States and certain other countries. The most severe effect was to reduce production from OAPEC sources by five to six million barrels a day, more than 25 per cent, but, with the lowering of political tension, the production rate improved in early 1974 and the embargoes were lifted in April 1974. The oil producers had shown, however, that they could adhere to a common policy—whether, as OAPEC, to vary production or, as OPEC, to vary the cost of oil by a variety of devices—and their solidarity as a cartel surprised and profoundly disturbed the industrialised, oil-importing countries.

A NEW STRATEGY FOR ENERGY

In these changed circumstances, a reappraisal of the Community's energy policy was urgent and was duly made. In its original form it appeared as a communication from the Commission to the Council of Ministers in June 1974, 'Towards a New Energy Policy Strategy for the Community.'[3] It built on the foundations of the earlier document, to which reference has already been made, 'Guidelines and Priority Actions under the Community Energy Policy' (April 1973), and dealt with both long- and medium-term objectives and policies for their attainment. Inevitably it had a certain eagerness, almost a missionary zeal about it, a willingness to set optimistic targets that subsequent experience has had to modify, but it remains, in principle, the cornerstone of Community energy policy and expounding its philosophy and proposals in some detail is worthwhile.

BASIC PHILOSOPHY

The change in the Community's energy supply situation was so far-reaching that the objectives of energy policy had to be adapted. The experience of the latter part of 1973 and its repercussions were seen as an incentive to the Community to reduce its dependence on imported energy as much as possible. Vigorous action was needed both to guarantee greater security of supply and to prevent violent changes in energy prices, which always jeopardise the effectiveness of investments undertaken and call in question the wisdom of the path that economic development has followed.

The objective of developing more secure energy resources obviously raised the problem of the relative prices of the various primary energy sources. Although action taken by the authorities can to a certain extent improve the supply situation, the benefits of such actions can be put at risk unless there is an adequate policy on prices. In this field, as in others, several factors had to be taken into consideration. First, the energy sources that were to be promoted had to be available at the lowest possible price, as an incentive to potential users. Second, the producers would have no interest in making the investments necessary for the future development of production if the profitability were too low. Lastly, special attention had to be given to the role that the consumers themselves can play. Although the increased costs of energy may put a brake on demand in the short term, this effect may well tend to weaken in the long term. It was therefore essential that the consumers were confronted with their collective responsibility to make better use of energy resources, which would be in shorter supply and would cost more than before. However, the substantial increases in the price of imported crude not only raised issues in the field of energy policy but also raised questions about the adaptation of the economic structures.

The deterioration in the balance of payments was causing the most concern. If there were to be the same quantities of oil available as before, the trade deficit would immediately result in an increase in the external debt of the Community. In the longer term, the factors of production would have to be redeployed to meet, internally, the increased costs of energy, and, externally, the need to increase income from exports. The scale of these adjustments would be quite different for each Member State. The differences in their initial situations and in their medium-term prospects were strikingly large. They depended essentially on the balance-of-payments situation before the energy crisis, on the scale of crude oil imports relative to total GNP, and on the availability of alternative energy resources in the near future at a competitive price.

Thus the gap to be filled so that equilibrium could be restored in the balance of payments was much larger in some member countries than in others. In other cases, the very limited availability of indigenous traditional energy resources meant that there was little hope in the near future of reducing the degree of dependence on imported energy, and that a special investment effort must be made to promote the development of nuclear energy.

These disparities are both valuable and hazardous for the Community—valuable, because satisfactory cooperation among the member countries would make for a fairer sharing of sacrifices over a period of time, to the benefit of the more exposed countries; and hazardous, because there is a danger that a difference in situations and prospects may lead to divergence in the policies and priorities of the individual member countries, the consequences of which would be to wipe out the potential advantages of a unified common market. To mitigate this risk, a Community energy strategy must be launched as soon as possible.

This strategy must aim at two objectives: a unified market and security of supply. The two are closely linked: only if the solidarity between the Member States—reflected in the principles of sharing the burden and of free movement of goods—has been seen to function without hindrance in normal conditions can such a bond have its full impact when supply difficulties arise.

THE LONG-TERM OBJECTIVES

A reasonable long-term goal (i.e. by the year 2000) in the Community energy policy seems to be an energy supply structure relying mainly on two components: nuclear energy and gas.

NUCLEAR ENERGY

Compared with other energy sources, nuclear energy is clearly the best solution for the large-scale production of heat either for electricity generation or for industrial uses. This is because of its ready availability, adaptability, ease of transport and storage, and relatively minor impact on the environment. For these reasons (bear in mind the small relative part played by fuel costs in the total costs) nuclear energy can potentially offer a high degree of security of supply, even if the Community itself has only limited resources of uranium ore. More than for most of the other energy sources, a policy of diversifying sources of supply and establishing stable relationships with the producing countries could rapidly reinforce that security. Of course, the development of nuclear energy will have its difficulties, but none seem insurmountable, provided that the necessary action is taken quickly enough and pursued resolutely (in technology, environment, sites, waste products, financial capacity for investment, industrial capacity, the training of qualified manpower, and public reassurance on safety aspects).

At least 50 per cent of the total energy requirements around the year 2000 could be covered by nuclear energy. Apart from industrial uses and electricity production, nuclear energy could have an additional advantage, that of making an increase in hydrogen production possible.

GAS

The gas obtained from a variety of primary sources (natural gas produced in the Community or imported from non-member countries, as well as oil or solid fuels transformed into synthesis gas) could cover nearly 30 per cent of energy consumption, mainly for heating buildings and for industrial processes with particularly demanding conditions (high-temperature processes, metal processing, synthesis). Over and above its inherent advantages as regards pollution and the rational use of energy, gas also offers in the long term the advantage of an additional outlet for nuclear energy: the infrastructure for transporting gas could gradually be used for distributing hydrogen or synthesis gas produced by means of heat of nuclear origin. In thirty years time, therefore, if the Community concentrated on creating an energy economy based on nuclear power and gas, it would be left with only a very limited dependence on coal and oil. Although coal and oil products would be used to some extent for gas production, non-conventional energies (particularly solar and geothermal energy) could begin to play a small role by that time, so that coal and oil used according to the 'classical' techniques might by then be meeting only a quarter of total needs.

The achievement of these long-term aims, set forth in orders of magnitude, depends on a whole set of conditions, the most important of which are as follows:

1. The necessary action must be taken immediately. In particular, the energy research and development programme must be intensified and accelerated so that the technological problems still to be overcome may be solved in good time.

2. Action in pursuit of these objectives must be compatible with solving the serious short- and medium-term problems that arise, notably those of security of supply. Such action must be sufficiently flexible to adapt to changing circumstances.

3. Finally, these objectives can only be realised if, at a stage when decisions are more advanced, account is taken of the consequences their implementation might have on the natural environment and the quality of life (e.g. pollution, scarcity of natural resources, increased intensity of land use).

THE OBJECTIVES FOR 1985

NEW HYPOTHESES AND CONSTRAINTS

In drawing up a new energy supply strategy for the next ten years, the Community found it necessary to examine the validity and continuing reliability of those basic hypotheses which had hitherto been considered the most likely. Four main factors required consideration:

1. *The rate of economic growth*, insofar as it affects energy demand. The predictions of economic growth justified the adoption of a hypothesis for the growth of GNP of less than the average annual rate of about 5.0 per cent previously accepted for the period 1970–1985. Nonethe-

less, the relatively high rate of 4.5 per cent was assumed to ensure that the energy requirements had not been underestimated.

2. *Substitution and its effect on demand.* The new price relativities between the various energy sources would bring about changes in the demand for most of them. However, account had to be taken of a series of constraints characteristic of energy consumption, namely that certain consumer sectors could not change from one source of energy to another or could only do so by gradual steps, for technical as well as economic reasons. In practice, as an example, sectors such as the iron and steel industry and motor transport offer little flexibility in demand even in the medium term, whereas the production of electricity can be based on several different fuels, and the capacity to adapt is therefore greater. Thus these demand factors limited manoeuvrability in drafting a strategy for energy supply.

3. *Rigidities in supply.* Some sources of energy would have to be used regardless of the circumstances, either because they are by-products of certain production processes (e.g. coke-oven gas or refinery gas) or because the investment to be authorised must be based on long-term prospects of profitability (e.g. North Sea oil, natural gas, possible new coal mines). Other sources have greater flexibility and would make it possible, for example, to take measures to achieve greater security of supply.

4. *Investment.* It was clear that despite the considerable increase in oil prices, the future development of prices of substitute sources of energy was still very uncertain. The latter could compromise future investments, which, while fulfilling the needs of a reinforced security of supply, could become less profitable owing to economic fluctuations. The energy supply strategy must set out to increase the flexibility of demand and develop those sources of supply having the most flexibility; however, this double approach would only be implemented over an extended time scale. As far as technically and economically possible, use must be made of energy forms with a high degree of security of supply, where a demand exists that could absorb them (either immediately or gradually by means of certain structural adaptations). The balance of the energy requirement to be covered from more uncertain sources should correspond as far as possible with the most flexible part of the demand.

The plan should include quantified targets that would constitute a framework of action, as outlined in the following section.

STRUCTURE OF THE ENERGY BALANCE SHEET IN 1985

In view of the restrictions on a new energy supply strategy, as described above, it appeared reasonable for the Community to set the following goals for the next few years, on the demand side and on the supply side.

DEMAND

First, the implementation of a deliberate policy on achieving more efficient use of energy, reinforced by the effects of price increases, should make it possible to reduce by one percentage point the average rate of annual increase in demand between 1973 and 1985, without reducing the economic and social product obtained by means of the energy consumed. Total internal energy consumption would then be approximately 10 per cent lower than the figure originally envisaged.

Second, as soon as it can be done without increasing dependence on oil, electricity consumption must be encouraged, so that 35 per cent of total energy would be consumed in this form, compared with the present figure of 25 per cent. This would establish the largest possible market for nuclear energy. This expansion must, however, be gradual and compatible with the objective of stabilising and then reducing the consumption of petroleum products in power stations.

SUPPLY

First, nuclear facilities would be expanded, to produce up to one-half of the electricity needed after the mid-1980s. The objectives should also consider the extension of nuclear power to production of industrial heat. It appears possible, subject to attainment of certain prerequisite conditions, to have a total available capacity of more than 200 GW.

Second, solid fuel consumption must increase, making use of domestic production, which would have to be stabilised at least at the present level, and maximising the use of imported coal, for which stability of price and supply would be required. Third, the potential high demand for natural gas must be met by an increased supply, both from within the Community and from outside, provided that the necessary economic conditions could be fulfilled.

Finally, oil consumption would be concentrated mainly on specific uses, i.e. for motor fuel and for certain applications as raw material. Consumption of liquid fuels for other purposes would be limited roughly to the amount available as by-products of refining the volume of crude oil needed to meet the specific uses. Strengthened by more efficient use of the energy available, this trend to substitution would gradually halt the increase in crude oil requirements. Slackening of the growth rate would continue until 1978–1980, and by the mid-1980s it should be possible to hold the demand for crude oil at a level barely higher than that of 1973. By this time, the arrival of new sources (North Sea) should significantly reduce the share of present suppliers in the overall supply of the Community.

SUMMARY OF THE ORIGINAL 1985 OBJECTIVES IN THE 'NEW STRATEGY'

ENERGY DEMAND

1. To reduce estimated consumption in 1985 by 10 per cent in relation to the amount initially estimated for 1985, by the more efficient use of energy.
2. In step with the development of nuclear energy, to increase the consumption of electricity, which should in 1985 represent 35 per cent of energy consumption (25 per cent in 1972).

ENERGY SUPPLY

1. To limit to 40 per cent (63 per cent in 1973) in 1985 the degree of Community dependence for energy on outside sources.
2. *Oil*—(a) To limit to 40 per cent (60 per cent in 1973) the share of oil in the overall energy supply, and (b) to limit to 75 per cent (98 per cent in 1973) the degree of dependence on outside sources for oil supplies; this implies production of 180 Mtoe (million metric tones of oil equivalent) in the Community. The pattern of demand would also change, in particular by reducing consumption of heavy fuel oil in power stations.
3. *Solid fuels*—(a) To maintain the absolute level of current production (for coal, 180 Mtoe or 255 Mtce), increase imports (31 Mtoe in 1985), and maintain the share of solid fuel in the overall energy supply at more than 15 per cent (about 23 per cent in 1973); and (b) to shift demand in power stations as often as possible toward coal wherever nuclear energy cannot be used (i.e. replacing oil products and natural gas).
4. *Natural gas*—To make extensive use of this source of energy; its

share in the overall supply should increase from about 12 per cent in 1973 to 25 per cent in 1985. This will entail (*a*) at least doubling Community production (115 Mtoe in 1973), and (*b*) for the most part; using imports from various sources. With respect to demand, the use of natural gas in thermal power stations, and perhaps in certain industries, should be discouraged.

5. *Nuclear energy*—To ensure coverage of 50 per cent of electricity needs in 1985 by nuclear energy. This implies an installed capacity of at least 200 GWe for electricity production (plus 20 GWe for other uses).

THE EVOLUTION OF THE OBJECTIVES

It is evident from the foregoing that the principles in forming the 'new strategy', stripped to their essentials, were

1. to reduce total demand for energy as far as possible while maintaining a respectable rate of economic growth;
2. to switch final demand for energy into some fuels and away from others;
3. to reduce dependence on imported sources of energy; and
4. to increase production of indigenous sources of energy.

We have already said that the document was in some respects optimistic about targets and objectives. This had already been realised by December 1974 when the Council Resolution adopted, as an import-dependence target, not the 40 per cent in the New Strategy, but '50 per cent *and if possible* 40 per cent by 1985' (our italics). Table 8.2 shows the actual figures for 1973, the initial forecasts for 1985, which were updated for the Community of Nine in January 1973, and the objectives for 1985, as adopted by Council, at the 50 per cent and 40 per cent import-dependence levels. Table 8.2 also shows, set against the objectives, the latest Member State forecasts and we discuss these in a later section.

The specific objectives were now the following:

ENERGY DEMAND

1. To reduce the rate of growth of energy consumption for the Community as a whole in order to achieve by 1985 a level of 18 per cent below the January 1973 estimates; this percentage may be

TABLE 8.2 European Community—total primary energy needs,[a] 1973 and 1985

Fuel	1973 realisations		1985 initial forecasts[b]		1985 objectives[c]				1985 forecasts[d]			
					50% import dependence		40% import dependence		High imports case		Low imports case	
	(Mtoe)	(%)	(Mtoe)	(%)	(Mtoe)	(%)	(Mtoe)	(%)	(Mtoe)	(%)	(Mtoe)	(%)
Solid fuels	220	22.2	175	10	250	17	250	17	215	16	215	16
Oil	614	61.8	1160	64	720	49	600	41	745	55	695	51
Natural gas	118	11.9	265	15	270	18	340	23	235	17	245	18
Hydroelectric and geothermal power	27	2.7	40	2	45	3	45	3	35	3	35	3
Nuclear energy	14	1.4	160	9	190	13	240	16	120	9	160	12
Total	993	100.0	1800	100	1475	100	1475	100	1350	100	1350	100
Breakdown of total												
Indigenous production	364	36.7	640	36	800	54	900	61	590	44	690	51
Imports	629	63.3	1160	64	675	46	575	39	760	56	660	49

Notes: [a] Internal consumption + exports + bunkers.
[b] Source: 'Prospects of primary energy demand in the Community (1975–1980–1985)', supplemented by an additional estimate made in January 1973 for the new Member States. (Official doc. no. 8415, European Publications Office, Luxembourg.)
[c] Adopted by Council Resolution, 17 December 1974 concerning Community energy policy objectives for 1985.
[d] Latest forecast by Member States, September 1976.

different for the various Member States, and, depending on circumstances, specific objectives may be set for saving energy in the shorter term.

2. To alter the pattern of energy consumption by progressively increasing the use of reliable energy sources and relying more and more on electricity as nuclear energy, in particular, is developed. The Commission feels that in this way electricity would cover 35 per cent of energy consumption by 1985.

ENERGY SUPPLY

1. *Solid fuels*:
(*a*) To maintain the level of the Community's coal production (180 Mtoe by 1985) under satisfactory economic conditions,
(*b*) To increase the possibilities of importing coal from non-Community countries (40 Mtoe by 1985), and
(*c*) To raise brown coal and peat production to 30 Mtoe.
2. *Natural gas*:
(*a*) To step up Community research and production (land and underwater deposits) to obtain at least 175 Mtoe, and if possible 225 Mtoe, by 1985, and
(*b*) To secure imports of 95–115 Mtoe from non-Community countries.
3. *Nuclear energy*:
(*a*) To provide power stations with an installed capacity of at least 160 GWe and, if possible, 200 GWe by 1985.
4. *Hydroelectric and geothermal power*:
(*a*) To establish and develop sites for the production of hydroelectric and geothermal power to provide 45 Mtoe.
5. *Oil*:
(*a*) To restrict oil consumption where it can be economically replaced by other energy sources,
(*b*) To accelerate research and Community production (land and underwater deposits) at least 180 Mtoe by 1985, and
(*c*) To cut back imports from non-Community countries to 540 Mtoe (640 in 1973) according to national prospects; the attainment of objectives proposed by the Commission for other energy sources would enable this to be further reduced to 420 Mtoe. The percentage of imported oil in the total energy requirements would be 38 per cent and 28 per cent, respectively (61 per cent in 1973), or 75–70 per cent of oil consumption (98 per cent in 1973).

6. *Other sources of energy*:
(*a*) To ensure by a technological research and development policy that traditional forms of energy are better exploited and, in the long term, replaced by new sources of energy.

IMPLEMENTATION OF THE OBJECTIVES

In furtherance of the energy policy objectives adopted in December 1974, the Council of Ministers affirmed in two resolutions,[4] the broad means by which the objectives should be attained. It commissioned a wide-ranging enquiry into the rational use of energy in order to achieve the energy conservation target of 1985 and it spelled out in some detail, on the supply side, the principles to be followed in the solid fuel, nuclear, and hydrocarbons sectors if the various production objectives for coal supply, nuclear-generated electricity, and indigenous oil and gas production were to be achieved and dependence on imported energy satisfactorily reduced.

We said in the Introduction that implementation of the energy policy objectives was largely a matter for the Member States, to be achieved by harmonising their own energy policies to that end. Member states report at frequent intervals on the progress made toward the achievement of the objectives. The first summary of these national reports was made by the Commission in January 1976 from reports made in September 1975. At that time, total energy demand was estimated to be about 3–6 per cent below the objective for 1985.

The Commission noted that the Member States' current forecasts of energy consumption for 1985 coincided to a large extent with the Community's objective of reducing dependence on imported energy to 50 per cent. In this sense, the forecasts could be considered encouraging, yet uncertain, disquieting factors remained:

1. The current forecasts of Community production in 1985 (solid fuel, hydrocarbons, and nuclear energy) were lower than the objectives adopted by the Council.
2. The Member States' current forecasts for 1985 coincided with a 50 per cent dependence on imports, but only on the hypotheses that efforts directed toward the rational use of energy would be effective and that a higher rate of economic growth than forecast would not create a stronger growth in energy demand.
3. The forecasts did not appear to make it possible to reduce dependence on imported energy to 40 per cent by 1985.

The Commission also noted that even though the installed nuclear capacity for 1985 would be below the objective of about 200 GWe, spectacular progress would be necessary to achieve it, and that there were problems to be resolved in order to realise the forecasts. Serious effort would be necessary with respect to financing (with construction costs rising rapidly) as well as increasing the capacity of the nuclear construction industry and the availability of trained personnel. Perhaps even greater efforts would have to be made to supply the plants with a satisfactory flow of fuels, especially natural uranium, which could be in short supply between now and 1985. Considerable efforts would therefore be necessary to reduce the risks associated with production and utilisation of nuclear energy, as well as to obtain public support for rapid growth in the number of nuclear sites and to maintain public confidence in nuclear power.

Revised 1985 forecasts were made by Member States in September 1976; these are summarised in the right-hand columns of Table 8.2. The difference in total estimated energy demand for 1985—1350 Mtoe against 1475 Mtoe—appears startling, but this is explained by the economic recession of 1974–1976. The Community's energy demand in 1976 was only 936 Mtoe, less than 1973, and to achieve 1350 Mtoe in 1985 from the starting point of 1976 implies an annual energy growth rate of 4 per cent, accompanied by a GDP annual growth rate of 4.5–5 per cent.

A return to economic (and consequently energy) growth is therefore confirmed by the latest forecasts from the Member States. What gives cause for concern is that the latest figures for indigenous production confirm the earlier (1975) trend, i.e. a failure to live up to the objectives. It is true that even under the (more realistic?) high-imports case, dependence on imports is lower than in 1973, but at 56 per cent it is still unacceptably high. Coal, and hydro and geothermal power production are below their objectives, and only by assuming the most favourable circumstances for indigenous production of both gas and nuclear energy (the low-import case) can we hope for imports as low as 49–50 per cent of total energy. The implications of this situation were pointed out by the Commission[5] to a meeting of Energy Ministers in October 1976, in the following terms:

These forecasts assume an annual economic growth rate of $4\frac{1}{2}$–5 %, a figure which Ministers might regard as the lowest allowing reasonable social and economic progress. Failure to achieve this growth would ease our energy problems—but in an unwelcome way. The reasons for this disappointing prospect are several. It will be difficult to sustain domestic coal production because of increased costs and a prospective reduction in power station coal requirements. Unless more coal-fire generating stations are ordered, coal-burning capacity might fall by some 30 GWe by 1985. Oil and natural gas production may fall short of earlier expectations.

The main change, however, is that nuclear programmes have gone forward more slowly than earlier planned, partly because of technical and environmental factors and partly because of a fall in electricity demand which may prove to be only temporary. In mid-1974, a nuclear generating capacity of 176 GWe in 1985 was forecast. Current forecasts amount to 125 GWe, of which almost 90 GWe are currently operating, being built or on order: *for at least 35 GWe decisions are still to be taken.* If shortfalls in the supply of nuclear electricity are to be met by increasing oil imports, this will jeopardize further the reduced dependence objective and help to strengthen oil prices.

Looking at the short term, as a result of the economic recession, we were able in 1974 and 1975 to show a falling demand for energy and oil; but consumption in the first half of 1976 was 9 % higher than a year earlier, and the trend is continuing. With an oil price increase likely by the end of this year, this rising trend is a matter of serious concern. An upturn in oil imports will certainly be a heavy charge for the balance of payments. If, in addition, the price of oil is to rise, the terms of trade will also deteriorate. All this will certainly compromise the efforts of Member States to restore stability to their economies.

A COMMUNITY ENERGY POLICY NOW?

Following the lead of the European Council of Heads of Governments, which met in Rome in December 1975, the Commission proposed in January 1976 a balanced package of measures to help achieve reduced dependence on energy imports, the Community's main objective. The principal components were

1. agreement in principle to
    (a) lighten the financial burden of cyclical stocking of coal,
    (b) extend and improve the existing aid scheme for coking coal and coke,
    (c) adopt a safeguard system to protect domestic energy sources, including oil, against a precipitate drop in imported energy prices (minimum safeguard price), and

(*d*) grant Community aid for oil exploration;

2. a Euratom loan scheme for financing nuclear power stations and fuel cycle installations; and

3. further studies on

(*a*) promoting the use of coal in power stations, and

(*b*) guarantees or loans for new energy investments in cases where special difficulties arise.

TABLE 8.3 OECD: net imports of crude oil and refined products, by volume and value, 1973–1976

Country	1973 (10^6 MT)	($ m.)	1974 (10^6 MT)	($ m.)	1975 (10^6 MT)	($ m.)	1976 (est.) (10^6 MT)	($ m.)
Belgium	30.8	678	28.7	2388	25.5	2308	27.0	2457
Denmark	18.5	407	17.6	1464	16.4	1484	17.0	1530
Germany	144.9	3188	132.1	10991	122.6	11095	132.0	12276
France	128.8	2834	126.4	10517	102.5	9277	118.0	10856
Ireland	5.6	123	5.4	449	5.1	462	5.0	445
Italy	103.8	2284	102.9	8561	88.5	8009	97.0	8924
Luxembourg	1.7	37	1.6	133	1.3	118	2.0	186
Netherlands	40.2	884	35.8	2979	21.6	2860	34.0	3094
United Kingdom	113.4	2495	111.5	9277	88.7	8027	78.0	7098
Total Community	587.7	12930	562.0	46759	482.2	43640	510.0	46866
USA	30.7	7066	303.3	2608	289.7	27086	320.0	30400
Japan	282.5	5932	266.6	21894	245.2	21681	255.0	22950
Other OECD Europe	148.6	3269	149.5	12408	131.4	11826	140.0	12880
Other OECD	(4.5)	(99)	5.0	415	17.0	1547	20.0	1840
Total OECD	1315.0	29098	1286.4	107559	1165.5	105780	1245.0	114936

Need for action on this package was re-emphasised at the October 1976 meeting of the Council of Energy Ministers, as was the need for action both to conserve energy and to ensure the security of imported energy supplies. Energy conservation presents great difficulties, but it is cheaper than new energy investment, which is calculated to absorb 25 per cent of the total industrial investment of the Community. As for securing our imported supplies of energy, the Community has been for some years the world's largest importer of oil, and we need to foster good relations with the oil exporters (OPEC) as well as cooperation with other industrialised countries.(The Community's relations with oil producers are dealt with in a later section of this chapter.) Other energy supply problems exist: For example, there is danger of a shortage of uranium in the early 1980s. One of the major suppliers, Canada, could limit exports, and Australia has yet to decide whether to export natural uranium and if it does, how much to export. Some other supplies might become insecure for one reason or another. Under these circumstances, it is important to promote uranium exploration and to continue discussions with the major uranium-producing countries with a view to obtaining secure supplies.

It is true that action was taken on two of the points in the package in December 1976. First, the Council recorded its agreement on the establishment of Community machinery to safeguard the unity of the common market in the case of supply difficulties, i.e. on rules for exporting crude oil and petroleum products from one Member State to another; it did not agree, however, on the second part of the mechanism, i.e. to set a Community goal for reducing energy consumption in the event of supply difficulties. Second, it agreed to extend the time period for aid to coking coal beyond 1977, but the level of future aid must still be decided.

Nevertheless, whatever difficulties we find in implementing individual parts of the present Commission package, major efforts are necessary to reduce dependence on external supplies. We also need to reach early agreement on measures to establish our refinery capacity and uranium supplies. Faster progress on all fronts is badly needed to make Community energy policy a political reality, both internally and externally.

INTERNATIONAL RELATIONSHIPS WITH CONSUMERS

The events of 1973 and subsequent years, briefly described in our opening sections, had effects similar in kind, but varying in degree, on all energy-importing countries, most of whom took individually what action they could to protect themselves against the much higher cost of imported energy and its dubious security. It was not surprising, however, that the major consuming countries should have some ideas about cooperation between themselves on these matters and, on the initiative of the United States, a conference was held in Washington D.C. in February 1974 to discuss the problems that had arisen or were likely to arise, and to suggest possible solutions. The conference was denounced as 'confrontational' by some of the oil-producing countries, and one of the participants, France, had so many reservations about the possible outcome that she dissociated herself from the results of the conference and, in this respect, from her Community partners who remained convinced that action in this area was needed.

THE INTERNATIONAL ENERGY PROGRAMME

The result of the Washington Conference and subsequent work was a draft Agreement on an International Energy Programme, which was produced in Brussels on 21 September 1974 with the support of eight of the Community countries—Belgium, Denmark, Germany, Ireland, Italy, Luxembourg, the Netherlands, and the United Kingdom—Canada, Japan, Norway, and the United States. The Programme is designed to cover both long-term energy needs and a possible emergency in oil supplies; it will also promote cooperation between members and the oil-producing countries, other oil-consuming countries, and the developing nations.

The Programme aims in particular

1. to develop and put into effect a long-term cooperative programme to reduce dependence on imported oil;
2. to promote cooperative relations with oil-producing countries and also with oil-consuming countries who are not members of the International Energy Agency;
3. to develop a common level of 'emergency self-sufficiency' in oil supplies, common restraint measures on demand, and measures for the allocation of scarce oil supplies in an emergency; and
4. to develop an information system on the economic aspects of the international oil market

THE INTERNATIONAL ENERGY AGENCY

The Programme is implemented by the International Energy Agency (IEA), which was established as an autonomous body within the framework of OECD in November 1974. It has, at present, 19 members: the 12 listed above, plus Austria, Greece, New Zealand, Spain, Sweden, Switzerland, and Turkey; all are members of OECD. It has a Governing Board, and its work is conducted by four Standing Groups on (*a*) emergency questions, (*b*) the oil market, (*c*) long-term cooperation, (*d*) relations with producer and other consumer countries. The participating countries are represented on the Governing Board and in the

Standing Groups and there are two advisory bodies from the oil industry: the Industry Advisory Board, which deals with emergency questions, and an Industry Working Party on matters connected with the oil market. The Agency has a full-time Secretariat, based in Paris.

THE COMMUNITY'S RELATIONS WITH THE IEA

Article 72 of the Agreement on an International Energy Programme states

1. This Agreement shall be open for accession by the European Communities.
2. This Agreement shall not in any way impede the further implementation of the treaties establishing the European Communities.

The Community, however, has not applied for membership pending any reconsideration of the French position, but has been given 'active observer' status and plays a full part in the work of the IEA, at all levels. Working alongside the eight Community countries that are members of the Agency, it tries at all times to express the Community view and it is also charged with the duty of keeping France fully informed of what is happening in the Agency. In its relations with the Agency, the Community is particularly vigilant over any proposed action that, applied within the Community, could be construed as being contrary to the Treaties. Proposals for emergency sharing of available oil, with their implications for possible control of oil trade between member countries, might be assumed to present difficulties in this respect, and the application of the Agency's emergency rules within the Community is a matter of some complexity. The rules on holding emergency stocks, too, are not identical for the Agency and the Community.

INTERNATIONAL RELATIONSHIPS WITH ENERGY PRODUCERS

The Community is seeking every means of establishing more stable relations with the oil-producing countries, if possible in the form of concerted action that will provide a better guarantee for the security of our supplies. The Community is playing a very important role in several initiatives that have been undertaken. The idea of economic cooperation between industrial and developing countries has existed within the Community for a number of years. On 1 April 1976, the Lomé Convention became effective between the Community and 46 African, Caribbean, and Pacific countries, some of whom, particularly Nigeria, are oil producers. Negotiations are currently under way on cooperation agreements with the countries of the Mediterranean basin, and they should lead to the establishment of a free-trade area within a few years. In addition, a dialogue has developed between the countries of the Arab League and the Community; although its objectives are far more general than that of developing our relations as regards energy, it does touch on this topic. More generally, there is the North-South dialogue—the Conference on International Economic Cooperation—involving 27 countries. The Conference ended in early July 1977 on a somewhat disappointing note, dashing the Community's earlier hopes for a successful outcome.

THE COMMUNITY AND THE CONFERENCE ON INTERNATIONAL ECONOMIC COOPERATION

Parallel with the development of the International Energy Programme, discussed above, grew a desire to have some means of discussing energy problems, especially because no suitably specialised forum existed for international energy discussion. In April 1975, France took the initiative in arranging a conference—known as Kleber I—in Paris to explore the possibilities for setting up an international energy conference between oil producers, industrialised countries, and developing countries that import oil. It was almost a complete failure. The oil-producing countries had already, in the Solemn Declaration made in the OPEC Conference at Algiers in March 1975, forged links with the developing countries for oil, other raw materials, financial problems, and development; the oil producers refused to countenance a conference on energy alone. In September 1975 another meeting (Kleber II) made headway by extending the proposed scope of the conference, and in December 1975 the Conference on International Economic Cooperation (CIEC) met in Paris and set up four Commissions—Energy, Raw Materials, Development, and Finance—to review the problems and make recommendations, if possible by the end of 1976. Membership of the Conference was confined to 27 countries or groups of countries. Eight of these are industrialised countries: the European Community, Spain, Sweden, Switzerland, Australia, Canada, Japan, and the United States. The other 19 are, broadly, developing countries: Algeria, Argentina, Brazil,

Cameroun, Egypt, India, Indonesia, Iran, Iraq, Jamaica, Mexico, Nigeria, Pakistan, Peru, Saudi Arabia, Venezuela, Yugoslavia, Zaïre, and Zambia. It should be noted that seven of the 19 are also important members of OPEC—Algeria, Indonesia, Iran, Iraq, Nigeria, Saudi Arabia, and Venezuela—and account for about 80 per cent of OPEC oil production.

From the Community's point of view, an important early decision was that the Community should be represented at Community level and not by the Member States separately—that it should, in fact, speak with one voice. In the Energy Commission, the Community was represented jointly by one representative of the Council of Ministers, the chairman of the Energy Working Group of the Council, and by one representative of the Commission, the Director General for Energy. The Community played an important part in CIEC so far as energy was concerned, both in public debate and in fashioning the concerted policy of the Group of Eight industrialised countries.

The early sessions of the Energy Commission were devoted to analysis and fact finding and much progress toward mutual understanding was made. The 'action oriented' phase of the second half of 1976 was much less successful. Problems encountered in other Commissions, notably that of indebtedness, impeded progress in the Energy Commission and early attempts to find common ground in such difficult areas as pricing were not promising. Nevertheless, with the early resumption of the CIEC in 1977, there were real hopes that with new impetus advances on all fronts might be made; that help might be given to the Group of Nineteen to move toward realising the New Economic Order; that the industrialised countries might receive assurances about the security of energy supplies; and that all aspects of energy policy of common interest to producers and consumers might be considered in some form of meaningful ongoing discussion. Not all of these hopes were realised at the final CIEC ministerial meeting (30 May to 2 June 1977), and no forum was established for energy consultation.

THE COMMUNITY'S SPECIAL RELATIONSHIP WITH ENERGY PRODUCERS

With CIEC, the Community was one of the Group of Eight, discussing energy and other problems with the Group of Nineteen, composed of rich oil-producers and relatively poor developing countries. The Community also has, in its own right, close relations with energy producers and developing countries, and it is to some examples of these that we now turn.

The Lomé Convention

As mentioned briefly above, the Lomé Convention, between the Community and 46 African, Caribbean, and Pacific (ACP) countries, entered into force 1 April 1976, and another three countries have joined since. Oil accounted for one-third of the Community's imports, by value, from ACP countries in 1975. The effect of the Convention on trade was to give ACP countries free access to Community markets. Since crude oil is zero-rated under the Common Customs Tariff, the Convention confers no particular advantage on Nigeria, an important ACP oil producer, as a crude-oil exporter to the Community. If, however, the oil producers among the ACP countries follow the current fashion and develop refining capacity, free entry for their refined products into the European market would be a decided advantage. There are many other aspects of the Convention that offer great advantages to the ACP countries, e.g. institution of a system for stabilising export earnings and proposals for industrial cooperation; in general, these are not directly connected with energy policy, but the goodwill generated should not be overlooked.

The Maghreb Agreements

Arrangements between the Community and the Maghreb countries (the Arab West) of Morocco, Algeria, and Tunisia have a long history. Agreements concluded with Morocco and Tunisia in 1969 were aimed at the eventual establishment of a free-trade area. They guaranteed free access to the Community market for almost all Moroccan oil and Tunisian industrial products, and privileged treatment for certain agricultural products. Algeria, as an independent state, made its first overtures to the Community in 1962, but trade arrangements continued in rather haphazard fashion for a decade until the Community's overall Mediterranean policy was defined in 1972. Parallel negotiations were then started with the three Maghreb countries and, although long drawn-out, were successfully concluded in January 1976.

The aim of the agreements is to establish 'wide-ranging cooperation' between the Community and each of the Maghreb countries, in the areas of economics, finance, technology, trade, and labour. Provision has been made for interim agreements to be concluded so that the trade arrangements can be implemented as quickly as possible. The agreements are of unlimited duration: they endow the 'overall cooperation' planned with the scope necessary to resolve any longer-term development problems.

The institutional machinery to be set up should make it possible to assess the results achieved, define certain measures more closely, and, where appropriate, propose new measures. A Council of Ministers, assisted by a Committee of plenipotentiaries and, if necessary, by specialist committees, will provide a vehicle for an ongoing dialogue, and there could also be contacts between political representatives. Lastly, a specific timetable has been laid down for examining the results of each agreement and any improvements to be made, first in 1978 and second in 1983.

On energy, in particular, the agreements with Algeria and Tunisia envisaged cooperation to foster participation by Community firms in programmes for exploration, production, and processing of energy resources and to ensure that long-term contracts for the delivery of petroleum products are properly performed. On trade in energy products, there is a temporary volume restriction on exports of refined petroleum products to the Community; these products enter the Community duty-free, subject to a ceiling that is raised by 5 per cent annually and that will finally disappear no later than the end of 1979.

Proposed Agreement with Iran
A framework agreement for commercial and economic cooperation between the Community and Iran is in the early stages of discussion. The precise shape and content of the final agreement are still matters for negotiation, but a preferential agreement is not envisaged. Entry of Iranian refined petroleum products into the Community on a preferential basis would therefore have to be under the system of generalised preference. This implies that any advantages granted to Iran would also apply to all other developing countries. It is possible that Iran, through planned expansion of its refining capacity, may have 15 million tons of refined products available for export by 1982, although details of the timing of refinery construction and the probable destination of exports are, at present, far from clear. The problem for the Community is how to accommodate imported refined products—e.g. from Iran—without jeopardising the profitable future of the Community's own refining industry, which is, at present, the subject of careful study.

As well as cooperation in trade, including trade in petroleum products, the proposed agreement with Iran also envisages mutual economic cooperation in many fields, such as industry, technology, energy, the environment, and employment. To bring this about, a diversity of means will be suggested including technological exchange, mutual investment, and joint ventures.

The Euro-Arab Dialogue

The Euro-Arab Dialogue originated in initiatives taken after the Copenhagen Summit of December 1973 to foster closer ties between the Community and members of the Arab League. Its purpose was to promote close cooperation in all fields between the two regions, e.g. industrial, agricultural, financial, cultural, and social matters.

Political difficulties delayed the start of formal talks, with the result that the General Commission (the Dialogue's managing body), instituted in July 1974, met for the first time in May 1976 and had a second meeting in February 1977. There were three earlier joint meetings at senior officials' level during 1975 at Cairo in June, Rome in July, and Abu Dhabi in November). Considerable progress was made in organising the Dialogue. Seven broad areas of cooperation, not including energy, were defined (industrialisation, infrastructure, agriculture, trade, finance, science and technology, and social and cultural matters), and committees, jointly chaired by an Arab and European delegate, were formed to draw up and implement work programmes for each. It was agreed that these committees would, where appropriate, create specialised work groups staffed by experts from national administrations and/or industry to 'examine in practical detail specific areas for cooperation.' The Arab League secretariat and the European Commission were made responsible for the distribution of documents and information and some funds have been made available.

The industrialisation committee, meeting at Abu Dhabi in November 1975, decided to set up a specialised group concerned with the oil-refining and petrochemical industries. In his introductory address, the Arab co-chairman, Mr Mahmoud Riad, stressed that the development plan for these industries would be of central importance in discussion at the Baghdad Conference in December 1976 of the 'strategy of Arab industrial development to the year 2000'. He also drew attention to the need for parallel progress in assuring markets for Arab industrial production. The other main initiative in the energy field was the decision by the Science and Technology Committee to exchange information on solar energy and to examine possible joint research projects.

The terms of reference given to the Oil Refining and Petrochemical Group were to analyse present and future capacities and requirements in Arab, European, and world markets so as to identify areas of 'complementarity' and to specify within them major projects for early development. A preliminary paper was tabled by the Commission on oil-refining capacity and demand, based on figures provided by the Member States. For their part, the Arabs provided a list of existing and proposed refineries amounting to a trebling of distillation capacity from the present level of 120 million tons/year to 375 million tons/year. In written comments on the commission's paper, the Arab experts rejected the contention that the principal problem was the surplus of distillation capacity and pointed instead to the growing shortfall of gasoline production capacity and the need for investment in conversion plant. For such energy-intensive processes, they suggested, the Arab producing countries were, by virtue of their abundant reserves of natural gas, the logical location (an argument that would apply equally to petrochemical plants).

It has therefore become clear from these early meetings that the Arabs regard the construction of oil refineries and petrochemical plants as an important and urgent aspect of the regional cooperation envisaged by the founders of the Dialogue, and as the basis for their future industrialisation. It is equally clear that although energy in general, and trade in crude oil in particular, were excluded from the Dialogue, there is a strong indirect energy element through refining and petrochemicals and, to a lesser extent, through the possibility of solar energy research cooperation.

CONCLUSIONS

Within the foregoing perspective, let us recall the main principles of the energy policy that the Community wishes to follow. The Community must

1. reduce its total demand for energy as far as possible,
2. switch final demand for energy into some fuels and away from others,
3. increase production from indigenous sources of energy, and, to the extent that these are successfully accomplished,
4. reduce its dependence on imported sources of energy.

In implementing this policy, the Community, both by its own efforts and by exhorting the Member States to carry out Community policy, will need to have regard to the internal and external aspects of the energy systems of member nations. Internally, 1979 will be spent consolidating certain parts of the work programme already adopted; the following parts are of outstanding importance:

1. the vigorous implementation of measures for the rational use of energy,
2. a re-examination of objectives, including objectives for 1990,
3. the protection and promotion of investments,
4. promotion of use of coal in power stations, and cyclical stockpiling of coal,
5. oil-refining capacity; surplus distillation capacity; compatibility with structure of product demand,
6. imports of refined petroleum products,
7. oil stocks, their location and financing,
8. support for hydrocarbon research and exploration projects,
9. solving problems of nuclear fuel supply.

At the same time, it is hoped that Member States will, where applicable, vigorously pursue their nuclear electricity construction programmes and their plans for production of oil and natural gas. Nevertheless, when all possible efforts have been made on internal policies, the Community remains, in any of a range of plausible scenarios, heavily dependent on imported oil and gas for about 50 per cent or more of its total energy needs.

Externally, because of this continued dependence on imports, the Community will need to consolidate its relations with energy-producing countries, through multilateral contacts as in CIEC or possible consultative arrangements that may follow from CIEC, and by extending its own cooperative relationships with energy producers in the general context of improved economic and trading relationships with the rest of the world. By such means, it will be seen to be in the interests of the energy-producing countries, no less than those of the large industrialised consuming countries, that sufficient energy is produced to meet the world's needs during the present transition period, during which it is hoped, an over-reliance on hydrocarbons will gradually give way to an abundance of renewable sources of energy.

NOTES

1. This chapter expresses the personal views of the authors and not necessarily those of the Commission of the European Communities. This work (with some changes) originally appeared as an article (The European Community—An Energy Perspective') in *The Annual Review of Energy*, No. 2 (1977) 343–64.
2. *Bulletin of the European Communities*: Supplements 12/68, 11/72, and 6/73.

3. *Bulletin of the European Communities*: Supplement, 4/74.
4. Council Resolution of 17/12/74 on a Community action programme on the rational utilisation of energy, and Council Resolution of 13/2/75 concerning measures to be implemented to achieve the Community energy policy objectives adopted by the Council on 17/12/74.
5. Community Energy Policy: document COM (76) 508 final, 30 September 1976.

9 Conclusions

PETER COFFEY

In this book, most of the important economic policy areas of the European Economic Community have been examined. In some fields, as we have seen, the Community has been successful; in others, its performance has been disappointing. However, in all sectors, the Common Market has now arrived at a crossroads. The fundamental question which remains to be asked is: what basic policy options should the EEC now adopt? Should the Community become protectionist, for example, or should it become more 'open'? In answering these questions, most of the contributors suggest that a threefold approach should be adopted. They propose that the Common Market place a greater emphasis on quality since the adoption of such a policy is more suited to the Community's levels of education and training. Also, such a policy implies that the EEC can become more 'open'. This is precisely the second general proposal running through most of the contributions. The Community should thus align its pricing systems and policies more with world levels. These two aforementioned policy proposals imply a third one, a greater degree of Community cooperation and coordination. Indeed, the general feeling is that at no time in the history of the European Economic Community was the adoption of such a policy more necessary. This call for increased cooperation and coordination between the Member States does not imply the creation of Community cartels or protectionist organisations but rather the creation of an environment which will lead to a more efficient use of scarce resources.

Thus, Professor Josling, in his chapter on agriculture, whilst not under-estimating the considerable achievements of the Common Agricultural Policy, does consider that the Community should take more account of world agricultural prices. This aim was in fact stressed at the famous meeting at Stresa in 1958. Professor Josling also calls for a more flexible internal system which could lead to a better flow of products both within the Community and between the Common Market and the outside world. Such a flow, he considers, would be more appropriate to the Community's needs. In order to achieve these basic aims, he stresses a four-point plan. Firstly, the quality of information being passed on to farmers should be improved. Secondly, major shifts in the price levels for products should replace the present unrealistic annual price reviews. This would imply a system of more realistic 'target prices'. Thirdly, the EEC should pay more attention to the poorer and smaller farmers on the basis of a social cost-benefit appraisal. Fourthly, Professor Josling considers that some modification of market regulation instruments is desirable.

In a similar vein, Professor Jacquemin stresses a policy of quality and of 'product differentiation'. He contrasts the major economic expansion of the first decade-and-a-half of the Community's history with the stagnation experienced since 1975. He also observes two contradictory movements within the Common Market at the present time. On the one hand, there is an attempt to maintain the decentralised market forces inherent in a competitive economic system. On the other hand, there exists a desire for collaboration between the private and public sectors. These contradictory movements give Professor Jacquemin much cause for concern. Thus he suggests that the Community should maintain as much competition as possible. Where 'national measures of intervention and planning agreements' may be necessary, these should be coordinated at Community level. In any case, where major structural changes may necessitate public intervention, such changes may be facilitated through common social and regional policies. Finally, he is opposed to protectionism and considers it indispensable that the EEC should adopt policies of quality and of 'product differentiation'.

The editor's chapter on Social Policy is in some ways a natural complement to the contribution on Industrial Policy. The editor points out that, until quite recently, the EEC did not have a dynamic social policy since the two basic aims in this field were the free movement of workers and a common policy concerning the social security benefits to be enjoyed by migrants in receiving countries. It is true that the main visible organ in this sector was and is the Social Fund, but, until recently, no excessive demands were placed on its facilities. The situation has changed dramatically since the advent of the energy and economic crises. This changed situation has led to the launching (in 1974) of a Social Policy Action Programme. Despite the laudable aims of this programme, the editor does not think that it goes far enough. In fact, he stresses the lack of attention which is paid to poverty and youth unemployment in the European Economic Community. Thus, he calls both for more common economic projects (like the European Airbus, for example) and more dynamic social policies. In the latter case, the editor considers that greater resources should be allocated to the Social Fund and that by, say, 1990, the Community should aim at the provision of minimum services (doctors, dentists and other facilities) throughout the Common Market. The achievement of these aims should lead to an improvement in the quality of the lives of the inhabitants of the EEC.

The successful achievement of many of the aims described in the first three chapters will depend to a very large degree on a successful fiscal system. In his contribution on Fiscal Integration, Professor Prest sees the fiscal aims of the Community as being mainly twofold. Firstly, the common taxes, VAT and Corporation Tax, should facilitate the removal of obstacles to trade and the free movement of factors of production—essentially removing any inducements to invest and produce in any one area of the EEC rather than in any other. Secondly, common taxation policies should lead to the adequate financing of the Community Budget.

At the outset, Professor Prest stresses that tax harmonisation does not necessarily imply the adoption of an identical tax base and rate structure in all member countries. In examining the VAT, he considers that the present tax, using a partial destination principle, works very well and that although the Neumark Committee's proposal for the adoption of a restricted origin principle may be desirable in a unified taxation system, its use in the foreseeable future would be quite unrealistic. Turning to the adoption of a Community Corporation Tax, Professor Prest finds that the Common Market is on much more difficult ground since the aim of such a tax must be capital export neutrality. The Commission has thus come down in favour of an Imputation System and recommends tax rates of between 45 and 55 per cent. But the real final aim of tax harmonisation is the financing of the Community Budget. Hitherto, this budget has been very modest (about 0.7 per cent of Community GNP). Now, as from 1 January 1978, up to 1 per cent of the yield from VAT in the Common Market may be allocated to this budget. Further, since the European Parliament now has a voice in the budget (as from mid – 1977) one may expect changes in this field. These changes imply the taking of major decisions about the future. If, as the editor suggests, the Community assumes additional social and economic responsibilities, then Professor Prest foresees increases in the percentage of the revenues from VAT being allocated to the budget. Equally, this implies that the fundamental question of the redistribution of income within the European Economic Community will, sooner or later, have to be faced. This is likely to cause a major upheaval within the Community.

In examining the Community's trade and monetary policies, the editor concludes that, whereas the former has on the whole shown remarkable consistency and success, the latter has been little short of a disaster. In its external economic relations the Community has defined fairly clear policies for the Third World (more explicitly, Africa), the Mediterranean and Eastern Europe. Also, it has successfully undertaken major international trade negotiations and created a large free trade area in Western Europe as well as a huge preferential trading area with the ACP States. Now, the editor observes, the Common Market does indeed find itself at a crossroads. Whilst on the one hand it is actively associating itself with the conclusion of international commodity agreements, it is, unfortunately, on the other hand, much tempted by protectionism. The editor stresses the danger of the Community succumbing to this temptation since, whilst such a capitulation would lead to a temporary respite for 'lame dog' industries, it would, in the long run, make the Common Market less competitive internationally. Instead, the EEC should emphasise quality and 'product differentiation'—a policy much more in keeping with its level of education and training.

If the situation regarding trade is both successful and critical, only the latter can be said about the progress made towards the achievement of an economic and monetary union—whilst the complete lack of a common international monetary personality is little short of a scandal. The editor believes that, in its bid for an economic and monetary union, the Community probably put the cart before the horse. Now it is suggested that more modest steps be taken, such as the creation of a form of European Payments Union. However, the editor insists that these considerations do not prevent the introduction of a 'Europa' for use between official institutions. Indeed, the amount of intra-Community trade militates precisely in favour of such a policy. Also, the creation of this currency would help the Common Market to find a common international monetary personality. This European personality has never been needed more than at the present moment as the world faces international monetary chaos.

The natural complement to competition and social policies would seem to be well-integrated transport and regional policies. Unfortunately, the Community's record in both these fields is, to say the least, somewhat disappointing. In examining Transport Policy, Professor Bromhead states quite bluntly that although one of the aims set down in the Treaty of Rome was the adoption of a Common Transport Policy, this has not, in fact, materialised. Such a policy is highly desirable—indeed necessary—in a customs union since it is basically concerned with the removal of obstacles to free movement and of distortions to trade. Thus the Schaus Memorandum laid down the basic tenets of an 'integrated system' (1961) and two years later an 'Action Programme' was accepted. However, even now, this programme has not been fully achieved. Further, Professor Bromhead expresses concern at the problem of payment for infrastructure. In this field many studies have been made, but by 1977 nothing positive had emerged from the search for a common system for infrastructure, except a recognition that a serious policy in this direction was an essential part of a market/competition policy. Thus Professor Bromhead is forced to conclude that, although one can see numerous minor achievements—such as safety and market regulations—and despite the very full communication made on Transport Policy by the Commission in 1973, the EEC is as far away from achieving a common policy as ever. The Community urgently needs a basic transport infrastructure and transport energy policy.

Happily, the picture regarding Regional Policy is somewhat more satisfactory. Although any Community policy in this field is at best complementary to national efforts, a strong regional policy becomes an absolute necessity because of the EEC's moves along the road towards economic and monetary union. Further, as Professor Paelinck and Mr Molle point out, it is desirable to reduce regional imbalances since failure to do so prevents an economy from making optimum use of scarce resources and thus keeps wealth below par.

Although regional aids have been organised in one form or another by the Coal and Steel Community, the European Investment Bank, the Social Fund, and the Agricultural Fund, systematic moves towards the formulation and adoption of a regional policy are of very recent origin. Also, the Regional Fund did not see the light of day until 1975. Equally, the first major systematic EEC analysis of regional development had only been made in 1971 (extended in 1973) when the Community also launched its first general schemes for coordinating regional aid.

The two contributors are very concerned about the regional question since there is an increasing divergence between the rich and the poor areas of the Common Market. This is a particularly serious situation since we are living in times of reduced economic growth. Thus they suggest a more analytical approach to the problem. Professor Paelinck and Mr Molle propose that, following a basic study and analysis of problem regions, moves should be undertaken to modify the 'profile' of these regions to make them more attractive for investment and living. The editor considers that this policy (probably the most correct one) will necessitate a more dynamic approach and the allocation of greater resources to the weaker regions, though he would personally favour—as an indispensable prerequisite—the transfer of some of the industrial, economic, and political centres of decision-making to these areas.

The last policy area to be examined was energy. Here, the collaboration of members of the European Commission, Messrs Brondel (Director) and Morton, was invited and accepted.

In their chapter, our colleagues stress and analyse the problems associated with the elaboration and application of an energy policy in the EEC. At the outset, they underline the fact that such a policy has a non-binding (exhortatory) effect on the Member States. Further, they point out that whilst the Community's original energy policy of obtaining 'a cheap and secure source of energy' remains basically unchanged, the background to the application of such a policy has radically changed. Thus, whilst before 1973/4 the main reliance of the EEC was a ever-increasing one on oil, thereafter it changed to a heavy reliance on nuclear energy and gas. However, this change had to be made whilst simultaneously trying to achieve an equilibrium between reasonable prices for consumers and adequate profitability for producers—to induce the latter to make the required capital investment.

Thus one can now speak of a 'New Community Strategy for Energy'— until 1985. This may be described as aiming at efficiency and a reduction in demand (whilst maintaining growth), substitution between different forms of energy, a reduction in the Community's dependence on outside energy sources and an increase in the production of indigenous sources of energy.

Messrs Brondel and Morton do however place the Community's energy policy in an international context and they, correctly, see it as forming part of the external economic policy of the EEC.

This is a very appropriate point at which to begin one's concluding observations about 'Economic Policies of the Common Market' because suggestions made by Messrs Brondel and Morton do underline the Community's important links with the outside world and the necessity of making a choice between protectionism and 'openness'. The European Economic Community does then stand at an important crossroads in what is a new world economic and political order. The Community faces an immense challenge, partly through the combined energy and monetary crisis, and partly through the fact that many third-world countries are in the process of rapidly replacing the EEC as major producers of industrial products. Internally, in the industrial, social and regional fields (to mention only a few) the Community faces urgent problems of restructuring. However, the Common Market possesses considerable advantages in its technological know-how, training and education. Further, the existing Community institutions, given clear policies and adequate means, are perfectly capable of both initiating and coordinating restructuring policies. The very worst choice for the EEC would be to lapse into a policy of protectionism for 'lame dogs'. Instead, the Common Market should opt for policies of quality 'production differentiation' and a gradual move towards 'openness'. In two years' time, we shall be able to discern the path chosen by the European Economic Community.

Index